FREELANCING

FREELANCING

Adventures of a Poet

Hugo Williams

faber and faber

LONDON · BOSTON

First published in Great Britain in 1995
by Faber and Faber Limited
3 Queen Square London WC1N 3AU

Photoset by Wilmaset Ltd., Birkenhead, Wirral
Printed in England by Clays Ltd, St Ives plc

A CIP record for this book
is available from the British Library

ISBN 0-571-17575-9

2 4 6 8 10 9 7 5 3 1

Our freedom as free lances
Advances towards its end;
The earth compels, upon it
Sonnets and birds descend;
And soon, my friend,
We shall have no time for dances.

Louis MacNeice, 'The Sunlight on the Garden'

Contents

ix

Introduction

A funny sort of life poet-journalists led in the early 1990s. They seem to have been blown hither and thither by a series of sudden shallow enthusiasms, no sooner taken up than laid aside, forever. There doesn't seem to be any plan or purpose to it. Where is it all heading, you ask yourself. I ask myself.

I had thought of calling the book *All Over the Place*, as the best description of its contents. One minute I'm in Central America with Judas Iscariot, the next I'm back at prep school. One minute I'm going out dressed as a woman, the next I'm staying home railing at 'Glucovision'. An article about Bruce Chatwin is followed by one about haircuts. Another about teaching creative writing is followed quickly by one about trying to buy drugs. Perhaps I should have called the book *Attempted Possession*, writing being like the drug you can never quite find. If anything is the subject of the book it is the search for one. Better luck next time. My only excuse is that all these things happened to me. It's my little world.

Reading the pieces all together I'm most conscious of the different speeds with which they move down the page. This may just be a question of quality, but it speaks to me vividly of the varying moods with which I related to deadlines, all the way from debonair to desperate. In some I can as good as see my heart beating. Writing is my definition of happiness, but happiness, when it doesn't write white, writes slow. (Unhappiness writes slow too, come to think of it.) I have sometimes flirted with approaching deadlines to the point where I was really asking for it, suspender belt and all. This hidden personal drama constitutes a more intimate aspect of the book than some of the autobiographical pieces. I only hope it will be the gear changes rather than the intrusive presence of the writer all over the place which the reader most objects to.

Having written two travel books and decided that travelling was the activity most like dying, in the way that it leaves an empty space behind where your life used to be, I had always thought it would be a good idea to write a travel book about staying home. After all, I knew more about it and I liked it more. In fact, as a freelance writer who worked at home, I knew *all* about it. I was an *aficionado*. But then, what was it *really* like? Was it the things I did? Or was it the things I only thought about? Was it the stories, or the spaces between the stories which affected me more? If the latter, what was the point? Hadn't I better write poetry?

Of course, one could never consciously embark on such a work. One would become a hermit, fearing to go out lest one came upon new material. One would never catch up. I am usually a year behind with my own difficulties as it is, never mind having time to go out and look for more. If I was ever going to make a start I would have to not know about it. Even in my worst nightmares, I could not find myself writing a book. The possibilities of that idea would have constituted the kind of writer's block that doesn't even bear flirting with. No, what we have here is a rearguard action, backs to the wall. 'I come on walking off stage backwards' (Lowell).

I only managed to get the travel books done by arranging for someone to be expecting something each week; in the first case Mrs Jolly, famed typist of Charing Cross Road, who always typed in blue because it didn't hurt her eyes so much; in the second, Xandra Hardie, a friend who happened to be working at Jonathan Cape and let the sections pile up in her office without even thinking about a book until we all felt stronger.

In the case of this one, it was Isabel Fonseca who was waiting for my columns at the *TLS*, so the trap of beginning was camouflaged by a realistic flooring of deadlines and temporary breathers. A book was the last thing either of us had in mind. Still is, really. (The column was later edited by David Sexton, then James Campbell, both of whom I'd like to thank.)

Isabel had had the idea of a weekly column, something vaguely literary, to be written by a roster of writers, subjects to be decided by consultation, length about 750 words. She had trouble thinking of a title and in the end used 'Freelance', because it was the subject of my own first effort (page 1). I liked the logo of those early columns – the title in a battered typewriter face, which further seemed to illustrate the freelance predicament. I can make out traces of Isabel's original concept in the earlier of these pieces.

Gradually the other writers found better things to do, preferring to leave a little something still at the bottom of their respective barrels. I scraped on and scraped by. I found I liked the short form. It suited my attention span and it almost fitted into my week. Like me, it could survive on almost, but not quite, nothing. If I stayed home one week, rereading teenage letters or wondering idly what it would be like to live next door, I made a conscious effort to be more professional next time. An article about my wife's childhood in Alsace would be followed more toughly by one about a tour of Vienna 'In the Footsteps of the Third Man'. One about family share-outs by a more general interest piece about Siamese twins or the terminology of roistering.

Isabel left the *TLS* and it became Ferdie Mount I reported to. I thought he would be more strict, but he turned out to be more tolerant and let me do more or less what I liked, to the point where my life actually seemed to make sense: I was writing about it. At first, my guiding principle was never to go out looking for material if there was any lying around at home. After all, why should a column be about *additional* experience? Wasn't what happened to me in the normal course of events interesting enough? I soon discovered that it wasn't. I discovered that writing a column is like having a small excitable dog to look after. At first it is sweet. Gradually it develops a life of its own. It gets hungry. It gets sick. It gets bored. Sometimes it's all too much, but the great thing about having a dog is that it likes to go walkies and in the end so do you. You look forward to it.

What About Pleasure? Where Does that Feature in the Freelance Hierarchy?

Coffee is the drug of the chronic freelance. It reproduces, for money, the state of anxious chaos that exists in his room, his brain, his work schedule, his bank account and his love-life. It also causes him to nod off at his desk from coffee-shock, a condition characterized by damp, cold feet. Balzac drank thirty pots a day. Proust, according to Redmond O'Hanlon, wrote all his books on bull's adrenalin, hence the curtained room to preserve the speedfreak's brittle, laser-beam constructions.

'Coffee is darkness', said Nietzsche, who believed that writing should be done walking around outside: 'Never give any credence to a thought conceived while sitting.' I was born three cups of coffee under par, but when I read what Nietzsche wrote, I decided to buy a lighter variety, only to discover that it is actually stronger than the full roast, being less cooked. It makes my heart beat visibly under my shirt and causes bladder and bowels to work overtime. If I'm not jumping up to turn over the Screaming Blue Messiahs or put the Dimplex up a few degrees as my blood temperature drops, I'm leaping upstairs to produce an eyeglass full of decaffeinated liquid ten times a morning. I sometimes think I'm nothing more than a machine for taking the colour out of strong brown drinks. I wonder does anyone else experience the same thrill of anticipation at the thought of going downstairs for a big bowl of sugary cereal, after writing one sentence?

A freelance collaborates with his deadline much as the people of Lyon did with Klaus Barbie. Deadlines are lifelines. You have a little affair with them, fraught with betrayals, recriminations and brinkmanship. They glow with a strange attraction: the light under the door that isn't there when you open it, only another door, another deadline. As you run your left hand repeatedly through your hair to appease an approaching showdown, scurf and hair follicles shower on to the desk-top and into the typewriter, causing it to jam and print double. Now every 'I' or 'e' has to be plucked back from the page by hand. Typewriter ink smears your fair copy. Knowing that your piece always somehow gets written, you wonder idly what would happen if you sat there doing nothing this time around. Under your desk, you stamp and kick a large hole in the carpet, as if you were running away from something in your sleep. It looks like an abandoned rat's nest down there. One day you kick your way clear through the floorboards into the wiring and electrocute yourself in mid-sentence. You wake up with a start, imagining it was all a bad dream. Then you wake up again.

What to do first? The report to Eastern Arts on my residency at Stevenage Comprehensive (no money till it's done), or the liner notes for a friend's new album? Check my American student's parodies of Cavafy, or do my accounts? Start my article for *Departures*, or watch TV for the *New Statesman*? A horoscope from a friend this morning advises me to 'set aside *a lot* of time for your poetry, rather than doing too many less worthwhile things for money'. On my desk lies the example of my brother's first novel, *Talking Oscars*, begging me to be gentle with it while blushing at its recent acceptance by Heinemann for a three-year sum.

And what about pleasure? Where does that feature in the freelance hierarchy, supposing you write about TV for a living? Your writer chappie thought he was such a clever little fellow, not working, but writing for a living. Look at him now, poor chap, hunched to his scrap-pad seven days a week, watching Australian soap operas with a hunted look in his eye. His blood pressure's the lowest you can have and still register. He's been advised to build up his cholesterol. He can't get heavy enough rock 'n' roll to keep his heart ticking over. The only crystals he owns are the ones in his shoulders.

I'm reminded of that funny little man in Oxford Street with the tall sandwich-board advocating beans, raw vegetables and sitting;

less red meat, violence and sex. Without meaning to, I seem to have
become one of his disciples.

[8.1.88]

Green Carnations and Author-Baiting

Your reluctant columnist, dwelling needlessly on the state of the
carpet under his desk for his last effort, was only too happy to eat a
couple of literary banquets last week on your behalf.

Waiting in the courtyard of the Old Brewery in Chiswell Street to
welcome guests to the Whitbread Book of the Year Dinner were two
magnificent grey drays, manes combed, harness polished, name-
plates gleaming: 'Pride' and 'Prejudice'. Which would win the day?
Or would they pull together? In the Gents, Christopher Reid was
trying to fix a black tie round the shaggy throat of Bernard McCabe,
there to represent Seamus Heaney should he win the £18,000 prize.
Having wished every success to one of the judges, Judy Cooke,
reading her as 'short-listed' on the menu, I found my name on table
thirteen next to Raman Subba Row, President of the England
Cricket Selection Board, who told me he had once, aged ten, run a
small south-coast railway station for several weeks while its master
was away drinking. It was Raman who went out to Karachi recently
to persuade our chaps to complete the test series, rather against his
and their better judgement, I gathered. When I noticed the Hon.
Colin Moynihan, our Sports Minister, talking to Miss Gaie Morris,
Captain of the England women's cricket team, I began to wonder
what the finalists were going to be judged on.

Round about pudding – a cricket-ball with green sauce – there
were big-screen videos of the short-listees talking, followed by
readings of their work by actors. Francis Wyndham looked the best
writer present, but he may have wondered, as I did, how a mere 'Best
First Novel' could ever triumph over anyone in the 'Best Novel'
category, a position occupied by Ian McEwan. Surprise of the
evening was the now fully-Yeatsified image of Seamus Heaney,

3

forty-eightish, half-frames balanced at the end of his nose and no reading matter within miles. Craig Raine's theory was that Irishmen turn into their fathers earlier than we do.

Heaney characterized the 1980s as 'shoulder-shrugging and elegiac', which seemed about right, but Ian McEwan thought the pace of change was so great he didn't want to be 'tied in' to 1987 and needed the 'wider canvas' of the future. The film of eventual Whitbread winner Christy Nolan showed him seated at his type-writer while his mother Bernadette held his head from behind and guided his 'unicorn stick' to the right letter. Her acceptance speech contained an unexpected endorsement of David Alton's bill to reduce the abortion limit from twenty-eight to eighteen weeks.

'I was never really into bindings', said Francis Wyndham as he fingered his expensive-looking consolation prize after the show. It must have been a strange, but very lifelike sensation to get back your book coated in leather and smelling of goat's cheese when the jackpot had seemed so close: 'Look, do you mind, I've read this one.'

The guests for the *Sunday Express* Book of the Year Lunch in the Wilde Room at the Café Royal were given green carnations as consolation prizes for giving up their day to watch this rather more down-market author-baiting. (The emphasis was on 'readability'.) I took my wife along, thinking it was a buffet, but it proved to be a sit-down, with place-names and finalists shared out among the tables like an away team at school, so she had to go home with the carnation. Ronald Hardy, our table's contender, whose book was described by one judge as 'very long', was nearly in tears at having been teed up so effectively only to be sliced into the rough at the last minute.

A fact not impossible to credit is that readers of the *Sunday Express* include '20 per cent of the people who buy book tokens'. On this occasion it was Brian Moore, Malibu-based author of many 'ultra-readable' novels, whose *The Colour of Blood* was chosen to see the colour of their money. If a film is made of it, the last scene, according to Monica Dickens, 'will rank in screen lore with Glenn Close in the bath in *Fatal Attraction*'. I got that from the fully written-up hand-out we were given on the way out. I suppose they must have quickly burned the ones for William Boyd, Noel Virtue, Mary Wesley and poor Ronald Hardy.

[29.1.88]

His Word against Mine

On my way to chair a poetry workshop in South Acton I leave all my books behind on a bench at Highbury and Islington. I get out at Gospel Oak and wait for another train going back. My books have gone. No one has heard of them. I see a door marked 'Private', knock and go in. There is a whole different world in there, relaxed and degenerate, in contrast to the busy platform outside. It has a carpet, a cat and a fine old dead clock with only one hand. In the corner sits an old man reading one of my books. 'Oh, thank God you've got them', I say. 'I'm supposed to be doing a reading in half an hour.' The old man looks up from the book and asks, 'You the author of this?' I say I am, but that I wrote it some time ago when I was quite young. 'Young eh? Heh! I don't know how they get this stuff printed. I mean it's so, you know, personal. I mean who wants to know how you shave and everything? If you want to write an interesting book you should write a book about me. I've been round the world four times on a submarine. I was interviewed by Billy Graham.' I say I'd really like to, but I am already late. 'What you see here', says the man, indicating his snug domain, 'is as much a microcosm of anything as anything is. It's my belief that we mortals are tenants left here on Earth by some buggerin' absentee landlord, to look after his estates for him while he's off evicting people from their homes on the other side of the galaxy. Interested? I knew you would be. All that wishy-washy stuff, "O Lord, make haste to help us", that's not going to make any impression on people like that. What you need is something much more like a word of command. Do this! Do that! I know from my experience in the war that people prefer you to be firm with them in an emergency. Take a look

5

around you. How would *you* like to live and work in this hell-hole?' 'I'd love to', I tell the man. I can hear a train arriving and am foreseeing some difficulty in getting all my books back into their carrier bags. 'The only thing is,' says the man, 'Your book isn't exactly what I'd call . . . correct me if I'm wrong, but isn't a sentence supposed to have a verb? What's "keroot" mean?' I dash for the door with my books under my arm. 'You forgot your Pomagne', comes the man's croak.

I am an hour late for the workshop and my garbled apologies undermine my credibility in advance. My students have moved their desks flush with the master's desk and are smiling at one another. Several of them are drunk. One has a bowie knife. I pile my books in front of me like sandbags.

The tricky thing about the creative writing industry is the more or less accepted notion that everyone's opinion, even on matters of grammar, carries equal weight. You have to be incredibly diplomatic and charming. 'Tap dancing' I call it, but there is another word for it. Before long I am locked in mortal discussion with an unhinged Welshman who has written 'Like a rough speck / of dull brown / dust caught / in a gold ray / of last sun / the small bright / kitten jumps / over the Dutch / clog into / the old wood / basket.' I read this over to myself but I can't for the life of me see the point of it. All of a sudden poetry itself seems the most pointless exercise imaginable and I try to explain this to the Welshman, who insists on taking it personally. 'Yes but WHY isn't it any good?' he howls. Why indeed. I want to know myself. I search in vain for an absence of main verb. I add up the adjectives and lose count. I mention Black Mountain poetry. I think of running outside and burying the poem in the garden, but first I ask other people what they think of it. They quite like it. They say it is visual and moving. It captures the movement of the kitten through the air and into the basket. I have to agree with this and end up retracting everything I have said and apologizing to the Welshman for going 'OTT'. I start to think I quite like the poem myself. 'After all', says the Welshman unbearably, as he shop-soils a copy of one of my books, 'it's really just your word against mine, isn't it?'

6

'Right', I whimper. I have picked a little hole in the plastic cup I am holding and Pomagne is running down my trousers.

[11.3.88]

The North Devon Farm Museum

Monday. Arrive at the Arvon Foundation in Devon to teach a 'closed' course with Alexis Lykiard of sixteen teenage boys and two girls from a Bromley comprehensive. Everyone has brought a music system of some kind. To ban or not to ban? Alexis is pro-ban. I mediate in favour of personal stereos only, ghetto-blasters to be limited to a 'loud hour' between six and seven o'clock. This is my first mistake. Before long even the duty master has on his walkman and is hissing with a 'Sixties Mania' tape; I can just make out 'Leader of the Pack' by the Shangri Las. He shouts that five boys are here to write, the rest are 'plonkers'.

Tuesday. The staggered consultations go gradually out of sync; by the end there are three fractious SAS types with headphones and shag spots sitting on my bed waiting to present their 'character sketch' of a big brother in the Navy before dashing off to the pub.

After dinner, the tutors do their reading. I read from my mucky American book and forget to read ahead. Quick as a flash, Tony puts up his hand to ask the meaning of 'sodomize'. 'Bugger', I tell him. 'Anal intercourse', says the teacher. We have both fallen into the trap. Later, schoolgirl Nathalie writes a piece of public porn to 'embarrass' cute Ghanaian Reg: 'As Nadine rose in climax, she gave Reg her all, but knowing he would leave as suddenly as he arrived she held on tightly, refusing to let him use her again, but it was too late . . .'. Reg replies in kind.

Wednesday. The boys doing school work on 'that patriotic cunt' Rupert Brooke. I try to defend him against Wilfred Owen, but can't quite remember why 'The Soldier' isn't imperialistic, so give them a prose paraphrase of 'Adlestrop' to turn back into a poem. Paul writes: 'Steam from a valve / Shot into the air / Rare flowers were

7

dancing / Without any care / The empty platform / With no one at all / With trees all around / Wild birds singing their call.' Reg conceives a nightmare Adlestrop in which 'I moved close to the rail / To have a look down / I fell and my legs were trapped . . .' All the birds and flowers of Oxfordshire burst out laughing as the train bears down on Reg: 'All hope was lost / and triumph was theirs.' Later, we have our 'Adlestrop Revisited' reading and each poet's manhood runs the gauntlet of his coeval's scorn. I unveil the original: the students aren't impressed.

Thursday. Giggles and huddles and headphones. Snatches of song-lyrics from the lips of passing walkpeople. Bully-Bully! Walking back to happiness with you oo oo . . . Alexis and I drive fast in the opposite direction to the strains of Fats Navarro on his car stereo. 'The North Devon Farm Museum' is closed, but the farmer opens up and takes us round: vintage steam engines, mantraps, hand biers, rubber 'funeral shoes' for cortège horses. 'Know what this is?' He holds up a spiked nozzle. 'That's for inflating veal carcasses to separate the skin off 'em.' Another device is for 'extracting pig's toenails'. Alexis and I feel we could find a use for these items back at the house, but the farmer refuses to break up his collection.

Favourite poem night. Tony has made an exhaustive study of the poetry library in his search for prurience and come up with a stinker called 'Song of a Phallus' by Ted Hughes. 'Belly', 'winkle', 'sod', 'bollocks', 'turd', there's a giggle on every line, not to mention a fine scatter of flesh particles: 'hacker', 'brat', 'whack', 'maw', 'axe', 'guts', 'bastard', 'guts', 'blood', 'axe', 'gore'. The poem might have been written especially for him.

Friday. I score my first popular success at the farewell reading with Paul Muldoon's 'Whim': 'Once he got stuck into her he got stuck.' At which the rather game English mistress mutters 'If we'd done it my way we could have walked out of here.' The reading is followed by satirical take-offs of myself and Alexis. Fixed smiles are in order. Alexis leaves early.

Saturday. Car, bus, train and tube back to Islington reading *Owning Up* by George Melly and thinking of all the heroic also-rans lounging in those café photos featuring Rimbaud or Gauguin. Who are we all, I wonder? I don't think I'll finish the book somehow.

[26.2.88]

Wendy Cope Makes Cocoa for Hugo Williams

17 March. Meet Wendy Cope at King's Cross in order to journey north to read at the Newcastle Literary Festival. We two TV columnists – she for the *Spectator*, me (now sacked) for the *New Statesman* – have read and exchanged moans together before, last year at King's Lynn. I tell her that a *column* column is harder because you have to go out and live in order to glean your material, an unpleasant new experience for me. Wendy says she must remember this when next straining at the controls. (Her favourite programme is *LA Law*.)

We discuss Fiona Pitt-Kethley's recent appearance on *Comment* on Channel Four in which she bemoaned the financial lot of the poet and lambasted her publisher for gross stinginess: 'Chatto's my pimp. / My cut is 5 per cent / (well in arrears). Clause after clause decrees / I earn less still and part's kept back for years. / I'm published now, so spin-offs come my way – / performances – I'm paid from fifty to / a hundred pounds for every one night stand. / Some buggers think that I should do it free' ('buggers' changed to 'scrooges' for C4). She goes on, 'Last year I made about two thousand net . . . I'm 33 and can't afford to rent / the smallest bedsit on my salary / I live with Mum . . . / What should I do? What chances do I have?'

With the financial support of the Council for Racial Equality, Fiona is currently suing the Arts Council for racial discrimination: all last year's applicants for an Arts Council grant had to be black, so she was turned down. We try to think of other authors who have written against publishers and can only come up with Byron – in letters – and Cyril Connolly in *Enemies of Promise*: 'As repressed sadists are supposed to become policemen or butchers so those with irrational fear of life become publishers.'

For the past seventeen years my wife Hermine has been writing a book called *The Tightrope Walker*, a historical work which includes her own adventures on the wire and elsewhere. For this she has received as an advance a sum £50 smaller even than the OUP are paying me for my own collected poems, although I must admit that my own deal includes the unexpected gratuity of a publication-date postponement – always life-enhancing. To help pay for some of the reproductions in her book, Hermine has taken on a job delivering the *Islington Chronicle* from door to door at £2.03 for 163 copies, the £2.03 to be paid into a building society to avoid mugging, says a Mr Grace. I wonder how many delivery women he has lost in this way.

The Newcastle reading has been announced as 'Wendy Cope Making Cocoa for Hugo Williams', but there is a plentiful supply of wine and the room is crowded. The occasion takes on a weird life of its own when I attempt to gloss the phrase 'permanganate of potash'. People can barely wait till the interval to press on me their experience of this chemical, with which, it seems, everyone in England was dyeing their face a streaky yellow in the late 1950s. (I thought I was alone.) There seems to be a difference of opinion among the audience as to whether its true application is for gargling, childbirth, or athlete's foot. Somebody asserts that she used to wash lettuce in it in the tropics. Just as we think the subject has faded away, a woman stands up at the back and states that she was working in a hospital in Bournemouth when a black woman was brought in who had been washed up on the beach. It wasn't until the permanganate dye started to wear off that they realized it was a white woman. They knew it was permanganate of potash because they had some in Maternity. They tried some on their own faces after that, but with limited success.

The woman sits down and there is a stunned silence, during which I try to figure out and answer her 'question'. With perfect timing she stands up again and delivers her *coup de grâce*: 'It took some time to wear off.' At which the reading breaks up in order for individual discussions on the matter to take place elsewhere.

[25.3.88]

Soho Revisited

The bar of the Poetry Society looked like the Pillars of Hercules in the late 1970s, each old face with its layer of newer respectability to operate out of: Richard Boston, Jonathan Raban, Craig Raine, Simon Gray, Al Alvarez. As Michael Hofmann observed in last week's *New Statesman*, 'few under the age of thirty-eight will think of Ian Hamilton, the reviewer and television bookman, the self-effacing biographer of Lowell, Salinger's injuncted ghost-buster, as a poet.' Yet the reading he gave recently to launch his collected works, *Fifty Poems* (Faber), or 'perms' as he would say, suggested that his kind of high-intensity lyric might prove salutary in these back-of-the-Cornflakes-packet days.

Far from relaxing his minimalist grip in the intervening years, Hamilton has actually trimmed several of the poems still further: the ten-line 'Windfalls' (1964) now presents only its initial four-line fly metaphor, moving it, strangely, away from neurosis and towards the apocalyptic. 'The Recruits', from the same period, loses three of its twelve lines, among them the once-admired but now no-longer-quite-possible 'At the trees, loafing in queues, their leaves rigid; / At the flowers, edgy, poised'. How one had strained to get that 'loafing in queues' sort of thing into one's work. Now it's lopped forever.

I worked at Hamilton's *New Review* in the mid-1970s, through that wonderfully seedy doorway in Greek Street long since obliterated by the new twittification of Soho. I started as Arts Editor and ended up as motorcycle messenger, my preferred role. (I later went professional.) Ian wanted the best and it had not been easy trying to get through to, say, Tom Stoppard to ask him to be our theatre critic for what amounted to babysitting money.

Two years after the *New Review* finally gave in to the recession in 1978, the Comic Strip started up on the other side of Soho in the Boulevard Theatre of Raymond's Revuebar. Odd to think of them as part of the same period, but perhaps they were on either side of a cusp. In 1981 Hamilton wrote a piece in the *London Review of*

Books about these bad new boys in which he speculated on their future – and, incidentally, on that of Soho itself: 'It is hard to see how The Comic Strip can "make it" without cleaning up and thinning out their best material. Already they are moving into the area of "alternative success". It need hardly be said that television will try to turn Alexei Sayle into Les Dawson.'

As we watch our repeats of *The Comic Strip Presents*, this may seem prophetic, but even Hamilton could not have guessed that seven years later leading Comic Stripper Rik Mayall, along with coevals Stephen Fry and John Sessions, would be appearing in the West End production of *The Common Pursuit*, the play Simon Gray wrote (and has re-written) about Hamilton and his set. It is currently previewing just outside Soho at the Phoenix.

Lunch with Alan Ross at the *London Magazine*, where I worked even longer ago. After eighteen years he has still not replaced me, so I sit down at my old desk and wait for him to finish work. He now runs single-handedly the operation he started twenty-seven years ago. He turns round manuscripts at the door, for which their owners are pathetically grateful.

This morning Alan has had returned as unsatisfactory a copy of *The Loiners* by Tony Harrison. The woman writes: 'For some unknown reason, whether it is due to conditions of storage, the print, colouring etc, I have done nothing but sneeze violently since I opened it. I tested this as I was out of the house this afternoon, but as soon as I returned and picked up the book I started sneezing again. Strange, I know, but there it is. I trust you will forgive my returning the book.'

One has heard of 'the sneeze in the loins' – maybe sneezing at *The Loiners* is the literary equivalent, brought on by reading, say, number X of Harrison's 'From The Zeg Zeg Postcards':

> Oooh aggghhh
> Oooh aggghhh
> *Sannu da zuwa*

(NOTE: *Sannu da zuwa*: Hausa = 'Greetings on your coming'.)

[8.4.88]

Rhyme, Reason and Arts Council Bursaries

Saturday. The Grand National. I find it impossible to choose between *The Times* and the *Telegraph*, let alone pick a winner at Aintree. Rhyme 'n' Reason seems to be the sort of thing my life is lacking in, so I give it my backing to the tune of £1 each way.

Can't they afford a starting gate? The horses won't line up properly and get off to a very unfair start, with R&R well back and not mentioned at all for the first five minutes, so to hell with it. I am in the kitchen sulking when I hear his name for the first time. The poor chap has fallen over and got back up again, bless him. I didn't know they could do that. He must have got that badge saying 'Falling over gets you accepted' because he and I never look back. He takes a bit of a beating towards the end – the recommended ten strokes being well and truly exceeded – but it's worth it from my point of view because I win £15 and have my faith in animal nature restored.

Tuesday 11 a.m. I attend the Arts Council meeting to announce the winners of this year's Poetry Bursaries and its plans for literature. I'm sitting between Pete Morgan and Fleur Adcock, who are among the short-listed, the others being Dannie Abse, Ken Smith, Carole Satyamurti, Tony Flynn and Michael Donaghy. We talk about survival. Pete practically lives off his vegetable plot in N. Yorks. Fleur spends more and more time in her north London garden, but fears the lead from exhaust fumes getting into her lettuces, although the blackberries can probably be washed. She lights a cigarette with her usual amused defiance, as she may well do with £5,000 in the balance.

Outlining the Arts Council's plans for the future, the new Literature Director, Dr Alastair Niven, late of the Africa Centre, says the highest priority will be given to encouraging children to take more interest in books, which can't be bad. A £15,000 Translation Fund has been set up with special emphasis on works in East European, Scandinavian and Asian languages. There are also the

Arts Council Allen Lane Foundation Literary Dialogues, to be funded by the ALF to the tune of £6,000, in which two literary figures will discuss something important in public. (A catchier title is being sought.)

Niven has appointed Brenda Layton, manager of The Other Branch Bookshop in Leamington Spa and a part-time research student in race and ethnic studies at the University of Warwick, to write a report on black literary presses currently operating in England: a growth industry if review copies of poetry are anything to go by. 'We believe that some of the best writing in English is happening abroad', says Mr Niven. He sounds a keynote for the coming year in his closing squib: whether the Arts Council's new plans are fresh air or hot air, he knows from his experiences in the tropics that rich and exotic fruits grow in hot air. No budding Philip Larkins being looked for just now then?

It is time to check the runners in the Great Bursary stakes. All the finalists were of equal merit, we are told, so personal need was the deciding factor. (When pressed, one judge felt unable to describe how personal need had been judged, except to say that it had been related to future projects.) The lucky three are Ken Smith and the two ladies, all of whom think it is a bit tough on the others, going home hungry after three weeks of tenterhooks, even if they are able to put 'Arts Council Short-listed' on their CV's – an ambiguous privilege perhaps.

The thinking seems to have been that the prestige of Arts Council short-listing is a form of compensation in itself and the tension generated might well have drummed up some press interest for them. I can't help feeling that their method has transferred 'personal need' from the winners to the losers. Next time they might set aside the odd thousand for the runners-up. But then, as Niven says, 'We're strapped for cash.'

All this is probably sour grapes: I felt a bloody fool sitting there as your panting paparazzo when I could have entered the race myself. After all, if Rhyme 'n' Reason could get up off his arse . . .

[22.4.88]

14

Five Go to Israel

Sunday, 24 April. Off to Israel with Blake Morrison, Wendy Cope, Michael Hofmann and Craig Raine, guests of the Friends of Israel Trust. As soon as the juddering jumbo's 'Don't Worry' sign pings on Craig gets out his walkman in order to die listening to his opera *The Electrification of the Soviet Union*: agony before, during and after the Russian Revolution, according to Wendy, who mollifies her own death pangs with Marzene and A. E. Housman. She has on a personal inflatable neck-pillow, like a goitre, which she wears about the place with a slightly silly smile.

Tel Aviv is a Bauhaus town in the sense that Tommy Steele is a rock 'n' roll singer. It's the Chinese whispers version. My 1963 and 1972 memories of the place are blurred by shopping malls and materialism.

Monday. Meet our guide Amnon Ahi-Nomi, a highly anecdotal ex-radio personality, a sort of chain-smoking lay Rabbi for Israel. He takes us for a walk on the Dizengoff and the first thing I notice is that the uniforms have changed: a more serious ugly khaki now, guns over shoulder like handbags. No one holding hands any more. 'The crime rate here is the same as Switzerland', says Amnon. 'The army is very easy to stay out of, but there are many in detention centres because they refuse to serve in the occupied territories.' He shows us an embarrassing new fountain like a multi-coloured humming top, which belches flames and plays Ravel's *Bolero*. Red flags are out for the First of May in this socialist country, as later we shall see black ones for the Palestinians' 'Twelve Days of Anger'.

Dinner with Israeli poets. Natan Zach, a major lyric poet and friend of Lowell and Davie from his days at Essex, has withdrawn from the Chairmanship of next month's International Literary Festival to mark the 40th anniversary of Israel, in protest against the Army's treatment of Palestinians. The reprisals after they themselves shot an Israeli schoolgirl were the last straw. Günter Grass has also withdrawn. 'This is no time for festivals in Israel', wrote Zach, and had his front door smeared with excrement.

Tuesday. Craig steps out of the hotel and treads on a small bird, but we tell him not to worry as it was almost dead anyway. Off to the Negev in the limo, we practise spotting Carmels, the fibreglass Israeli car, now defunct. We see one being eaten by a camel. I think the catch-phrase for the tour is going to be 'All this used to be desert out here': a familiar chorus.

We visit the hilltop Negev Monument to the war of 1948, a vast, pee-smelling abstract adventure playground with war lessons inscribed for the kids. At the Yad Mordecai kibbutz we see the open-air reconstruction (with recordings) of how in 1948 settlers held off the advancing Egyptian tanks with one machine-gun and assorted foreign rifles, buying six invaluable days for Tel Aviv with fifty of their lives. More heroic Jewish survival – from the Romans this time – in the first century Hazan Caverns. We creep and wriggle through the passageways to see the oil-press and wells where they hid. Wendy eagerly declines.

Reading in Tel Aviv with Hebrew and English-language poets. Wendy's poems aren't funny in Hebrew apparently, but a Miss Herman tells us she presented forty-five poems in praise of England to Mrs Thatcher, who cried.

Wednesday. Calamaris and rosé at Abu Christie's beside the port at Acre, gunfire across the bay, kids snorkelling at our feet. We visit the underground Crusaders' City, discovered in 1947 by an Israeli terrorist who fell through into the massive Knight's Chamber while trying to escape from a British prison built on top of it. 'So that was the first time the fleur de lys was used, I wish my flash was working', says Wendy. Amnon explains that the Arabs tend to think of Zionists like the Crusaders, 'They'll stay for a bit, then we'll push them back.' Bearded Craig buys an Arab headscarf and turns into Mustapha out of *Tintin*. 'Craig, when did you have your charisma bypass operation?' Amnon advises him to take it off for the kibbutz where we are due to read tonight.

[13.5.88]

Mudlarks

27 April. Wednesday. This is the life, rolling along in a limo with four friends, Craig and Blake and Hofmann and Wendy Cope, our only worry who gets to sit next to the patched window, smashed last week in Nazareth, we are told, by a Palestinian stone. 'Are we going to Nazareth, Amnon?' 'Don't worry, Hugo', says our trusty guide. Some confusion from Craig between the West Bank, the Left Bank and the South Bank, but as long as Melvyn's in charge we should be all right.

As we approach the lush surroundings of Kibbutz Kfar HaNasi, where we have come to read poetry, it is easy to understand why the average Israeli factory worker – probably oriental – resents the comparative luxury of the kibbutzim, which are almost exclusively European (in this case British). Although it is apparently poor, a concert hall is being built there – by Arab labour. I suggest, unkindly, that the true division in Israel is between Orientals and Europeans, not Arabs and Jews, which unleashes a storm of justified protest from dear Amnon.

On arrival we are allotted a host and within minutes I am drinking lemon tea with a family from Sheffield who after fifteen years seem rather depressed by it all. Having no money, they cannot visit England unless someone sends them a ticket, although there is a travel grant for the young. 'Life deteriorated when they allowed TVs into the place, then telephones. We used to sit on the lawn after work and talk excitedly, now people just phone each other. At least we aren't allowed videos.' They have got a new hammock, but only one hook.

The reading is poorly attended, mostly old-timers who cannot hear and miss the declamatory style. Craig gives me the giggles badly when I read a highly inappropriate (but detailed) poem about flared trousers. It serves me right when an English teacher asks whether with free verse it is the editor who puts in the line-breaks. I say only with Michael Hofmann's poems.

We repair to our shared cabins and spend a hot sleepless night raided by mosquitoes and amorous cats, haunted by distant explosions on the Golan Heights. Blake and Craig sit up drinking whisky and smashing the adjoining wall. Michael puts his head under the pillow.

Thursday. We leave the kibbutz for our next engagement in Jerusalem. After the Mount of Temptation Restaurant where we buy Dead Sea Moisturizer Cream, some of our heads are banging as the big old Mercedes swerves and the *Hamsin* blows like a hair-dryer on hot. We check into the kosher Windmill Hotel in Jerusalem and rebuild our spines in long baths. At the reading later the Jewish poets are full of agony and ecstasy. We must seem very cool with our little images and jokes.

Friday. The Holocaust Museum. 'We see the Holocaust and the birth of Israel as *one* story', says Amnon, who insists, unlike most guides, on showing us round the horrors, albeit with tears in his eyes. The exhibits begin with a suitcase, banjo and lampshade made out of Torah scrolls. The later human-skin lampshades speak for themselves by their absence.

Saturday. Masada and the Dead Sea. Amnon says Lot's wife was the only woman to reach salinity before she reached senility. He explains the three Jewish complexes: Zionism, the Holocaust and Massada, the last being that it must never happen again that self-destruction is the only way out. The last time I came here they were still taking recruits up onto the plateau to swear the oath of allegiance. Michael wants to run up the path instead of taking the cable-car, but we always discourage his youthfulness.

Before going into the Dead Sea we daub each other all over with the black mud recommended by the Queen of Sheba. I wallow out to an explosion-shaped salt-tree and climb on to it. On top is an old copy of the *Daily Mirror*. Everyone in cracking form as we cruise home to Jerusalem. 'Look at that trampoline', said someone, and with so much poetry about I was quite surprised to turn round and see an actual trampoline.

[20.5.88]

This is Your Life

My brother looked very handsome in his dark green frock coat when he worked at Fortnum and Mason in the 1960s – a pre-figuring of his part as Captain James Bellamy in the Edwardian saga *Upstairs, Downstairs*, although on the other side of the master/servant divide. He was let off lightly by the floor manager when he sold someone a dummy pot of caviar, but he had to leave within ten minutes when he told a rich account customer, 'We say "please" and "thank-you" when we're asking someone for something.'

Meeting a friend there for tea nearly thirty years later, he was surprised to see fellow actors Nigel Havers, Gareth Hunt, Ian Ogilvy and Colin Baker (Dr Who) all working there, humping hampers and wearing the Fortnum's uniform. Surely they weren't all resting? He turned a convincing shade of pale when a shadowy figure stepped forward and spoke those worrying words, 'Simon Williams, This Is Your Life . . .'. Personally, I had my doubts about the look of bashful amazement on his face.

Anyone who has ever had anything to do with the programme will know that the only person who isn't deeply involved with it for months is the 'subject' himself. There's plenty of money about, and plenty of researchers paid to go to the ends of the earth and hang on your every word. I told mine I thought I had a piece of old vinyl torn off the kitchen table of the house we'd all grown up in, and she waited happily for half an hour while I failed to find it. Nothing is too much trouble, but of course it is our silence they are really asking for.

I did consider telling him. After all, what are brothers for? Mightn't he want to get a haircut, change his socks, put his affairs in order? In the end I thought it would be more of a worry pretending not to know. He himself only wondered why he hadn't heard from any of his friends recently. It was as if he'd died in order to become the guest of honour at his own memorial service.

At the run-through the day before, my mother, flown in from

Portugal for the occasion and stashed in a safe-house out of the way of the children (who can't be told), couldn't resist mentioning the name of Danny Blanchflower. There was an appalled hush from the dedicated workers at the memory of the only subject in thirty years to have told them to stuff it, sending months of teamwork up in smoke and leaving his nearest and dearest, childhood sweethearts, service pals, mortal enemies, everyone, waiting expectantly back-stage – not to mention a studio audience of 800. There was nervous amusement round the conference table and polite requests for us all to leave our scripts behind until tomorrow.

For the show is indeed scripted, right down to the last comma and camera angle. Your fumbled family anecdotes are compared, rationalized, condensed, and then skilfully incorporated into a half-hour comedy show by writer Roy Bottomley. Later, you get to learn his version of events by heart. I'd always wondered why guests seemed to know the presenter personally. This is because their scripted fondnesses, prefaced by 'ENTER, GREET & SIT' (for family) or 'ENTER, GREET & STAND' (for celebrities) invari-ably start off, 'Well, Michael, I first met Jimmy . . .' etc. When I received my script I didn't at first recognize my story of a black leather Cisco Kid outfit and real horses, because the game had been imaginary. After some word bargaining and a promise to end on the same cue-word, the story was rewritten by Roy, the page retyped and restapled into the thirty-page script. Likewise, my mother said she couldn't call my brother her 'tiny little darling' just because he was two months premature. She'd rather say he'd ruined her Ascot. Fair enough. Home in chauffeured cars to get our beauty sleep.

Next day, the cars picked everyone up again and ferried us all to the studio, where there was much waiting, everyone walking about repeating their lines and swigging hospitality. Did I want some powder on that spot? Was I wearing that jacket? Never mind, it wouldn't show up on camera. Meanwhile, my brother was being surprised in Fortnum and Mason. Men with walkie-talkies were alerting the people in the studio to his approach. It was time to gather in the wings.

On a tight row of camp-stools sat Jean Marsh, David Langdon and Nicola Pagett from *Upstairs, Downstairs*, Maureen Lipman from *Agony*, Andrew Birkin and Hayley Mills from my brother's childhood. In the distance we could hear the warm-up man teaching the studio audience to laugh and clap. They would soon know all too well, because we were having a technical hitch.

Wine was served in the wings and people started going to the lavatory again. The children were delighted and kept saying 'Look, the screen's gone green, it's gremlins.' The dogs didn't like it and my mother, perched on her stool, wished they would get on with it. Her adrenalin was peaking. 'I don't think he's famous enough to be on *This Is Your Life*, do you?' said his son Tamlyn.

All this time my brother was being kept talking in the star dressing room. They don't like to give their subject time to think what might be about to hit him, and take a childlike pleasure in causing maximum shock. Ten minutes is normal. But we had to wait over an hour. Finally, I heard my pre-recorded voice saying 'Hey, Pancho! Fetch de horses!' and the presenter saying: 'The Cisco Kid of years ago, of course your brother.' I entered, greeted and embraced, muttering as I did so, 'You knew, you cunt', which was picked up on his lapel-mike. It was suppressed by the mixing board but is still just audible on the video. I did my piece all right, but it's a moment no one can fail at because the audience isn't allowed to stop clapping until you sit down.

Most memorable for me was Andrew Birkin, director of *The Cement Garden*, who had lent an 8mm film he made with my brother when they were teenagers, my brother's fee being a love-scene with Andrew's sister Jane. We saw a summer-hazed clip of a kiss in a boat on a lake, then the present-day Jane speaking from Paris, remembering those 'precious last days of childhood'. Yes, the past is another country.

[30.12.94]

21

British Year at Sarajevo

On the plane to the Sarajevo Literary Festival with a bunch of British poets I sit next to a beautiful American girl who is studying modern British poetry in London. Perhaps she has heard of Douglas Dunn or Peter Porter? David Harsent? Christopher Reid? Kim hasn't heard of any of us. I feel it is my duty to set her straight once and for all about the Plath/Hughes thing she is mostly interested in.

Sarajevo – the town that grew up round a gunshot. Our cavalcade passes the spot where Princip shot the archduke – his footprints in the sidewalk like a film star's. Hotel Europe. Collapse of poetic bonhomie as it gradually emerges that three rooms have been booked for the five of us. Inward groans and outward smiles until it is decided that the conference of Eastern Bloc economists are better suited to doubling up. (Yugoslavia has an inflation rate of 180 per cent. Unemployment is about a third.)

Tuesday. At breakfast a terrifying Titoesque waitress shouts at me because I do not want coffee *or* tea, only juice. She punishes me by bringing a roll with no butter *or* jam. A press conference at the Writers' Union. A big smoke-filled room with not a few glum local poets round the edge. One of the Russian visitors is a 'semeye-dissident' with a bad limp; his compatriot and minder a rotund and oratorical State Poet with arm gestures and wild protestations of good will. I breathe the fragrant breath of Dijana as she whispers her translation. In between poets I get to my feet and am horrified to find my move interpreted as a desire for utterance. I hear my name and country being announced as I scurry for the loo: a first black mark for Britain. The Bosnian poetry reading. Peter Porter gallantly volunteers to represent us, his theory being that if you don't understand what they're saying you don't have to listen. He is more experienced at this kind of thing than us: a Commonwealth Studies veteran.

Wednesday. Breakfast. Tito cuffs me round the ear and brings me a dry roll. 'Today you are basically free', says Mario Susko, our translator and guide. We scour the Old Town for trinkets (not cheap). In the evening the Contemporary British Poetry Reading is introduced in Serbo-Croatian by our Ambassador. All I catch is 'There was a young lady from Bude / Who ran down the street in the nude'. I hold my breath for 'A policeman said what'm / Magnificent bottom / And smacked it as hard as he cude', but the Ambassador restrains himself. During Douglas Dunn's 'Troubles' poem a very bad Polish poet who looks like Oliver Hardy walks out of the room with his friend. 'Another fine reading you've got me into!' At which David Harsent offers our host country a strong little lesson in manners through our smiling interpreter. The sound crew drown everything with a long-running slapstick routine which climaxes in the downfall of an aspidistra.

Thursday. Breakfast. Christopher Reid has the idea of ordering coffee *and not drinking it*! All is forgiven. Butter and jam galore. A reading at the University, nearly all girls, who laugh and cry at all the right places and would be nice to meet afterwards. To our surprise they all file out of one door while we go through another for coffee and politesse with the (all male) Faculty.

Twenty or so big fat poets on a tiny stage for the International Reading, which promises to be a bummer. Slender Chris our volunteer representative. Oliver Hardy and the State Poet flail the air once more. 'I am just going outside and may be some time,' says Douglas. A sit-down banquet with speeches, embracing and leather presentation folders. I somehow manage not to kiss the president of the Writers' Union on the lips and score another bad mark for Britain. Since it is British Year there is considerable translated pressure on us to do something *heart-warming* for once. I have a strong feeling that bad behaviour is about to be extracted from us by force, but even Douglas doesn't know any songs. I suggest 'God Save the Queen'; instead, he invents an old Scotch toast, 'Whisky and Freedom!', which seems to get us off the hook.

[10.6.88]

23

Old Etonian Anxieties

Terribly keyed-up and over-excited finally to be asked to go down and read for no money to the Eton College Praed Society. At dinner beforehand I even get a chance to prove to the young gentlemen how much I know about rock 'n' roll – and I think I am right in saying that they were impressed. Yes, over there, in 1956, the Bardotesque Miss Sullivan introduced Etonians to Elvis Presley. I'll be reading my poem about that later. As it turned out, I read my poem about that and so many other aspects of misplaced adolescent nostalgia that I had to be stopped and thanked. 'We very much appreciate your generosity in giving us so much of your time, Mr Williams, but some of the boys have to be back in their houses by lock-up, which is at ten.' It seemed I had missed the last train from Windsor and had to be driven all the way to Slough, where I waited nearly all night for the milk train.

The Eton poetry society is named after the much-patronized Winthrop Mackworth Praed because the more prestigious Shelley was sacked for atheism. Personally I prefer Praed, 'that inquisitive man with a notebook' as someone remembered him, 'ever open to furnish contributions to the inevitable album that every fair one cherished in those days'. One of the best poems I know about the passing of youth is his 'School and Schoolfellows' – 'That I could be a boy again, / A happy boy at Drury's' – a piece as rich in period feeling as anything by his fan John Betjeman.

A hundred-year-old photograph of Drury's, Praed's old house, covered in snow – 'a rambling place that stood empty and unwanted for years until it was eventually replaced by the School Library' – turns up in Danny Danziger's collection of Old Etonian rumi-nations, *Eton Voices*. It makes me feel old, but not as old as Nicky Haslam, who regrets not having been taught how not to age fast at school. 'Until ten years ago the English hadn't any idea how to wash their hair! They just didn't do it and people got bald by the time they left school.' I remember being sent on a boy-call to Haslam's room in about 1956 and while I was waiting for an answer and boggling at the ostrich plumes and ocelot curtains, the clock chimed for school and Nicky dabbed his hairbrush in a box of chalk dust to give his hair just that distinguished air he now dreads. 'I see people I went to school with and they look like Harold Macmillan – practically crumbling to bits with grandchildren. It's too, too frightening.'

It is interesting to note who the icons were then. 'Cool was the thing', says Mark Heathcoat Amory. 'Glen Kidston had this gaunt white face and always dressed in black and he was very cool and didn't say much. "There you go" was his phrase. "There you go, man." ' Strangely, Lord Gowrie produces identical admirations: 'Guy [sic] Kidston was cool, to the point of not being wholly there a lot of the time.' He mentions another rebel OE, the writer and magician Heathcote Williams: 'He was rebellious and difficult and he has remained a sort of alternative writer, with a certain kind of Etonian charm which shimmers over the surface of the prose.'

Williams's latest production, *Whale Nation* (Cape), is mostly free from shimmering Etonian charm, being a long poem and documentation on the subject of whale genocide. Unlike Kingsley Amis, who once said he thought turning whales into soap sounded like 'quite a good way of using them up', Williams is passionate, if late, in their defence. 'The poem is overwhelming', writes Ted Hughes, 'brilliant, cunning, dramatic and wonderfully moving, a steady accumulation of grandeur and dreadfulness.' There is accumulation here all right, and piles of glossy colour pictures and research, but any poetry (or humour) is inhibited by Williams's relentless decent-mindedness, aimed presumably at Kingsley Amis. Or am I just jaded? I remember meeting him in some high-jump semi-final thirty years ago (a name confusion). We meet again in the lists of the Stratford Poetry Festival next month. I wonder will he jump higher than me again, make me disappear, or just kill me with a look? I'll let you know.

[15.6.88]

What the Dickens

Author's proof. Some pencil notes. Original wrapper. Partly unopened. Small spindle hole in corner. Such are the erogenous zones of the love objects in a bibliophile's anxious, humid world. At Sotheby's recent auction of English Literature and History a silver dish engraved with Charles Dickens's initials went for twice its estimate of £500 because the great man had himself broken one of the handles. His ivory-handled folding picnic spoon and fork, the first incorporating a corkscrew, both with his crest and initials, together with an autographed certificate by his sister-in-law – ' "I certify that this ivory picnic spoon and fork was always used by Charles Dickens when travelling and from the time he went to live at Gads Hill until his death and that it has since been in my possession and used by me". Signed, Georgina Hogarth' – went for £1,250. Ah, but where's the certificate authenticating Georgina Hogarth? And what happened to the knife? Perhaps Charles threw it at Georgina?

Anxiety to possess such items must stand in inverse ratio to an enthusiast's self-respect. If, for example, I could lay my hands on that malacca cane of Somerset Maugham's perhaps I too might become interesting in some way that cannot be taken away from me, until, that is, they take the cane away.

Does an item's value at auction constitute an index of its owner's literary standing? Half a film script of *The Naked Lunch*, along with various home movies of Burroughs' work by friends, was sold for a staggering £5,500 by one Genesis P. Orridge, who nevertheless had been hoping for £20,000. A first edition of what the catalogue called *Finnegan's Wake*, signed by the author – and with its pages suitably uncut – also failed to live up to expectations (£1,100 on £2,000). The star of the show, 'An important archive and working library of Lawrence Durrell', including many unpublished works, some jointly written with Henry Miller, was 'expected to prove something of a literary event', but didn't. When the daunting bundles came on the stand, £80,000 proved too sanguine an estimate for the listless

Sotheby's regulars, whose cautious £20,000 had caught wind of the wordy pair's waning readability ratings.

Puerility (or general interest) would seem to be at a premium in the scavenger's po-faced profession. What we like are indiscretions, lapses of taste, details of gross bodily inadequacy. What we get are excuses. Dickens had at least four on sale at Sotheby's last week, all of which sold over the odds. His 'pressure is so great on Fridays . . . it is quite out of my power' had a peculiarly contemporary feel, I thought, and might be useful to quote at some future date. One could less plausibly re-employ James I's all too human 'exhausted by the accidents of forreine warres, and inwarde rebellions', but Oscar Wilde's strangely credible stroke of having to take his folks to a fancy dress ball is definitely one for the book. If one were petitioning A. E. Houseman one would feel no pain at all at his elegant 'While I was at University College I was in a measure compelled to read things to the Literary Society now and then; but I am escaped even as a bird out of the snare of the fowler, and shall never do it again.'

When an excuse of our own is called for it is tempting not to miss the opportunity for some veiled impertinence. Gandhi's absurd vow of silence was the perfect pious put-off: 'The silence on Mondays is a blessing which I prize even though at times it seems to be inconvenient.' Is there any reason why our own silent day should not be a floating one? Evelyn Waugh's knee-jerk 'Alas, impossible' has just the right note of needling hyperbole. Robert Graves, referring to his biography of T. E. Lawrence, dazzles us with logic: 'All I write I am sending out to him to blue pencil so I can't spare the time to visit you.'

If anyone is considering a career as a weekend painter, historian or PM he should take care, like Winston Churchill, to leave behind him when he dies a sketch of a pig, done blindfold, while drunk. It went for over a thousand.

[29.7.88]

A Festival Too Far

Off again to attend a literary festival, at Budva, a holiday resort in Montenegro. Would I mind getting my air ticket in London? They'll pay me back in sterling when I get there.

No reference is made to this arrangement on the long drive from Dubrovnik to Budva, but the poet-organizer Radomir Ujarevic is a bearded charmer who recites poetry while he drives and says he will make me famous in Yugoslavia. He gives me a pass for demi-pension in the government's Hotel Splendid. Later, my presence on Radio Budva is announced with 'Colonel Bogie'.

Day Two. The 'Poetry Square' is like an open-air room, with raked seating occupied by passing holiday-makers. Tonight's poet is Branca Lucak. He sits for long moments under stifling spotlights, inspected by several hundred docile eyes. He riffles some papers in a relaxed manner and says he has five books at home, which he was unable to bring along with him today, but he will read from these pieces of paper he has with him, if he can just find them. I am so pleased this sort of thing goes on in Yugoslavia as well as at The Poetry Society. I think of the bafflement and violence such open exhibition of poetry would cause in one of our own seaside resorts. But philistinism is not a problem here. The promenades are lined with bookstalls selling Milan Kundera, Henry Miller, Charles Bukovski, Erica Jong and Dzordz Orvel.

A film crew from Titograd gradually destroy's Lucak's long poem about 'Stalinka', a girl named for the former politician, then dismantles early during his poem about Zola Budd, a popular figure here. Radomir appears. He says he has got the dinars for my fare, hundreds of thousands of them, but cannot find enough pounds in Budva. He'll keep looking. When am I leaving exactly?

Day Three. The outing to Sveti Stefan (Sweaty Stephen) – the island village which was destroyed in the 1979 earthquake and has since been reconstituted as a sterile four-star hotel-village. Clients include the young Titos, who do nothing for their floundering country but squabble over property. The beach is 'Reserved for the use of Hotel Guests Only' – a fact our communist guide seems curiously proud of. Her mother, who has a law degree, makes £80 a month working five and a half days a week. (Someone else tells me this is an average wage.) She thinks there will soon be civil war between the Serbs, who speak Serbo-Croatian, and the Croats, who speak Croato-Serbian. No sign of Radomir.

Day Four. I meet the Russian poet Vyacheslav Kuprianov and make so bold as to pass on a joke I have heard. Why is the Montenegran always late for work? Because he has to transfer all his medals from his pyjamas to his overcoat. Vyacheslav is brave about this. He doesn't twitch a muscle. Instead, he hands me a large, rough bundle of translations of his poems, one of which is called 'How to Become a Penguin'.

My own reading later is tightly organized and chaotic. People go on talking to me right up to the last minute so I am nothing like ready. Where is the lavatory? A tiny picture of a man's shoe turns out to have been a tiny picture of a woman's shoe. Why is it that all over the world lavatory seats won't stay up?

Just before I go on I am introduced to Nina, Radomir's girlfriend, the most beautiful woman I have ever seen, on or off the screen, and told she will be introducing me, interpreting my comments and reading the translations, one of which is about a girl peeing on my face. I myself am to read only the first verse of each poem, as no one will understand them. This is unforeseen and causes me to wither inwardly. I can't look at her. I can't look anywhere. I seem to ask her if she has ever met me before, as if I might not remember this. Everything is ugly. My poems, which are not like Yugoslav poems, are prosy, offhand and flat. And that is how she reads them, with a casual, dismissive air and the occasional toss of her gorgeous hair. She is certainly winking at people.

After the reading, Radomir says will it be all right if he gives me my air fare in Deutschmarks.

[9.9.88]

Fred Green's Red Biro

I first met Fred Green at the Mary Ward Poetry Group in Queen Square, where his poems were considered too old-fashioned by the organizer and he was not invited to become a member. I got a letter from him recently saying he was seeking a Poetry Editor to 'collate and edit' his MSS prior to publication. Would I be interested? I agreed to take a look, but could see at a glance that his careful Copyright Registration Numbers, patient mailings to major publishers, optimistic waits while they 'took their time deciding' were all a waste of time in the face of poems that denied the existence of the twentieth century. From over a hundred Housmanesque items I selected eighteen or so and advised him to go for some sort of pamphlet publication. We met in Soho so that a drink or two could mollify this advice.

Fred Green is a neat, close-cropped, grey-haired man of fifty-six. He was wearing a blue windbreaker, striped tie and grey trousers. Cycle clips would have completed the picture of a gentle, rather pre-war character, who currently earns his living working in a hospital in Streatham. His father was a journalist on *Reveille* before the war, he told me. 'Inspirational stuff for the troops. "Straight Shooting by Tommy Gunn", that was him.' Ex-marine Jimmy Green also wrote leaflets for Oswald Mosley, until he was arrested and taken in for questioning. Fred had been happy at elementary school, where they chanted poems and made leaf collections, but afterwards the competition was too much. 'I didn't have the same relationship with life. I was interested in Gilbert and Sullivan.'

He left school early and worked briefly as a messenger for the Westminster Bank. National Service in Rhodesia was followed by a trip to Canada. 'I got my contacts through the Church of England Council for Resettlement, who put me in touch with the Port Chaplain of Montreal. I started to write poetry when I heard a report about an execution which was about to take place.'

Fred decided to go to New York for two years before going home.

He stayed ten, got married, joined a poetry group which met on a deserted pier of the East River, got divorced and by 1972 was back in England working on trade magazines, 'writing news and features in the food field.' In 1982 he took voluntary redundancy and since then has spent 'more time looking for work than doing it – temp work mainly and concentrating on sending out poems.'

He had some accepted by *Dowry* and *Wayfarers*, but mostly the news was bad. 'When *Envoi* send you a rejection slip,' he told me, 'it's always a sensible one. They work on a unanimity principle. They seem to vote on them. If you send them five poems you get a rejection slip from five different editors, which I think is very complimentary. I had a very good rejection slip from the *New Hampshire Sunday Times* once, which I kept, "These poems are too serious for our readers". A rejection slip should help you to go on, change and grow. I don't keep rejection slips if they say something blasé like "Sorry" or "Regrets". I got one once which just had a rubber stamp with the word "Wow!". You don't know what he means. Stamped right on the poems.'

Nowadays Fred rides down to Brighton on his Honda to write poetry in the Library above the Museum. 'I have a code. I use a red pen and a green pen and I use these for getting the lines right and the emphasis right. I underline them with a ruler and that helps me when I come to switch them around.' He also makes weekly visits to Oxford to the Old Fire Station Workshop, started by Andrew Motion. 'As a result of going there I totally re-wrote a villanelle using the coloured pen method, totally altering the line sequence and the title.'

His ambition is to get all his poems published in a book, to be called simply *Poems*. 'You see something called "Pink Sails" and there's nothing whatever inside about "pink sails". I feel cheated. In a play or a book you're bound eventually to come across a *reason* for the titles, like *The Old Man and the Sea*, for instance: supposing he wasn't there?'

Fred's spirits were by no means dampened by my critical wet blanket. His next poem, he said, was going to be about a cattle market. He'd written to the *Farmers' Weekly* and they'd sent him a photocopied list of all the towns where they still have cattle markets. 'I'm going to check out the terminology. You've got the terminology, you've got the cries and you've got the smells. If I can get all that in I've got the makings of a really good poem . . .'

I last saw Fred Green walking jauntily off down Greek Street, his bulky MSS, heavily blue-pencilled by me, clutched firmly under his arm. I wondered if my own step would be as jaunty if someone had just put a blue pencil through most of my life's work. I hoped it would.

[30.9.88]

A Walk through *The Waste Land*

Meet outside London Bridge station to go on a centenary 'Walk Through The Waste Land', a tour Eliot himself liked making in his later years, although he would go in Mary Trevelyan's car. Our guide Maire McQueeney has brought along her husband and little daughter to monitor her performance, which is uniformly excellent. I have got my undergraduate daughter with me to explain the references. We reckon about six people will turn up Sunday morning, but Maire, a diminutive New Yorker, is surrounded by thirty or so people only too keen to hand over their modest £3. Of the couples present, one spouse is invariably wide-eyed and willing, while the other looks as though he has been ripped untimely from his lie-in.

We stand on London Bridge, seeing it all anew. Up till 1750 this was the only place you could cross the Thames dry-footed, so Dante would have passed this way on his rumoured trip to Oxford. Eliot's London Bridge (John Rennie, 1830) has gone to Arizona of course, where a lake has been dug under it and red double-deckers take you from nowhere to nowhere, attended by Beefeaters.

On to Magnus the Martyr and the 'inexplicable splendour of Ionian white and gold', which they certainly haven't stinted themselves on. This is just the sort of High Table stuff Eliot would be converted to twenty years later, an Anglo-Catholicism so fruity it might as well be Roman to this visitor. The paving stones outside are all that's left of the approach to the original 'falling down' London Bridge, plus a very old piece of wood under the portico. 'Flowed up the hill and down King William Street' probably refers to seventeenth-century as much as twentieth-century crowds, since the hill in question, Fish St Hill, is opposite the original bridge, not the newer one.

We arrive at St Mary Woolnoth just too late to check the authentic 'dead sound' on the final stroke of eleven. The church is closed at weekends, having 'a weekday ministry', to alleviate the stress in City workers, of whom Eliot should surely be the laureate. Outside Lloyds Bank we peer at the subterranean grille beneath which he toiled from 1917 to 1925. 1922, the year of *The Waste Land*, was a time of massive unemployment in Britain, yet the City, the dead heart of the inferno, went ticking on, a four-dimensional jungle which the poem seeks to imitate (both requiring a guide to get anywhere). Broadcasting had just started and Eliot mimics the disjointed sounds of a distant wireless. 'I could mention that having a two-year-old produces the same effect', says Maire. 'She's even got to the stage of reciting bits of nursery rhymes.' 'So has mine', I moan. 'Ah, but does she do "Tom, Tom, the Piper's son"?'

We have reached Bank by now and have stopped to look at the Royal Exchange. The courtyard was open to the public in Eliot's day and he may well have eaten his sandwiches looking at the first of twenty-four murals to be completed on the subject of ancient commerce, that of two Phoenician sailors, tin traders in Cornwall. Did he remember that Joseph of Aramathea is supposed to have been a tin trader and might have brought his nephew Jesus to these shores? 'And was Jerusalem builded here. . . ?' The courtyard today houses LIFFE, the London International Financial Futures Exchange, ultimate heart of the twenty-four-hour unreal global village, which, according to stipulations laid down by its royal host building, can be deconstructed and removed within forty-eight hours. What a pleasant order that would be to give! Maire says the last maternity unit in the City has just been closed down, enhancing still further the area's unreality.

We are standing at Eliot's tube stop – 'My heart is at Moorgate': a dedication to Keats, whose birth plaque appears above the Moorgate pub. Moorgate was where the Great Fire finally stopped and where people from 13,000 households camped out on the wasteland, waiting to start a new life: the poem's true theme, according to our guide. It is also where our tour comes to an end, allowing us to repair to the nearby Barbican coffee shop for our own regeneration.

[14.10.88]

A 'C' For Creative Writing

Dear Professor Williams, It wasn't until I arrived home two weeks ago that I found you'd given me a 'C' for Creative Writing. This surprised me, for I thought I'd improved a great deal with my song-writing. In addition, the goal with which I started, to open my mind and release the creative energy inside me, has been accomplished. That's why I'm surprised and disappointed that you found my efforts so wasted. My university will not accept anything less than a 'C' [he means a 'B', I think] to give me credit, so unless you consider my songs (the songs of a first-timer) a complete failure, I would greatly appreciate it if you would raise my grade to a pass level. The change can be made by writing to etc. etc.

What to do? My natural sympathy for winners of the wooden spoon award conflicts here with some spurious notion of fair play, not to mention sloth. I usually give everyone a 'B', unless they write a good poem, in which case they get an 'A'. X never opened his mouth and refused to budge an inch on his awful sub-Donovan ditties. He did, however, always turn up, so he got a 'C' for attendance.

Creative writing is big business. The University of Cut-Back has

34

had to acknowledge this strange new discipline in order to pack in those cash customers from overseas. Brand leader East Anglia is about to start a Creative Writing Centre. Even University College London has succumbed, although 'New Writing' is the nearest they can bring themselves to pronouncing the dread phrase. Of the mainstream writing farms, the Arvon Foundation is the best known, but there are other, holistic-type enterprises springing up, which cater for an altogether different bird. The Eden Centre in North Devon offers courses in 'Creative Development' including 'Breathing and Creative Thought', 'Re-Creative Writing' and 'Psychotherapy and Visualisation'. Their 'Right Writing Weekend' uses 'recent findings about the right side of the brain to help develop creativity and "letting go" in writing'. 'Emmy and Joop will welcome you', says the blurb, 'and offer a variety of additional skills, including guided walks, massage, counselling, healing and Bach flower remedies.'

I was booked to take a poetry course with the novelist Margaret Mulvihill on fiction. As the time got nearer, we started getting calls from the organizer warning how few people had signed for it, the final figure being an invigorating nought. Would we care to come down anyway, just to see the place?

Early days at the Arvon, when pairs of students and tutors would wend their way into the woods with blankets under their arms, are remembered with nostalgia by middle-aged hands, but when Margaret and I arrived at The Eden we found various books beside our beds: *Towards Celibacy* by Marion Myers, *The Tyranny of Sex* by Liz Hodgkinson. Creative Writing began in 1963, which was just too late for me.

Last year I stood in for the creative writing tutor at a very different 'Health and Personal Development Centre' in southern Spain, motto: 'There is only one religion, the religion of love. There is only one language, the language of love.' Courses on offer included 'A Course in Ecstasy' by Irene Feigham, 'Celebrating Spring' with Nicky and Davy Ramsy and '7 Days of Unconditional Love' with Angela Winner. Odd man out seemed to be 'The Way of the Warrior' by Leo Rutherford.

35

As soon as I arrived I knew I was there under false pretences. 'We'll spend time in play', said the blurb I inherited, 'using guided imagery, meditation and movement to help free the imaginative flow'. Luckily there was an alternative leader on the premises and I quickly fell in behind him. Every morning before breakfast we did T'ai Chi on the roof: The Archer, The Cloud and The Tortoise. The metaphorical summit of the week was supposed to be the climbing of a mountain, but just before setting out I twisted my ankle. I went half way up, but the unspoken verdict was that this was a metaphor of the level of my commitment to self-discovery. On the last day I did experience a shock of self-knowledge when I found myself holding hands round a very old olive tree. I don't think I can put into words what we were supposed to be doing. Empathizing with the tree? I'm afraid so.

[11.11.88]

Cobham Hall, Kent

I'm going down to read at a girls' school in Kent called Cobham Hall, where I used to live myself in the 1950s. In those days this vast Elizabethan 'H' belonged to the Earl of Darnley, a terrifying figure of about 6' 8", who stalked his crumbling domain in a patchwork smoking jacket, wielding a long-handled weeder like something out of *Struwwelpeter*. My six-year-old brother was the only one who wasn't intimidated. 'Hello, Lord Darnley', he piped when we were caught in the wrong part of the arboretum, 'still as tall as ever?' He was later caught playing doctors with the Earl's daughter, but my mother evened the score by catching the old boy helping himself to our coal. Notes flew back and forth. The Earl was into his third wife by then and evidently broke because the house was stuffed with all manner of distressed gentlefolk, defrocked priests, ex-military types and out-of-work actors like my father. Richard Gordon was scribbling his *Doctor* books. The Earl's son ran a daffodil farm and we kids made money bunching them for him. My mother would drive the lorry to Covent Garden. The whole thing was like a drawing-room comedy – and would eventually become one, written by my parents.

I travel down on the motorbike and arrive three hours early, thinking Cobham is as far away as it was when I was eleven. The house looks the same, but the famous grounds are littered with prefab outhouses. 'Dadd's Hole' is still there in the woods, where the painter Richard Dadd murdered his father, but the chalet where Dickens wrote *Little Dorrit* is gone, removed to Rochester Museum. I sit in the summer house strewn with the girls' cigarette ends and disposable lighters.

One of the girls, Tiffany Langdale, sent me some poems at the *New Statesman*, so I have asked her to take me round. We enter the house through various time-locks, down the 'Matted Corridor' where the Earl's tree-studies used to hang, up the stairs to our humble flat, now called 'Flowers'. My room has gone completely. The vivid chaos of the girls' dormitories easily overcomes my flickering projections of my grandmother with her bag of wine gums and cigarette ends, my father brooding, my godfather appearing dressed as Father Christmas driving the old London taxi he'd bought for us, my mother saying, 'What do you mean there's nothing to do? Get outside and get some air in your lungs.' It was so cold indoors we spent most of our time outside, building houses. Or we would creep into the Gilt Hall, where the huge ornate State Coach sat, and turn the handle of the barrel organ and run for it. 'Do you want to see the Gilt Hall?' says Tiffany. She opens the door ajar and I glimpse several acres of pink flesh twirling balletically.

It is time to report to the Headmistress's Study, once the Earl's drawing-room. We converse in instalments as dinner guests arrive and are brought up to date on my efforts at reminiscence. 'Hugo was just saying that he used to live in Flowers. . . .' Cobham's latest acquisition is the Sultan of Brunei's daughter and yes, she does actually have servants, a cook, a maid and a bodyguard, who live at the Inn on the Lake, once called Laughing Water, where we used to swim. I think of my father walking up the drive to catch the bus to

London to go to auditions for the first time in his life. We were paying £1 a week for our flat.

At the reading, there is a row of long-legged things in the front whose stretched-out legs reach right under my table, making me nervous. I hate it when I have to go into a room full of people and start unpacking and undressing in front of everyone. I needn't have worried. For once I have something concrete to present: Cobham Hall itself, as it used to be. I start by reading out the stage directions for Act 1 of *The Grass is Greener*, the play my father wrote about our time at Cobham, later filmed with Gary Grant and Robert Mitchum: 'The curtain rises on a small charming upstairs sitting-room in the private part of one of the stately homes of England. Through the long windows can be seen the dark branches of a cedar tree. It is early spring.' If it hadn't been night I could have pointed to the very tree.

[28.11.88]

My Brother's First Novel

The thriller is a paranoid art form and one peculiarly suited to actors, particularly those who, like my brother Simon, are driven by a deep-seated fear of unpopularity. As his older brother, I couldn't help reading *Talking Oscars* as an expressionistic autobiography, condensed into one horrifying fortnight in which everything in the world goes wrong for a successful young actor; a story in which I was myself the unacknowledged villain and oppressor, even though the 'Hugo' in the book is the hero's one ally. Supposing, I wondered, this 'Hugo' (a reporter) cracked under the rather unpleasant torture he is submitted to, if indirectly, by the author? What then? Might I revert to type? Might I have written a torture for him?

When I asked my brother about his chosen genre, he said straight away, 'Oh, paranoia's the source of everything isn't it? I suppose it's semi-autobiographical, but if I admit it people say, "Tell me Simon, how long have you been impotent?" '

38

I had thought he was lucky to get a £30,000 advance for a first book, even if he is a household name as Captain James Bellamy of *Upstairs, Downstairs*. I changed my mind when I heard the kind of punishing promotion campaign Heinemann is putting him through. For the past two months he has been racing up and down the country meeting the local press, attending Literary Dinners and doing local radio chat-shows. 'Often you don't know where you are. Green baize tells you it's the BBC, red formica means independent. They're sitting there lining up the next commercial with their finger on the disc and the headphones on, saying "I suppose you're tired of hearing this, but you're probably best known for your part in *Upstairs, Downstairs*. Any amusing anecdotes from those days?" You get about five minutes with Dire Straits in the middle and a bed sale on the end. I spend my time trying to steal back their copy of the book.'

Simon's an old hand at this game from his days promoting the series in America. He walked into a Dallas radio station once and the DJ didn't even look up from his turntable: 'Now Stewart, you're seeded 88th in this year's Open, your critics say your serve is way off target and this time next year you may not even be playing for the state. How'd'you reckon your chances tomorrow?' 'Well, Bob,' said Simon, 'I'm not too worried about my service at the moment because I've been getting into a bit of drama recently. It's been going quite well in fact and we've just been awarded an Emmy for the new series. . . .' The DJ lined up a record, took off his cans and said 'Who the fuck are *you*?'

In England PR people usually accompany their authors on the road to ensure against this kind of thing, but Simon prefers to make his own way, get there early, check into the hotel, then mosey over to the dinner in his own time. Literary Dinners are laid on by local newspapers or bookshops to coincide with a chat-show appearance. Guests pay £10 to hear an author speak and there is a bookstall at the back of the room for after-dinner signings.

Simon might start off a speech with 'The last dinner I did was the Gay Alcoholics Anonymous. It's nice to see so many familiar faces here tonight.' He goes on to relate how he nearly got a part in *Dynasty*. He rings up his old friend Joan Collins who is down with flu and not available. 'Never mind', he says, 'couple of days on her feet and she'll be back in bed in no time.' When he was rehearsing *The Last of Mrs Cheney* with Joan at Chichester a worried director told them both not to worry, 'It'll all make sense when we get to the thrust stage.' If there are any questions about mixing writing with acting he'll work round to 'Roneo Roneo, wherefore art thou, Roneo?' It's terrible stuff, but the most important thing is to make the book sound successful, so my brother apologizes for the fact that the fourth reprint isn't on the bookstalls yet, they can always buy a copy from him afterwards. 'You sign everything in sight', he said, 'that way they can't remainder them.'

[16.12.88]

Pope's Grotto and Sister Mary Michael

Alexander Pope would have been amused to see the dozens of little girls who pour through his beloved grotto every day on their way to music lessons on the other side of the Twickenham / Teddington road. 'Let the young ladies be assured I make nothing new in my gardens without wishing to see the print of their fairy steps in every part of them.'

The grotto was originally planned as a mere tunnel, but grew to become a symbol of all the romance denied to the crippled hunchback in his life. St Catherine's Convent has taken the place of Pope's Palladian villa, but the grotto miraculously survives. It must be one of the more exclusive sights of London. To see it, you have to make an appointment with Sister Mary Michael: 'Ring the bell on the door that says "Pope's Villa" ', she told me when I telephoned. The door was opened by the ancient but lively Sister, who ushered me through the convent and out on to a terrace overlooking the Thames. 'The house next door was bombed during the war', she told me, 'but the bomb spared that willow tree. It's the only offshoot of

Pope's famous willow, which was the first to be brought to England from China.' She threw her hands in the air. 'Excuse me, I've forgotten the torch!'

Pope was already famous when he moved to Twickenham in 1719, aged thirty, a Catholic barred by William III's penal laws from owning property within twelve miles of London. He was besieged with poetesses and poetasters:

> What walls can guard me, or what shade can hide?
> They pierce my thickets, through my grot they glide.
> By land, by water they renew the charge . . .

This was disingenuous of Pope, who preferred the fame of gardener to that of poet and allowed his servants to show his handiwork to anyone who called. It was a habit which would have disastrous consequences, for when Lady Howe bought the villa in 1807 she got so fed up with people knocking on her door that she destroyed all traces of her predecessor, devastated the gardens, stripped the grotto and built another house on the spot, earning for herself the titles 'The Vandal of Twickenham' and 'The Queen of the Goths'. That the grotto exists at all after 250 years of vandalism, encroachment and damp is something of a miracle, enhanced by the amused presence of Sister M., who knows it all too well, having slept there during the war. 'We would bring the blessed sacraments down here to protect them during raids. Bombs went off all round, but we were spared, thanks to Mr Pope.'

The grotto originally had chandeliers and the first glass mirrors to be made in England, at Isleworth. Pope set the place with 'pieces of looking glass in angular forms so that a thousand painted Rays glitter and are reflected all over the Place'. If Pope had been born this century he would surely have been an apostle of camp whose favourite TV programme was *Come Dancing*. 'It was a thing of great beauty then', said Sister M, looking round the dingy remains, as if remembering her youth. 'He used to sit down here and compose his poetry. Oh dear, here's another piece that's coming loose.' As she spoke, a chunk of grotto came away in her hands and was laid respectfully aside. We flatten ourselves against the wall as an avalanche of curls and cries hurtles through. 'And here is old Bounce', she tells me as we emerge past two stone statues of Pope's favourite dog. In thin shoes she conducts me over the wet grass of Pope's garden, now scattered with tennis courts and sheds. 'Do you think this is the original garden wall?' she asked. 'It looks like it to me', I tell her.

At first we cannot find the memorial stone erected by Pope's successor, Lord Stanhope. I take the Sister's hand as she negotiates the bits of broken masonry and branches. At last she finds what she is looking for and tries to decipher the inscription, picking at the moss for all the world as if we were coming upon it for the first time: 'The golden roof, the garden's scanty line. . . .' If anyone wishes to know the rest of what is written on the tablet they will have to make an appointment with Sister Mary Michael, whose spirit inhabits Pope's villa today just as freely as Pope's does her convent.

[6.1.89]

A Slight Improvement

It seems to be half-time already. Someone is coming on to the field with lemon slices. I pucker up my lips. A few years ago I was desperate to have a *Selected Poems* out, but now the lid is coming down on thirty years' production I find myself gasping for air. Give me one more year and I'll get it right! Perhaps it is no big deal to put a few slim volumes back into circulation, but one cannot help remembering how few poets have improved much after forty, if indeed they didn't get a lot worse. Is the mould set or can one still shrug free? Something tells me you really have to go for it in the second half just to stay on the same spot.

I had thought of calling my life's work *A Slight Improvement* after my best school report. The concept of improvement runs deep. We need it to come to terms with time: 'Every day in every way I am getting better and better'. Art, love, truth, fame, even good looks

42

and talent are within our grasp if only . . . But then Fate pipes up, reminding the Olympic Hopeful that he has a wooden leg. And 'a wooden leg is no excuse for wooden verse' as Kingsley Martin once reminded an agent.

Looking back over the work it is easy to see the various shifts, though whether these are my own or everyone else's is harder to say. One is away from metaphor and towards speech, another is away from the page and towards humour. The *Review*'s cleansing minimalism and the rise of the poetry reading acted as a hinge for these. Were they movements away from Poetry in the dubious search for a Voice? You start with no voice, but no stifling awareness of the fact. If you do acquire one, it may be accompanied by a hobbling self-consciousness. Awareness of this is the difficult card called 'Maturity'. Give me two new cards!

It is easy to patronize one's younger self; the struggle out of it leaves one strangely impervious to its charm. An early poem of mine about a pick-up has a mix 'n' match metaphor which raises a smile today: 'Both know they walk / Tightropes like duellists and to gore / The enemy is to fall on one's sword.' I had to fight with my right hand not to slim that down to something like 'Both know / They walk tightropes through air / And into each other's eyes.' But feeling is the one unfakeable part, the one unreproducible element. And thereby hangs my doubt about the upward mobility of it all.

Mercifully, the true state of affairs is hidden from us most of the time, though one does occasionally see through a chink in the safety curtain of friends and white lies that surrounds one. 'There was a moment in the 1970s when you looked like being the next thing,' said a friend once as he saw me off on the last tube from Notting Hill Gate, 'but somehow it never happened, why was that?' A number of possible excuses flashed through my head, but I had to catch my train. The fact that I wasn't willing to miss it in my defence was a sort of answer: caution, tidiness, self-preservation. (It is a consolation to my lack of wildness now that I was never wild then.)

My habit of containment and limitation may be in for just the kind of jolt one needs at half time: a field trip to Central America to

43

do one of the BBC's 'Great Journeys'. The world is divided up into different types of TV programme – Turkey is Holidays, Norway is Wildlife, etc. – and the BBC thought it would be amusing to send a non-current affairs man into a current affairs area and see what happened.

The truth is no one else wanted to go and I felt I owed it to this column to broaden my outlook and visit some of those Nicaraguan minister-poets on your behalf, if not the Death Squads. Even as you read I am setting out in my dirty white suit and crumpled panama to recce the Pan-American Highway from Texas to the Panama Canal. I have with me my copy of the indispensable *Bishop Amongst Bananas* by the Right Revd Herbert Bury DD (London, 1911). Also my Wiseman Survival Outfit, comprising wire, saw, compass, fire-lighting flint, candle, fishing kit, safety pin, pencil and waterproof instruction leaflet showing how to make a signal fire, dew trap and sundial. I have even obtained a 'waterproof and tearproof' notebook in case I feel miserable and creative at the same time.

[17.2.89]

Secret Undercurrents in Culture and Society

In the late 1960s the grip of the big studios on the film industry was temporarily prised open by Dennis Hopper's *Easy Rider*. In the 1970s, the monopoly of the big record companies was smashed by dozens of little 'indie' labels offering fair deals to bloody-minded punks. In the 1990s, according to Maxim Décharné, proprietor of Malice Aforethought Press (slogan: Buy our books, you bastards) and author of the self-published *Beat Your Relatives to a Bloody Pulp*, it is now the turn of publishing.

The second annual Small Press Fair in the Conway Hall, London, was bursting at the seams with literary arcanery: 'not just books: pamphlets, journals, tracts, zines, rags, *livres d'artiste*, cards, badges, etc.'. Also, 'poets, ranters, monologuists, contactees, mind-boggling performance art and lyrical barroom distraction from the quasi-stalinist Bing Selfish and The Idealists'.

The books themselves ranged from demure anthologies of poems on different counties, published by Margaret Tims of the Brentham Press, to *Lake Monster Traditions: A cross-cultural analysis* by Michael Meurger, published by Fortean Tomes, the publishing arm of *Fortean Times*. This marvellous little magazine of weirdness is edited by Bob Richard, among others, with what looks like an entire subscribers' list as special correspondents. One of these is the thinking man's hippy and prophet of green, John Michel, writing about a fossil forgery at the British Museum. At another stall, that of the Bozo Press, imprint of the fair's organizer John Nicholson, the first study of John Michel's work *An English Figure* is for sale, moderately priced, at £4.50.

It has to be said that there was a strong feel of the 1960s hanging over the proceedings at Red Lion Square, a cross between Kensington Market and the Indica Bookshop with the smell of joss sticks over the flying-saucer bookstall, which, needless to say, was doing a brisk trade. *Fortean Times* incorporates the section 'Strange Days', which I seem to remember being part of *IT*.

A more youthful, serious and expensive publication, 'not for sale to minors', is *Rapid Eye*, a glossy the *Observer* finds 'crucial', though to what they don't say. If the spirits of John Michel and Heathcote Williams hover over *Fortean Times*, those of Aleister Crowley and William Burroughs preside at *Rapid Eye*: the heavier end of the 1960s. 'This is a book about secret undercurrents in culture and society that are illuminating thousands of lives, yet are ignored or misinterpreted by the conventional media.' This 'user-friendly grimoire of cultural survivalist techniques' is out to 'crack the Western World's coded attitudes and drag the reader up a wild and imaginative route through magick, Art, sex, drugs, cosmology, Religion and anarchy'. Even without the wonderful, non-existent 'grimoire', this is cutely enough phrased to 'drag' in a whole new generation of experimenters and revolutionaries; at £11 it is cutely priced too.

It is perhaps unfair to suggest that the whiff of incense was a cultural constant at the Small Book Fair. The Pythia Press publish a book about Margaret Fell, founder of the Quakers. Primary House, a Quaker offshoot, publish various pacifist and educational works. The Aporia Press publish books by De Quincey. The Wellsweep Press were about to publish the Chinese poet Duo Duo when events in Tiananmen Square took a tragic turn. The poet saw shooting in the square, but escaped to the airport and caught the last plane out of Peking. The book was snapped up by Bloomsbury, but mysteriously published at the same price of £5, despite the difference of print run – 500 for Wellsweep, 10,000 at Bloomsbury – a fact which Wellsweep cannot explain; here, at least, is a case in which low-watt publishing very nearly short-circuited a big power station.

[6.10.89]

Tara Browne: A Lucky Man Who Made The Grade

The first verse of 'A Day in the Life' from *Sgt Pepper's Lonely Hearts Club Band*, the one that begins 'I read the news today, O boy / about a lucky man who made the grade . . .', refers to the younger son of the late Irish peer Lord Oranmore and Browne, a young man called Tara Browne, who 'blew his mind out in a car' in Redcliffe Gardens one night in 1966. He was twenty-one, a shining star of my generation, but a victim that night of LSD, although according to his passenger he was not too out of it to turn the car so that she escaped unhurt.

John Lennon affects detachment in the lyric: 'He didn't notice that the lights had changed / A crowd of people stood and stared / They'd seen his face before / Nobody was really sure if he was from the House of Lords . . .' But he knew Tara and it is clear from the song's elegiac mood, coming just after the jubilation of the title track's reprise, that his death stood for something in the life of the band, that it marked the end of the party and that nothing was ever quite the same after it. The last line expresses the mood of emptiness and disillusion: 'Now they know how many holes it takes to fill the Albert Hall.'

Or so I like to think, because that was the way I felt about Tara's death myself. Before it came the innocent phase of the 1960s: the twist, the mini-skirt, 'I wanna hold your hand'. After it, long hair, old clothes, psychedelia, the Underground, Altamont, the rock 'n' roll deaths. Before it, for me anyway, the carefree present tense. After it, fatherhood, responsibility, the future.

I met him in Paris in 1960. He was still living at home with his mother Oonagh Guinness and her new husband, Cuban shoe designer Miguel Ferreras. He was barely educated, having walked out of dozens of schools, and was currently being coached slightly by a friend of mine filling in before Oxford. He was fifteen, two years younger than me, but years ahead in sophistication and fun, dealing jokes and laughs, complicated insults and ridiculous boasts, from an inexhaustible deck, like a child delightedly playing snap. 'Promise you won't tell anyone.' 'All right.' 'I'm not telling you, then.' In his green suits and mauve shirts with amethyst cuff-links, waves of blond hair, brocade ties and buckled shoes, smoking Salems and drinking Bloody Marys, he was Little Lord Fauntleroy, Beau Brummell, Peter Pan, Terence Stamp in *Billy Budd*, David Hemmings in *Blow-Up*. I suppose he would have been the ultimate spoiled brat if it hadn't been for the charm. Something to do with his Irishness and the fact that he was not quite a gent. Something to do with that name. And then of course he died like James Dean in the full blaze of summer.

Girls loved him. All the white-gloved pre-debs at Paris finishing schools found their way to his mother's apartment in the Rue de L'Université, where they encountered their first taste of '60s hedonism, without mummy and daddy around to say no: drinks and cigarettes and staying up late, two American cars with a chauffeur to conduct them to the clubs and swimming pools. There was even fresh milk in the fridge, picked up daily by the Irish butler from the

47

American Embassy canteen, the only place you could get it in Paris in those days. Tara had all the latest hit singles sent from America and he would take a selection for the DJ to play at the Club des Etoiles: 'Running Bear', 'Rubber Ball', 'Cut Across, Shorty', 'You got what it takes', anything by Phil Spector, Duane Eddy or the Everley Brothers. If there was ever any trouble at the door about his age, he would stand his ground, explaining everything in great detail, paying for everyone. If there was ever any embarrassment about money, he would pretend to find a *dix mille* note in the street, which then belonged to all of us. He had one of the first car record players, which you could walk along with while it was playing, and after the clubs we took it to the Aerogare des Invalides and danced for the cleaners and airline pilots, keeping the photo-booth busy. Our childlike faces peer out of the little black and white squares, in ecstasy at our new-found freedom in the grown-up world.

At ten next morning, Tara's tutor would arrive at the flat to find bodies scattered everywhere and an hour later Tara's face, round as a bun from sleep, would peer out of a blanket, saying his Irish 'Sorrry, sorrry,' then collapsing in laughter. I seem to remember his lessons taking place in the back of the Corvette on the way to swim at Eden Rock, where Jean-Paul Belmondo waved to him. Did I imagine that all this was going to be part of my own future? I got a brush cut and a gold chain like Alain Delon and I made a point of not wearing any socks. These were the days of Godard's *A Bout de Souffle*: yellow-T-shirted American girls calling 'New York Herald Tribune' in the Champs Elysees, Edith Piaf's 'Milord' playing in Le Drugstore.

One by one the girls went back to London to begin their seasons. Summer came and Tara and I made our way to Majorca, where my parents and his father happened to have taken villas. Family Holiday time for the new sophisticates. Tara and my father facing one another warily over the heavily laden drinks tray. Would he like an orange juice or a Coke? 'An orange juice?' said Tara in the tones of Lady Bracknell. 'I'd rather have a Bloody Mary, sir. But do you mind if I make it myself?' The photos have him building enthusiastic sand castles on the beach: a novel activity. He was barely sixteen.

A year later he had set up in London with a girl called Nicky, met the Rolling Stones, opened a shop in the King's Road, passed his driving test and bought the fatal torquoise Lotus Elan in which he entered the Irish Grand Prix, driving it to and from the track. He let me drive it once in some busy street. 'Come on, Hugo. Put your foot down.' The thing was like a bullet from a gun pointed straight at his head. I had just got my first job and our ways were dividing.

There were out-of-time house parties for his pretty Paris friends at Luggala, his family's birthday-cake castle outside Dublin – 'With whom will you be sleeping, sir?' asked the butler, taking one's suitcase – but Tara was moving into heavier reaches of the social scene. He could hardly have failed to be a success in Swinging London, but he was a hopeless millionaire. His money and social susceptibilities made him the natural prey of certain charismatic Chelsea types, who soon turned him into what he amiably termed a 'hustlee'. Life is dangerous in such company and Tara's defences were skin deep. 'Never show anyone what you're feeling,' he once told a friend. He got his motto from an Oscar Brown Junior record: 'Act cool, be cool, stay cool.'

The last time I saw him was at his twenty-first birthday party – his last – when the Lovin' Spoonful, flying high on 'What a Day for a Daydream', flew in to Luggala for the occasion and we danced on a sloping lawn. The last time I heard his voice he was asking me to testify in his mother's latest divorce case against his stepfather who had once asked to get into bed with me. I couldn't be bothered and never heard from him again. His last letter, scrawled in South Sea Blue ink, can't quite disguise the fact that he never learned to do joined-up handwriting.

Why write about him now? Everyone has got some golden boy or girl in their youth whose death or sudden departure distils the period into the long party it should have been, but never really was. My time in Paris was only a few months, but it has a mythological feel to it now, because of Tara. He is the distorting glass through which the whole short period goes on haunting me, jokes and parties and girls standing in for all the adolescent doubts and fears for the future looming on the other side of the Channel.

The teens are so short compared to what comes afterwards and what came before. Looking back, you can't believe you did so much. You start in a little gang, a little knot, then slowly you straggle out into your lives, until you are miles away from one another, seeing everything differently. You take one of the strings and follow it back and there it all is, still happening, with certain tunes still playing at the Club des Etoiles, or La Discothèque in Rupert Street.

We have all come home safe and sound from the party, but Tara went on into the night and didn't make it home. The day he died his friends went out of date. (That is a thought he would definitely have agreed with.) Perhaps if he'd apologized just once for being born into the gold, he might have lived, but not so vividly, not so indelibly. When my first girlfriend was trying to find something really nice to say to me, the best she could do was, 'Your eyes are almost as nice as Tara's.' I remember being tremendously pleased and could hardly wait to tell him.

I tried to write a poem about him when he died. Twenty-eight years later it is still no good – yellowing quarto sheets typed on my first typewriter, corrections in an unformed hand. It didn't work because the details didn't add up to the sum of their glowing memory. The truth is that Tara himself didn't add up: he hadn't had time to. I looked at my record collection just now and realized that most of them were made after he died. How furious he would have been.

In my scrapbook of the period I have stuck a strip cartoon of 'BC', a prehistoric caveman favoured by Tara. BC is carving a memorial to himself and musing quietly: 'Posterity will not remember a man for his name alone. He must leave the world a lasting image, a title, a billing . . .' He erects the finished big stone arrow and sits down in front of it. Carved on the arrow are the words 'The Smartest Man In The World'. Now that was Tara Browne – a lucky man who made the grade.

[16.12.94]

Paul Muldoon's 'Cuba'

Term-time again and we university lecturers are dusting off our stone-washed 501's, Air-Pegasus trainers and Gross Moral Turpitude Tour bomber jackets. I have recently had my front teeth removed and been given a 'symmetrical' haircut. This means that I have got to face twelve potentially dangerous creative writing students on the University of East Anglia's prestigious Writing Programme (twenty years old last year) with a lisp and centre parting. An urgent mental note to myself: for God's sake don't mention these things in the first ten minutes.

From Norwich station I make my way out to the University, buy some sweets and coffee and check my tray in the English office. This will be where my students deposit their weekly poems for me to photocopy, but at the moment there is only a Course Grading instructions, a Style Notes and a letter from someone who doesn't want to take the course after all.

I find my seminar room and rearrange the furniture as for a dinner party of ten, two of whom I know won't turn up. Creative writing classes are like musical chairs in reverse: every week there is a wider range of seating to choose from and a greater sense of intimacy among those huddling together at one end of the room.

Thank God for photocopy machines! I make a great performance out of passing round copies of Paul Muldoon's 'Cuba', having failed to notice its topicality. Someone points this out to me and I say, 'Yes, but what else have you noticed?' 'Its Irishness?' 'Yes, it does have an Irish lilt to it, doesn't it. Anything else?' It has suddenly occurred to me that, aside from the poem's unassailable perfection, which I have already mentioned, there is very little to be said about it, but I go ahead all the same and draw attention to the remarkable way the poem has of not going on too long, a point which may not have escaped my invigilators.

There is a pause, during which we all admire the outstanding brevity of Paul's poem. All too soon it is time for me to speak again.

51

'I like short poems,' I begin. 'I always feel disappointed if I have to turn over the page, don't you? I mean, I think it's a *page* thing. A *time* thing.' (Even I am shocked by this.) 'Is that why you break up your own long poems into different parts?' asks an apparently guile-free student. 'To suggest they are really self-contained poems?' 'Yes, that's it,' I answer. 'But you have to have a few long ones in a *book*. Paul Muldoon . . .' I stop here, conscious that we need to introduce a new angle into the discussion. But what?

I notice a little beacon of light being held out to me by a distant but familiar figure in an adjoining lecture room almost ten years ago, when I was writer-in-residence here with responsibility for poetry readings. It is Andrew Motion, and his point, as I remember it, is that what you need to do in poetry, or what he needed to do, was lean two things up against each other in the hope that they become more than the sum of their mutually supportive parts: a public and a private narrative, say. Motion offered this as a modest put-down of his own poem, 'The Letter', which contains two interlocking stories: that of an English girl who gets a letter from her Forces sweetheart, and that of a German pilot who comes down in flames in a nearby field. I expound his theory to my students at as great a length as possible, not forgetting to point out the topicality of the poem and dashing to catch my train before anyone has time to object.

On my way home I remember an article by Dana Gioia in *The New Yorker* in which he recalls his time on Elizabeth Bishop's writing course at Harvard. 'She was a politely formal, shy and undramatic woman who wanted no worshipful circle of students and got none. "I am not a very good teacher," she told her students, "so to make sure you learn something in this class I am going to ask each of you to memorize at least ten lines a week from one of the poets we are reading." '

Her students could not have been more shocked by this indignity than if she had asked them to put on sackcloth and ashes, but they did what they were told. I pictured my own students with their 'Tell me about it' expressions and I heard myself asking them how they felt about the idea. It didn't appeal to them? In that case, how would they react to the idea of my learning the lines myself each week? They liked that better. 'Fine,' I said to myself. 'It seems to me we are beginning to understand one another.'

[15.2.91]

A Garden of Black and Red Sausages

As well as taking a poetry writing class at the University of East Anglia, I have creative writing students from an American college in London come to my house once a week for what is called a 'surgery', a strangely appropriate term in the circumstances. Anyone who has been in a room with seven heavy-duty Sylvia Plath-heads will know what I am talking about.

What happens in the surgery is that each student reads out the piece of Plathery he or she has written that week and the others try and talk the poet down from it with various wildly conflicting value judgements. Most of the time it is hard to work out what is going on in the poems. The students use airy, roundabout language and they don't give away any facts unless they have to.

My job is to strip away the layers of pretence and get them to confront the origins of the trouble, which often goes back to something like a burnt cookie in early childhood. The students are not always happy about this. They are not interested in cookies. They prefer the gravitas of introspection, which is more like real poetry. This is the central paradox of the creative writing movement: it is as if an alternative art form is trying to be born, what Yeats referred to as a 'terrible beauty', with me as appalled midwife.

Despite their artistic zeal, the students don't like coming here because it is hard to find and there isn't any central heating. I compensate for this by providing hot drinks and rugs and we always have a long intermission during which we study the lives and lyrics of early rockabilly stars. Lew Williams, for instance, who wrote 'Like a long, lean lizard, gonna drag, man, drag. Like a dog, I'm gonna shag, man, shag.' Or, as a concession to the Plathites, the great Johnny Ace, who shot himself dead backstage during a game of Russian Roulette.

Sometimes during these sessions I suspect the students would prefer a more 'structured' course with more charismatic leadership and a theory of poetics which amounted to more than 'I don't like this bit very much' (although I usually don't like any of it). One dissatisfied customer suggested warm-up exercises, physical as well as mental. He wanted us to lie down on the floor, the way they used to at USC. There isn't room to stretch out in my study, so I had to come up with something else for them to do. I was casting about for a suitable project for them to write about when I noticed two enormous cracks running down the wall of my study, the result of the recent freeze-up. It looked as though the entire fourth wall was about to fall into the street, revealing my unusual profession to any passer-by. How much was this going to cost me to put right, I wondered.

A week or so ago I had a call from someone at the BBC offering me £200 to write a fifteen-minute poem on the subject of food, to be included in a series called *Table Talk*, broadcast on Sunday lunchtimes. She sent me a tape of Redmond O'Hanlon's contribution in which he described eating cayman intestines in Amazonia and parasitic worms in central Borneo. I had been worried about how to live up to this standard when it occurred to me that I could get my Americans to write about their favourite meal, then run them all together and call it 'Ode to America'.

The results, when they came in, owed less to my inclusion of Lew Williams on the syllabus (his best known hillbilly boogie is the stomping 'Centipede' already quoted) than to Wagner's murderous 'The Ride of the Valkyries'. Three of the entries would have sickened even a hardened explorer like O'Hanlon. If you can imagine a dinner party cooked and eaten by Sylvia Plath during her 'Ariel' period, with the unseen presence of Ted Hughes hovering over the kitchen, that is what my contribution to the BBC's *Table Talk* sounds like: 'I am a garden of black and red sausages' etc.

At the end of the session, two female students found they were unable to get home on account of the weather and asked if they could stay the night. Not wanting to risk any nastiness in the kitchen, I got a take-away. Then the girls kipped down on my living room floor.

After they had tramped off into the snow next morning I found something heavy, soft and reddish-black wrapped in an old newspaper in my bathroom. At first I thought it was a foetus. Then I thought it might be the afterbirth. Eventually a friend went in and had a look at it and said it was the remains of a face-pack. I must admit to feeling strangely disappointed by this.

[1.3.91]

A Small-time Antichrist

For a few hair-raising weeks in 1989 I drove a car for the BBC. I had been selected as the 'subject' of a road movie about the Pan-American Highway, to be included in their *Great Journeys* series. Of course, I jumped at the chance of visiting countries like Nicaragua, El Salvador, Panama. Jumped with fear, that is. I had no knowledge of Central America, no experience of 'presenting' and no Spanish. Worse, I had seen Oliver Stone's film and read Joan Didion's book.

My first mistake was to set up a meeting with actress and old Nicaragua hand Charlotte Cornwell, who said I shouldn't go, that it was dangerous and that all her contacts were too busy doing important work to talk to someone who knew nothing about the Revolution. I had taken the trouble to find out what the capital of Nicaragua was, but Charlotte couldn't imagine me as cultural ambassador to Central America and by the end of lunch I was losing my grip on the concept myself. Depression followed. A friend explained that going away was an image of one's own death which I was simply mourning in advance.

The world is divided up into different types of TV programme. Portugal is holidays, America is comedy shows, Norway is wildlife, etc. The BBC thought it would be amusing to throw a non-current-affairs man into a current-affairs area and see what happened. Unfortunately the time-hallowed categories have a habit of reimposing themselves. The crew had gone on ahead and, by the time I arrived in Texas, had already filmed a Salvadoran refugee of such impeccable misfortune that I had, without knowing it, lost the game before I started.

There were nine of us sitting down to our first meal on the road. When the bill came, director Peter Dale said he'd pay and divide by nine later, would it be OK if he did this throughout? Idiotically, I objected. Silence fell. It was as if Judas Iscariot had kissed Christ on the lips. (My actor brother told me he'd been wanting to do the same for years but never dared because of what the lighting boys could do to you.) Peter came up to me afterwards and said if anything was going to upset the smooth running of the show he was going to jump on it, so I had better buy the crew a round immediately. I went to my room and sulked.

Odd that I should have identified with Judas because I was about to come face to face with him in a Guatemalan village. He was wearing a Stetson, dark glasses and a business suit and smoking a cigar. 'Maximon' is a small-time antichrist and clay window dummy who has been consoling the Indians for their losses since the sixteenth century when they decided, reasonably enough, that if Judas betrayed the white man's god he must be on their side and duly made a cult of him. One is expected to buy this genial con-man a drink, so his keepers tipped him back and I poured the bribe down his clay throat, a basin under his chair recuperating the overflow for later. After presenting him with three spivvy neckties we filmed him receiving a cerebral palsy sufferer who may not have benefited from our attention.

This was the high spot of the trip for me, but I was at a loss to know how to behave in that candle-lit hovel. There is a hole in the heart of armchair travelogues which is supposed to be filled by some colourful writer chappie but whatever else I am, I am not colourful and Peter finally lost patience with my listlessness: 'Hugo, you've got to DO something, otherwise we're buggered.' I rumba'd to the

Oswaldo Ayala band in Panama City, but it was too late: the camera averted its gaze. The last shot of me is from behind and seems to be illustrating the point that one's trousers get wedged half way up one's bottom in a warm climate.

When the film came out my brother was appearing in Iris Murdoch's *The Black Prince*. The BBC were doing a tribute to her and the cast agreed to go in and film one or two scenes. They kept my brother waiting all day, then, without apology or explanation, sent a message saying they wouldn't be using him. He walked on to the set and tore into the director in public. On his way out, regretting his outburst, he overheard a bemused cameraman telling an assistant, 'You think *he's* a prat, you should see his brother. I was in Central America with him for six weeks.'

[29.3.91]

Alan Ross's *London Magazine*

Alan Ross's *London Magazine*, Britain's longest-running and best literary monthly, is celebrating its thirtieth birthday. Ross took over *The London Magazine* from John Lehmann in 1961, dropped 'The' from the title, kept Charles Osborne as assistant editor and took me on as 'Advertising Manager'. I was nineteen.

At school in the 1950s, *The London Magazine*, along with Elvis Presley, was my talisman of independence. I had an order at the local Smiths and every week I would go in and ask if my copy had arrived. When I found a poem called 'Elvis Presley' by Thom Gunn, my head turned, my future was sealed. In 1959 John Lehmann accepted some poems of mine and a year later Alan Ross said if I found out a bit about printing I could join him when he took over the editorship. It was powerful medicine for a feckless youth with four 'O' levels and a possible opening as a waiter at the Savoy. I signed on at Brighton tech for six months, then moved to London.

The office in those days was a big sunny room at the top of 22 Charing Cross Road. Instead of a receptionist there was a hatch with a bell. Callers would ring and wait. I was supposed to slide back the hatch and repeat the person's name so that Alan or Charles could hear. A shake or a nod would dictate my delayed reaction to the visitor's often illustrious name. 'Christopher Isherwood?' 'Hello, Christopher! Come in.' At other times I had to go out into the hall and turn away would-be contributors, or Gerald Wilde scrounging half a crown. The paranoid, dandified Julian Maclaren-Ross would turn up with the latest instalment of his memoirs, hand-scripted in finest Bic, with illuminated capitals, for which he required payment. Someone was following him, he said. I had to go downstairs and pay his taxi.

I didn't mind touring the galleries on my motorbike each month (£25 a page), but my least favourite task was ringing up all the publishers – there were more than forty in those days. A magazine's 'advertising manager' is the only person a publisher's PR can patronize, but if we had a review of one of their books I was allowed to get a little bit heavy. If I succeeded, blocks would be delivered to our printer. John Fuller and Ian Hamilton borrowed my advertising contacts for their new magazine, *The Review*.

Once the ads were in, I had to measure the galleys and do the make-up, paste it up, type out a contents list and send it back to the printers along with authors' corrected proofs. Ten days later the page proofs would arrive for final checking. Another two weeks and finished copies appeared. It was a low-tech, hot-metal world with little old messengers labouring up from Harlow on the train. The most scientific piece of equipment was a gleaming, chromium coffee pot; still is, I hope.

As well as the magazine, Ross had a thriving imprint, with books by Tony Harrison and Paul Theroux among others. It seems impossibly long ago that young unknowns were actually encouraged to produce books, but I wrote one and so did my wife (*Life Star*, 1969). I remember getting the newly-instigated SBN number wrong on the latter: a thousand fly-leaves had to be torn out and new ones glued in by hand. I see it is still being advertised in the LM under 'Women's Studies' alongside Barbara Skelton's *Born Losers*.

The two authors met at one of Alan's parties and Barbara invited Hermine to stay in Antibes without realizing she had a baby. Hermine turned up furious at having to take a bus from the station and the two actually came to blows before Hermine got back on the bus.

After some years, Alan let me edit an anthology of poems from the magazine. I set about cutting up old issues until my desk was awash with verses by W. H. Auden and Brian Patten. Difficulties arose when a poem went over the page and a two-verse poem by Kingsley Amis made its appearance in a slimmed-down one-verse form which the author didn't appreciate. I apologized in person at the launch of a new bookshop in Regent's Park Road (Bookshop 85?). Amis decently said he could forgive the mistake; what he hadn't been able to take was Alan assuring him it was an improvement.

That was typical of Alan's piratical, partisan style, which I drank in. As often happens in offices, I started speaking and laughing like him, so that everyone thought it was him on the telephone. Even today, twenty years after leaving, I have to be careful to tone it down when I'm with him. If I write his name on an envelope, it still looks like his signature. Enough said. I owe him everything. Congratulations on the first thirty years.

[12.4.91]

Madrid, by the Hand of Goya

Goya, painter of torture and mutilation, might not seem the ideal subject for a theme holiday. (A keen packager would run into similar difficulties with the work of Francis Bacon.) But Goya has another, less well-known side, suffused with sunshine and youthful gaiety, more suitable for holiday-making. This lighter, pastoral phase precedes the 'Disaster' etchings inspired by the Napoleonic holocaust. I leave it to the reader to guess which aspect of his work characterized my own experience of 'Madrid by the Hand of Goya'.

The Spanish Tourist Board had organized a weekend promotion

for British travel journalists. I turned up at Gatwick Airport expecting to find a jolly bunch of freeloaders already half drunk, only to learn that all the other writers had cancelled at the last minute, leaving me as the sole representative. I asked the PR girl, who had been so nice on the phone, if she would mind if I, too, backed out of the arrangement. She replied that this would be impossible as there was a Welcome Reception being laid on by the Director of Tourism in Madrid. As a last minute contingency plan she and her fiancé were taking the place of the missing reporters. Her fiancé would write an article about Spanish wine for the Dan-Air in-flight magazine, *Flair*. She herself was doing research for Michael Aspel. I thought of making a break for it, but her fiancé was warning me with his eyes not to try anything.

What they had omitted to tell me was that the Reception in the fabulous new 'Puerto Toledo' – a 1930s fish-market converted into an up-market galleria – was to be attended by twenty-four Spanish journalists and art critics, invited to come along and meet their British opposite numbers. I hid behind the language barrier until it was time for a slide presentation of *Madrid Pittoresque* – fountains, pigeons, horse-carriages and sunbeams. At last, I thought, a recognizable world for me to cling to. 'What a magnificent Presentation,' I told the illustrious mayor, Lady Marta Gutierrez Renon, fingers crossed behind my back.

Early next morning I received a message from the PR saying she and her fiancé had to be back in London for rowing practice. They'd caught the early flight. After a brief sensation of unreality I found myself in an empty mini-van being taken on a compulsory tour of the monastery of San Lorenzo de El Escorial, an hour outside Madrid. 'Write down 16 courtyards, 88 fountains, 9 towers, 86 staircases, 2673 windows, 1200 doors,' said my guide Diego Ginez as he whisked me past hot queues to see a series of Goya tapestries. 'You can always tell Goya children by their round, red faces, always shouting, angry and wrinkled.' He lifted a barrier and showed me a commode, slightly stained, in Felipe II's bed chamber, from where a small door opened directly onto the High Altar of the Basilica.

Beneath this altar a staircase leads to an antechamber where Royal corpses are left for fifteen years until the flesh has fallen from their bones and they are ready to be permanently encoffined in the Royal Pantheon. The present King's grandmother is currently in this rather coy state of semi-undress. I asked to see her, but Ginez shook his head. When he conducted our own Queen round the Escorial recently she made no comment until she came to Felipe's throne, then she confided that she hoped the King hadn't had to sit in it for long as it looked most uncomfortable. She was awarded *no* points by Ginez for this *aperçu*.

Sunday. A free day. Up early to have my pocket picked at the *Rastro* flea market: street upon street of sunglasses and day-glo cycle shorts. Only one more day!

For the last evening of the Promotion the British travel writers and critics were to be fêted with a specially-produced 'Celebration of Goya' by a troupe of Flamenco dancers from the Madrid Ballet School, who burst into the reception rooms of the City Hall, clicking castanets and stamping their heels. What they did was superb, not Flamenco, but a series of earlier eighteenth-century dances, each of which ended in a freeze-tableau of one of Goya's sunny pastoral scenes. I could not help seeing them as scowling, red-faced children in postures of domination and agony. We British journalists were supposed to be photographed with the troupe and receive castanet lessons. Instead of a group photo, I was photographed individually with each of the dancers, then given a pair of castanets to go home with.

[10.5.91]

Could This Be My Wife? Would She Make it down the Stairs?

The copy of a tiny, roly-poly 'Venus figurine', said to be 25,000 years old, given to the Princess of Wales in Bratislava last week, made an ironical comment on her status as the world's foremost fashion goddess. Not only does its shameless amplitude mock our Western obsession with thinness, its provenance makes pointed reference to the passing of the golden age of womanhood (matrilineage), a revolution of which Diana is perhaps the ultimate disempowered example.

In primeval time it was said to be woman, in harmony with nature, who organized human life. These saggy-bosomed artefacts, unearthed all over Europe, were the world's first goddesses, but they brought about woman's downfall – what Engels called 'the world historic defeat of the female sex' – by arousing male jealousy of their powers over sex, fire and food. Henceforward, man would be god (and king). That Diana should have been photographed holding one of these forgotten deities in her hand was portentous. 'How An Ancient Fertility Symbol Captivated A Princess' ran the headline. Supposing it were true?

I learned the meaning of these chubby statuettes from my wife, who has just returned from Basel in Switzerland, where she has been giving a series of performance-rap-lectures on the subject of 'Mother-Right', in the very house, now a museum of Greek antiquities, of the nineteenth-century pioneer anthropologist J. J. Bachofen, whose book *Das Mutterrecht* coined the phrase in 1861. For her entry down the great staircase of the house, Hermine had made for herself a grotesquely padded costume, complete with outsize pendulous breasts, which transformed her into one of the bulbous, naked goddesses already mentioned. With the aid of projectors, puppets and scenic effects, her performance evokes the pristine world and sets it in the context of modern anthropology. Her rap includes the lines 'Men don't pray to prehistoric women,

men strive to please, strive to please prehistoric women, to get lovemaking time' – a thought which, to one man at least, has a modern ring to it.

When her tour was over, it seemed a shame to abandon the monstrous appurtenance in Switzerland, so she decided to freight it back to London and wear it to enter Andrew Logan's Alternative Miss World, held this year in the Business Design Centre in Islington. Logan is undoubtedly a royal figure on the contemporary art scene, part Warhol, part Disney, part Fabergé. A retrospective of his mirror-decked sculptures currently at the Museum of Modern Art in Oxford offers 'An Artistic Adventure, inspired by the globe, its various civilizations, the universe and beyond.' Here the gods and goddesses of ancient Egypt, India and Greece rub shoulders with the modern gods and goddesses of Logan's very social life today. There is a portrait-in-mirrors of Princess Diana, among others, a *son et lumière*, singing flowers, a cornfield, and hundreds more mythological creations, including all the bisected Host/Hostess costumes worn by Logan at each of his Alternative Miss Worlds since they began in 1972.

The theme this year was 'Air' – with trapeze artists for cabaret, Ned Sherrin and Sian Phillips judging. Among the participants was Miss Ts of Avalon, attended by the 'Neo-Naturist Cabaret', a tribe of naked women, men and children daubed in egg yolk and singing 'Somewhere Over the Rainbow'. There was a rustle of prudery from some of the corset-queens over the inclusion of nude children in this entry, but I thought they made a happy complement to my wife's outfit.

Naturally, the high spot for me was the appearance at the top of the silver staircase of what looked like an enormously fat naked woman with a tea-cosy over her face. Could this really be my wife? Would she make it down the stairs? I held my breath, as I have so often done in the past, as the wobbling mass teetered forward, hands held invisible inside preposterous breasts. I thought of the Princess of Wales, her skeletal form, her bashful glances, giggling as she clasped the little figurine, now magically migrated from Eastern

Europe to bestow its blessing on the occasion. Had the goddess come back to earth to be crowned 'Alternative Miss World 1991'? My wife's rap filled the cavernous spaces of the Business Design Centre (*née* Royal Agricultural Hall): 'Prehistoric women aren't immortal. Prehistoric women don't die and resurrect. Prehistoric women don't fly between heaven and earth. But their life-blood flows from generation to generation.'

[24.5.91]

Armand Dupuis, 1892–

We've been staying in Paris with my wife's grandfather for the funeral of the last of his children, my wife's aunt. At ninety-nine, he's in superb health himself, having outlived every known virus and built up a hundred years of immunity to the world. His flat in the 17e, with its graceful interconnecting rooms, is a creaking relic of the 1890s in which he grew up. Not a trace of modernity, let alone modern art, is allowed to disturb the ordered routine of his twilight. He rises at eight, puts on a three-piece suit, breakfasts at nine, reads *Le Figaro* for an hour without glasses, and so on, until it is time for him to retire at 8 p.m., firmly closing the shutters and drawing heavy curtains on broad daylight, his guests required to do the same. His mind is still percentage-keen.

We had taken an early train via Dieppe, not to be late for dinner on the dot of seven, and walked up the hill from the Gare St Lazare to the Boulevard de Courcelles. Even though he married us himself in his little *Mairie* in the country twenty-five years ago, he still delights in asking my wife 'C'est ton mari?' whenever he sees me. This time he was as rude as ever, staring repeatedly at my clothes and asking for translations of my French, 'Qu'est-ce qu'il dit?'.

Usually the first thing he says when he sees me is 'Vous avez une voiture maintenant?' But I had made a stir by arriving at his ninety-ninth birthday party on a motorbike, so he restricted himself to asking my wife 'Il n'a pas de col, ton mari?' I waved my arms in the

64

air and said 'Le voyage, le voyage', noting the heavy vest sticking up behind his own made-up bow-tie. As soon as we sat down to dinner, he poured me wine and I fell into another trap: 'Il boit du vin avec sa soupe, ton mari?' He was evidently highly amused by this barbarism. 'Qui fait la soupe chez vous?' 'Hugo,' said my wife. He looked at me with renewed contempt.

After dinner I begged her not to leave me alone with his deaf-aid, an economy model which suffers from piercing feedback as soon as a word is spoken. I needn't have worried. He turned his clear eyes on me and asked how old I was, remarking that I was only half as old as he was and had a long *chemin* to travel. This seemed terribly old, so I told him my father died at sixty-five. Nothing to do with it: his father was sixty, his mother forty-seven. It was during the First World War. He asked his commanding officer for twenty-four hours leave to attend her funeral and was given eight days in prison just for asking. 'Twenty-five years later I was a Deputé (MP),' he told me. 'I went to the Ministère da la Guerre where the officer worked, slapped his face ("une paire de claques") and left without a word. There was nothing he could do.'

I sat there, silenced by this vision of a younger man springing up before me, fists flying. I remembered how he had lost his job as President de la Commission des Douanes during the Occupation for refusing to vote for Pétain. My wife returned and told me I was to be accorded the honour of closing the shutters for him and saying goodnight to him in bed. After pretending to go to bed ourselves, we crept out like bad children to see a grown-up film.

On the following day the old man would be burying his last daughter, having outlived his last friend. And yet his life has been a sort of miracle. He served in the trenches throughout World War I. He had the dangerous job of stringing telephones from one trench to another: 'We felt reassured when we were given helmets.' Once he was completely buried by a shell, another time a mortar killed his driver and he barely had time to grab the wheel. He should have died many times, if not from bullets, from diptheria, jaundice, or an infected appendix. How strange it must have been, in that black hell, to have recognized his father's mare dragging a luggage van through the mud. 'J'ai eu la surprise de voir Palmyre, qui tirait le fourgon d'un régiment d'infanterie.'

The afternoon we left, a portrait in a heavy gilt frame showing him aged nine, wearing an Eton collar and jacket, fell onto the sofa where ten minutes earlier he had been resting. The string had not been renewed for ninety years. 'I should be dead,' he said. 'I should be dead instead of her. It isn't just.'

As we closed the door behind us we heard him telling his maid, 'Je vais mourir maintenant'. We couldn't help smiling as we remembered the vitamin pills laid out on the breakfast table. It seemed impossible that we wouldn't be going through the whole obstacle course again for his hundredth birthday party in August.

[7.6.91]

The Stoned Rubbish School of Poetry

I wonder how many people have an old folder hidden away labelled 'Stoned Rubbish' or 'Sixties Dope Poetry'? Not many, I hope, having just unearthed a pocket of my own work in the genre. 'The negs are coming from Halfwit,' I wrote in 1970. 'Either we print them in a week / Or else we wait / And Paul Harris will get them printed.' Even today, the poem acts like a stun-gun on my imagination. Note the line 'Or else we wait' – highly symptomatic of my way of life in those days, likewise the reliance on 'Paul Harris' to get anything done.

Another of my poems from this period contains the typical untruth, 'The house is full of bat-feathers, / Like the droppings of an eagle called Mr Tarty' and ends, disappointingly, 'Flight Officer Judith Patterson / Was brutalising Honest Jim Poke-Eye with a sponge' – clearly influenced by brand-leader John Ashbery's superior 'Darkness falls like a wet sponge / And Dick gives Genevieve a swift punch / In the pyjamas'. Naturally, I don't recall writing any of this, let alone typing it up with caps at the beginning of the lines, like Ashbery's. 'Don't you ever imagine,' I seem to have asked, 'When you are going down to your room / That a stranger is sitting there / With a better understanding than you?' Which, in my own case, would not have been difficult, as the poem, in its way, proves.

I contemplated publishing a selection of this material recently, as the work of a grotesque *alter ego*, but was checked in the enterprise by an anti-marijuana pamphlet I found with the poems, given to me by Aram Saroyan, poet son of William Saroyan. Aram is the New York poet who would put one word alone on a page: 'oxygen' was one of his, as were 'leukemia' and 'gum'. Occasionally he would put two, even three words together, as in 'farm eye month' and 'air rice fur'. His optical poems include the juddering 'lighght', as well as 'Picassc' and 'waht' (which is almost impossible to write). Perhaps his greatest poem is his own name, a magical thing, which may have influenced his career in some way.

I met Aram when I was staying with Tom Raworth in San Francisco in 1975. We had taken a hairpinning bus round the misty, beautiful mountains up to Bolinas, a strung-out, vague sort of place on a brushy plateau above the Pacific, where lots of poets lived in the 1970s. Aram, his wife Gailyn and their two children, Strawberry and Cream, lived in a ramshackle single-storey house under a big tree. The interior was sparse, new, struggling, heated by a hungry wood stove on which Gailyn cooked our meal, while we drank beer and Tom teased Aram about his fame-sickness. Bolinas, I gathered, had been a deliberate effort away from 1960s' madness, but the city life still leered and Tom and I smelt of it.

In his pamphlet, Aram described his life in New York in the 1960s: first room, deflowerment, writing plans, rise to fame and excitement, name friends and others and what they all thought: 'We related Clark's (Coolidge) work to the drip paintings of Jackson Pollock, my own work to the silk screens of Andy Warhol – isolating the familiar in a way that made it visible again. A Campbell soup can, or the word "guarantee".'

There is no doubt that Saroyan, along with people like Gerard Malanga, was one of the boys in those implosive days – young, handsome, dark, touchy about his father, making up jokes for Woody Allen like 'My friend has a contagious personality – after two hours with him you have to start taking his pills' (rejected), or 'The block I live on is so bad that on the 4th of July they use dynamite' (also rejected). But he wasn't the only one trying to turn and face the world by 1975, that final, fatal year of the 1960s, in which America fell out of Vietnam. 'My wife began to hate it when I turned on,' he wrote, 'When I left her for the other world, becoming *too* excited, too intense for the actual moment in time. After we had our first child, things became even more impossible. There was continual demand, and it had to be met. As the family became a tighter unit, marijuana had to be excluded.'

As I looked through my own attempts to be idiotic enough for inclusion in *The Paris Review c.* 1972, I had to agree with him. I let the yellowing bundle slip through my fingers into the bin and reached for my Guarana capsules, 'Dynamic Life Force of the Amazon Rain Forest. Recommended when advancing years slow our performance, When a demanding day lies ahead, When giving up smoking . . .' Let's see what sort of inoffensive garbage these mothers produce.

[21.6.91]

An Intimate of Robert Graves

It was with a sinking feeling that I learnt, in the car going there, that there were to be no drinks before my reading to the Crediton Writers' Circle in Devon. I set out my stuff as usual, smiled at the small audience and commenced the usual pseudo-confident introductions.

Ten minutes later, in came an elderly gentleman with an imperious air and a clear expectation that everything should stop while he settled into his usual place. I started reading again, but it soon became obvious from his loud sighs, which became groans, that my work was not to his taste. When I sat down, he was first into the fray: what were my views on rhyme? It was my turn to groan. I answered that I tried to avoid it, unless it came unconsciously and sounded right. In that case, he said, what was my definition of poetry? (Given that I had just finished reading, the question was a fighting one.) Memorable speech? Experience recollected in tranquility? What did it matter? All I could think of was 'a piece of writing in which there is something going on' – nearly adding 'Sir' in my humiliation. Had I ever written a rhymed poem? If so, would I mind reading one? Like a fool, I took the bait and read some laboured piece. 'Far better', thought my tormentor. 'Your other poems aren't moving because they lack the tension of rhyme. They're just prose.'

By this time the atmosphere in the Crediton Library had gone completely to pot; we sat around making desultory points about prep schools, which seemed only to justify my assailant's case that I was engaged in 'mere reminiscence'.

A few days later, a letter arrived revealing his name to be Harry Kemp, one-time intimate of Robert Graves and Laura Riding, 'with whom I served my apprenticeship as a poet in the Thirties', and enclosing something called a 'Report on Hugo Williams', 'a record of my findings' which he was planning to read to the Circle. 'Mr Williams' pieces', went the Report, 'are written at the lowest possible degree of commitment to any significant depth of thought or feeling. What is offered is, as Coleridge might say, fanciful rather than the product of the imagination. He seldom uses rhyme and measure because he does not view the poetic occasion as a *special* occasion.' The Report went on to categorize me as a 'modernist' who thought poetry was primarily 'self-expression'. My 'shapeless juvenilia' were 'an insult to the great rhyming poets of our century, Hardy, Cameron, Graves, James Reeves and Trumbull Stickney'. In a coy gesture he enclosed a handbill for his own privately printed *Collected Poems*, which he offered at the reduced price of £7.

I fell on this with glee and hastened to the Poetry Library, where, sure enough, a complete set of H. Kemp's poetical works were on file, 'donated by the author' and reeking of disuse. The first book fell open at a poem called 'How Poems Come', in which I learnt that 'They come most often when the moon / Riding the trees and house-tops / Signals the magic presence of the Muse'. In another, the poet is visited by the Muse in person, weeping for 'Lovely friends / Robert and gentle James / So lately dead / And witty Norman too, / Who once strayed with his sheep / Into my valley . . .' To which, Kemp answers: 'Today, a dire fate looms, / That of there being none / To praise you rightly, when / I too am gone. / For everywhere the young / Espouse as something new / An impotent *vers libre* . . .'

I have to admit that his poems are not all quite as bad as this. A workmanlike blend of dullness and knowing pomposity by a weekend Graves-ite, they are, however, hardly 'psychic disturbances' inspired direct by 'Mnemosyne and her Nine Daughters'. In an Introduction called 'Advice to Young Poets', he writes that 'Poets whose work is any good are *bound* to be neglected. The better their work, the more ahead of its time it will be . . .'.

When I read that, I found myself warming to the old fool and his idiot integrity. I began to see in this deluded curmudgeon an image of myself in thirty years' time, turning up late at obscure readings, sighing, loosing off broadsides, haranguing New Formalists about the primacy of natural speech, my interminable tirades in favour of Paul Muldoon or Michael Hofmann a pathetic plea for the reconsideration of my own long-out-of-print verses, my absurd doings the subject of derision in the columns of literary weeklies . . . Surely such derision would rebound on its perpetrator? Could we not agree on one thing, at least: 'Poets live by their feelings and must learn to trust them. Theories of poetry are of no consequence whatever' (Harry V. Kemp)?

[5.7.91]

Weldon Kees and the Academic Barbecues

The most battered book in my possession is *The Collected Poems of Weldon Kees*. A life's work curtailed by the author's probable suicide, they are as easy to pack as they are to read and would almost certainly accompany me to that musical desert island, preferably without the Bible or Shakespeare.

On 18 July 1955, Kees's car was found with the radio playing near the entrance to the Golden Gate Bridge, about which he had just finished making a documentary film. His body was never found. Today he is known for a smaller number of poems (about 150) than any other poet of comparable standing. Indeed, he is best known for just four, the strange and powerful 'Robinson' sequence, which pre-dates, pre-figures and, to me, surpasses the many hundreds of over-affected *persona* poems by his contemporary John Berryman, whose manner of dying he also pre-empted. Robert Lowell included Kees in the original published version of a poem about the self-destructive nature of his generation, although when he reprinted it in *History* he named only the poets he knew personally: Roethke, Berryman, Jarrell.

Born in Nebraska in 1914, Kees was a contemporary of J. D. Salinger and shared Salinger's pathological revulsion for anything phoney, a quality which may account for his continued survival among writers, as well as his critical neglect. He is absent from most anthologies, a notable exception being Conrad Aiken's *20th Century American Poetry*, which printed nine poems by Kees, more than any other poet after Eliot and Pound. That his work should remain unavailable in this country and usually out of print in America is absurd, but it says less about Kees than it does about the ignorance and isolation of the critical/academic sector. One wonders whether tenured critics read any poetry at all outside their formal programmes of study and research.

It was in trying (unsuccessfully) to persuade Oxford University Press to take on Kees that I first corresponded with Donald Justice, who edited him for Stone Wall Press in 1960 and considers him 'among the three or four best poets of his generation'. Justice, whose 'Sestina on Six Words by Weldon Kees' was the first (1954) of a growing series of homages by mostly younger writers, handed me on to another poet, Dana Gioia, editor of Kees's stories for Graywolf Press (1984) and tireless champion of Kees's poetry. Gioia, whose *The Gods of Winter* (Peterloo) is the current Poetry Book Society Choice, is another American maverick who probably won't be invited to the academic barbecues. West Coast Sicilian by birth, Stamford and Harvard by education, businessman by admirable preference, reluctant apologist for 'the New Formalists', he has become the *bête noire* of the writing course professors, whom he taunts unmercifully. His massive article in a recent *Atlantic Monthly*, 'Can Poetry Matter?', attacks the university-bred creative writing industry, which, he claims, has turned poetry into a sort of subculture in America, cut off from the mainstream of artistic life by mediocrity and vested interests. Graduate writing programmes, of which there are now over a thousand in the States, will, according to Gioia, produce 20,000 accredited poets over the next decade. A self-fulfilling, self-perpetuating mutual admiration network – the standard greeting between poets is now 'Where do you teach?' – the programmes have hijacked poetry as the raw material needed to stoke up those profitable critical boilers, the end product of which, like toxic waste, is getting poetry a very bad name.

Of course, the poetical un-dead defend their sinecures like cornered rats. Gioia's *Atlantic* broadside has generated hundreds of letters, 'which come in ominous bundles once or twice a week', he tells me. 'They faxed a set to my office, demanding another written response to publish in their August issue, following the one I wrote for July. They seem astonished that an article on poetry has generated so much mail – more than any other article they have published in two years.' He has even been manning a radio call-in show for students trapped Moonie-like in the creative writing scam, reassuring them that there is poetry on the outside.

How Kees, who earned his living in the real world, writing for magazines, taking photographs, making documentary films, learning to paint and play jazz piano, would have relished a war with the forces of institutionalized pretention. In a sense, his dark, pessimistic poetry is prophetic of exactly the creeping sickness Gioia has diagnosed.

[19.7.91]

The Good Old Days

I'm staying with my mother in Albufeira in the Algarve, in her house overlooking the beach. I swim before breakfast, work in the mornings, then we get in the car and drive to some other beach for the afternoon. 'Where shall we go today?' asks my mother. I suggest the name of a beach, then we go to the one she wants to go to.

Last night there was a robbery next door at Bizarro, a British bar that has loud music twice a week. Acrimony flies up and down the Esplanada because those who complain about the music failed to hear the break-in. The matrons sit on the wall in their dark clothes, regarding the hated bar with something like affection.

My mother has lived in Albufeira since the mid-1960s, when she and my father moved there to write plays. The Algarve was an outpost of swinging London in those days, with the usual mixture of pop stars, royalty and criminals, and my mother had the first 'boutique' in the area. Cliff Richard came in. So did ex-King Umberto of Italy. My mother invited him in for a drink and being royalty he preceded her up the little flight of stairs to the flat, where my father was awaiting the arrival of a plumber. A tall foreigner came through the door and my father ushered him straight into the bathroom, vigorously flushing the lavatory to demonstrate what was wrong. My mother arrived a minute later and there was much ho-ho over the Camparis.

Those days are gone. The idyll was flawed. My father found he had to be in the plays he wrote and they were constantly shuffling back and forth trying to get things put on, till my father died, exhausted, in 1969, and my mother lost heart in the shop. She stayed on in the Algarve, marrying, erroneously, an Englishman with a habit of driving his Rover over cliffs at night. Then she took up with a smooth Portuguese gentleman in an Austin Healey. One year I flew out to Lisbon, where Innho lived, and he picked me up at the airport and drove me down to Albufeira. The drive was a sort of trial by ordeal, which I failed. How fast could he go without killing us? How long could I sit there without screaming? I conceded defeat, begging, then commanding him to drive more slowly. He sped on through the Alentejo like some crazed knight errant on his way to rescue my mother from her tower. Unfortunately, her dining table is not so much round as oval and there is a perceptible 'head' to it. I won't say we barged each other out of the way, but we would have done if my mother hadn't placed me firmly in my father's seat, with Innho on her left. He couldn't speak. He wouldn't touch his avocado. He demanded ice-cream. Then he wanted a pea omelette instead of chicken. He obviously wanted to be smacked.

After dinner he unpacked a number of tiny cups which he said he had won for gymnastics as a young man, challenging me to produce some of my own. These cups were about one tenth the size of their English equivalents, but Innho was unaware of this as he proudly set out his acorn-sized trophies among the Copenhagen china on my mother's mantelpiece. When she asked if they were dolls' egg-cups, he flipped, seized a handful of them and dashed over to the window with the intention of hurling them into the sea. We watched as he drew back his arm, but we doubted his resolution. Sure enough, he lowered his arm and replaced the cups on the mantelpiece. Not long afterwards, he fired a pistol past my mother's ear, a shot which proved to be his parting one.

Over the years, as Albufeira changed from fishing village to international destination and the yobs took over from the trendies, my mother made a happier transition from 'Mrs Hugh Williams' to 'Donna Margarita', one of the enduring characters of the coast. She tried to write a bit, but prefers crosswords: 'Darling, what's another word for forgiveness?' Her white cat sits on her portable Olivetti to

74

keep itself cool and prevent her from doing anything they might both regret. This machine must be the same Lettera 22 they wrote their first plays on in the 1950s. I take a toothbrush and clean out a year's deposit of fur. Then I carry it up to the little terracotta room decorated with Stevengraphs. 'The Good Old Days' (a coach), 'The Present Time' (a train), 'Dick Turpin's Last Ride on His Bonnie Black Bess'. One year, when I was writing about my father, my mother delivered up several hundred of his letters, written from North Africa during the war. As I read, a blow-up of my father as Mr Darcy watched me through a long-handled spy-glass. He's watching me now.

[2.8.91]

The Colony Was for Lunch

'I met your father on the boat to New York in 1937, the SS *Washington*. We were both going to be in this Freddie Lonsdale play on Broadway, *Half a Loaf*. I'd heard he was going to be in it, so I got my agent to fix me an interview with Gilbert Miller, the director, who very sweetly gave me the part of someone's girlfriend. Ina Claire played opposite your father. Bubbles Ryan and Viola Keats were in it too. Far too many women. *Once is Enough* it was called here.

'He was surrounded by reporters when I got to the platform at Waterloo. They kept asking him to take his hat off, but he wouldn't. He'd cut his head out drinking the night before and his hat was tipped forward over his eyes. I was very cross. Everyone was being lovely, posing for the cameras, and I thought, there's a spoilt boy. I got into the train and said, what a dreadful young man. But Austin Trevor, who was in it too, said "We're all very fond of Tam you know", so I kept quiet after that.

'Luckily, I met a friend, Ian Galloway, on board. I was sitting having dinner with him on the first evening, drinking orange juice as always then, when a note came over from your father's table saying

75

"Champagne better than orange juice, why don't you join me?" I didn't have the Champagne, but I did join him. I told him I'd met him the year before in Le Touquet, but he said he didn't remember, or pretended not to. I'd flown over for the weekend in someone's plane with Heather and Prairie Field, fantastic names, rich pretty sisters from Australia, one looked exactly like Sylvia Sydney. I'd seen him on the stage when he was touring Australia when I was a girl, but never met him there.

'Anyway, in Le Touquet I bumped into Pat Levy from Sydney. He'd been slaving in Australia for years in order to take his wife to Europe one day. Finally, when he'd got enough money, she decided she didn't want to go. It always stuck in my mind, that. Pat asked me for a drink in the Casino nightclub and while we were dancing I said, "Isn't that Hugh Williams?" and like a fool he introduced us. Pat didn't know him either. He did it to impress me, I think. He married Nedra Ryrey later, who I'd run the three-legged race with at school. We sat down at your father's table, but he didn't take any notice of me at all. I was doing my nut trying to get him to light my cigarette, but he always said he didn't remember anything about it. And that was that until I heard he was doing this play in America. I think he thought he'd just spotted me sitting there at that table with Ian Galloway. Little did he know . . .

'When we got to New York it was evening, and Guy Middleton and Frank Lawton came down to meet the boat in their dinner jackets, straight from a party, and took us back to it with them. The Duke and Duchess of Windsor were there, all the Americans were falling over themselves, curtseying like mad. We made a point of just saying "Hello, how are you?" I suppose it wouldn't have done me any harm to have curtseyed, but I was young then.

'It was great fun in New York in those days. The Colony. The Twenty-One. The Twenty-One was an ex-speakeasy in a cellar run by Mac and Charlie Krindler. There was another place all black and white, very chic, zebra stripes everywhere, I forget the name. The Colony was for lunch. We used to have Daiquiris. You might buy a new hat at Hattie Carnegie's, then go to lunch at The Colony. Then

76

you'd change. We used to change at least twice a day in those days. I had this lovely hat from Hattie Carnegie's, soft white straw, pointed like a clown's hat with a big veil going right across one shoulder. In the evening, after the play, we used to go to the King Cole Bar under The Plaza where Nat King Cole played, or upstairs to the Dining Room where they had Eddy Duchin. Then there was the pianist Joe Bushkin, who was part of the Tallulah Bankhead set, lots of jokes and smokes . . . We were staying at The Gotham at first, then we went to The Devil, which was cheaper.

'I was having a wonderful time, but your father was always rehearsing with Ina Claire. I was furious because she took all the clothes for the play. It sounds blunt, saying I didn't like her. I had admiration for her, but she obviously wasn't having any rubbish from younger members of the cast. When she saw my dark blue wool suit she said she wanted to wear it in the first act, so I ended up wearing trousers, which was quite rare then, sort of bell-bottoms with a sailor's top, not bad. Everyone wore falsies in those days. I didn't, but some people did. They were made of celluloid or something. Once your father pressed Viola Keats's breast to see if she was wearing them and she had to put her hand inside her dress to poke out the dimple.'

[6.9.91]

Anthony Astbury

Publisher, prep school master, member of The Savile Club . . . Anthony Astbury wears a blazer and has his hair cut at Trumpers to disguise the truth that he is really a poet. 'If it hadn't been for Barbara', he tells me, remembering the girl who jilted him in Manchester years ago, 'the list might have read tennis player, insurance man, father of three. She was my Waterloo, Hugo.' 'She was the making of you, Anthony.'

We were talking in a pub in Fitzrovia, the spiritual home of this endearingly rakish figure whose subsequent life has been a homage

77

to his beloved literature. He was just back from staying in Devon with W. S. Graham's widow, Nessie Dunsmuir, whose poems he published, on his way to Norfolk to stay with George Barker, another of his poets. After twenty-five years, he is thinking of giving up his job as English master at Emscote Lawn in Warwick and coming back to London to start again.

The son of a grocer in Bury, Lancs, Astbury left school at fifteen in 1955 and joined the two thousand clerks working in the Manchester office of pre-Beeching British Rail. 'It was like an ant-heap. My job was to go down and get the files out of the cellar. I wanted to write, but I thought you had to go everywhere and read everything, only then would you be able to start. I read the *Encyclopaedia Britannica*. I did go everywhere with the P&O, but that was later and I only saw the sea.'

At nineteen, Astbury was a fair tennis player, handsome, athletic and in love. One day he went to a party and his girlfriend introduced him to an older man she said she was going to marry. There was a scuffle and Tony left Manchester for good.

He knew no one in London, but it was 1960 and the world was young. 'I discovered this coffee bar in Carlisle Street, The Partisan. One night I went down and heard something called a poet reading his work. I'd never heard of this. I knew Wordsworth, but it wasn't that common then. Actually, it was Bernard Kops. It wasn't so much what he read, it was his passion. He read with panache. Kops was reading this ghastly poem in this little cellar and I somehow responded to it.'

He was soon organizing readings himself, upstairs at the Lamb and Flag, or in the Museum Tavern: Rilke, Swinburne, then living poets such as William Empson, George Barker, David Gascoyne, W. S. Graham, John Heath-Stubbs. He was scraping a living at the usual tasks, *clothed* model, bookshop manager, ship's writer for a while, but by 1966, as London turned psychedelic, he'd had enough. 'The wear and tear within had been frightful' begins one of his poems from the period. His friend Peter Vansittart suggested he try teaching. 'He sent me to his old agency in Baker Street, they're gone now, Truman and Knightley, and off I went to Emscote Lawn.' The poem has an epigraph from Pasternak: 'The dreamer turned schoolmaster'.

The readings continued at a gallery he started in Warwick. Then in 1975 the Greville Press was born, named after Fulke, who built Warwick Castle. 'I only intended to publish small editions of a few people I admired – Barker, Gascoyne, a selection from Greville, but it's taken over my life.' One of his early books was an anthology of poems to Mary Queen of Scots, edited by Antonia Fraser. He wrote to Harold Pinter, asking him to read, and received a note which he still has by heart: 'To my surprise I find myself accepting your kind invitation . . .' It was the start of a long friendship, culminating in Pinter's offer of financial support. 'The man's a saint. He was paying it through a company, now he's got to pay it out of his own pocket after tax.'

Astbury runs the Press from his monklike room in the Lodge at Emscote Lawn. Photos of authors line the walls, poetry pamphlets are piled high on the single bed. 'I like it there, but these prep schools are turning out workaholics at the age of twelve. They're like tycoons, up at dawn practising their violins. Some of them follow you about, copying everything you do. The trouble is I've lost interest in myself recently. I'm a burnt-out case, Hugo.' I asked him what he would do if he left Emscote and he said he would come back to London and try to get a job in publishing. From dreamer to schoolmaster and back to dreamer again. 'David Wright keeps saying something has got to be done about me. He's going to send some of my stuff to *The Spectator*.'

The subject of religion never occurs with Tony, but at the end of a long evening he declared himself. 'The brevity of life and all the deaths and entrances make me feel there must be something more to it. That remark of Baudelaire's, "People who don't believe are lazy people".' He once published a cloth-bound list of his favourite illustrious dead, with some recent names added in his own hand. I imagine this most romantic and modest of Englishmen would like nothing more than that one day someone should add his own name to the list. It's not impossible.

[3.9.91]

The Damaged Dressing-Gown

I received a letter from a member of the Wivelsfield Poetry Society, asking if I'd been in communication with their Secretary recently and, if so, whether I had any knowledge of his whereabouts. He'd disappeared, leaving the Society's business in chaos, so she was writing to everyone who'd read there in the last year to make sure they'd been paid. I wrote back saying that I had been paid and that, by an extraordinary chance, I did have news of the Secretary. I'd bumped into him the month before at a writer's retreat in Wales. As far as I knew he was all right and would soon be back in harness. I didn't say what sort of harness he would be back in: the last time I'd seen him he'd been acting extremely strangely.

The writer's retreat was an olde worlde sort of place with beams, a 'poet's hole' and various other hazards, mental as well as physical, which the newcomer had to negotiate before he could feel at home in somewhere like the Quiet Sitting Room, let alone relax in the Writer's Block. The greatest of these, for me, was the Dining Room. Perched directly above my allotted place was a vase on a shelf; hanging over the middle of the table was a glass float in a net. If I hit my head on this float, I was told, it was liable to swing over and dislodge the patron saint of writing from his niche in one of the beams, which might bring me bad luck.

On the first morning I was trying to leave the breakfast table by simultaneously ducking my head, hunching my shoulders and shuffling to the side with my legs still trapped under the table, when I realized that my dressing-gown was caught under the leg of the bench. I would have fallen over backwards if it hadn't torn, releasing me to go staggering off across the room, clutching my dirty cup and plate. Nothing was broken, but my dressing-gown was badly damaged. This was worrying, because it wasn't mine. I'd found it hanging behind the door in my room and had assumed it was abandoned. I tried to tidy up the ripped hem with a pair of scissors and ended up taking off more than I intended.

When I came down to breakfast the next morning, the first person I saw was the Secretary of the Wivelsfield Poetry Society, who had just arrived by car. He didn't say anything, but stood staring at me as if he'd just seen someone who owed him money. I tried to remember what the Society had paid me when I read there. Had I asked too much? Had I added any unjustifiable expenses like buses or meals? It seemed to me that they hadn't even had to pay my travel expenses because I'd been doing another reading nearby. It crossed my mind that they hadn't really wanted me in the first place, but had been persuaded to try pot luck by the Southern Arts Literature Director, who was a friend of mine. From the look on the Secretary's face, I hadn't come up to scratch.

'That's my dressing-gown you're wearing', he blurted. 'I left it in my room last time I was here. I did ask if I could have the same room this time but obviously . . .' He must have remembered that the retreat operated on a first-come-first-served basis. Suddenly he noticed that the dressing-gown was shorter than it should have been. 'What have you been doing to it?' he shouted. 'It's ruined. I bought that at New and Lingwood. It cost me over £200.' I tried to explain what had happened, apologizing profusely, but he wasn't satisfied and said I would have to refund him in full. 'Surely it didn't cost *that* much', I said, trying to head off the confrontation by putting on the kettle. He followed me over to the sink. 'What do you mean *that* much? You don't know anything about it. That's Shantung silk you've been cutting up.' 'It certainly isn't silk', I said. 'It may be rayon. Anyway it's completely worn out.' I turned round to show him the back. 'Look, it's all faded along the folds, as if it's been hanging behind a door for years. Anyway, you left it behind.' The Secretary looked at me with hurt eyes. 'If I'm such a disgusting worn out old character,' he said, 'I'm surprised someone like you wants to be seen in it.'

I returned the dressing-gown, further trimmed, with £10 and a note of apology. I didn't surrender the room. I saw the Secretary about the place from time to time, wrapped in the truncated garment, mouthing vengefully. I couldn't write at all. I kept wondering if I should give him the room to make up for the dressing-gown. I had a beginning, 'A man in a white shirt came to the entrance of Ormond Court and lit a cigarette' and an ending, 'The man in a white shirt put out his cigarette and stepped down into the street', but I couldn't work out the middle. Note the transferred longing for departure. Note the nostalgic urban setting. Maybe retreat is not the best manoeuvre for a writer?

[27.9.91]

Before She Met Me

I realized recently that I have always set my wife's childhood in my own – a Box and Cox arrangement by which we share the same rooms, the same gardens, the same dormitories even, but are forbidden by time and space from meeting or touching, doomed to have led half our lives alone. We had taken the train to Colmar in Alsace, where Hermine spent the years seven to fourteen. She had never been back and I was keen to explore my shadow childhood in those years 'before she met me'.

First stop was the Lycée Camille Sée – vast, Germanic and seemingly abandoned. The builders were in, but no one was about, so we stepped over the debris of learning and back thirty-seven years to when she had last hung her coat on those hooks, obeyed that bell, plunged her hands in that basin. On the floor lay some notes in English on the meaning of the Dire Straits lyric, 'Telegraph Road', a song about time and distance as experienced by American immigrants.

Her time at the Lycée was brought to an end when she got into trouble for going to 'too many parties', the innocence of which can only be guessed at today. The teen breakout that was going on in England at the time (1956) was still twenty years away from provincial France, whose morals had more in common with Spain and Italy than America. Dates were not allowed. Clothes were personal prisons. Hair was cut short. As in the Spanish *paseo*, girls and boys walked endlessly up and down the opposite sides of a particular street, watching and hoping. If they were very good, little gatherings were permitted after lunch on Sundays: tangos, waltzes and *paso dobles* on the radiogram. 'We were all Jeunesse Musicales de France in the hope of sitting next to someone interesting at concerts. My only record was *La Nuit Sur Le Mont Chauve* by Saint-Saëns. There was an Audrey Hepburn contest.'

The atmosphere in that little Catholic backwater must have been explosive, so the hatches had to be battened down. At the Couvent de L'Assomption, where she was sent as a punishment, they weren't allowed to talk during break, only to play. 'On the rare occasions when talk was permitted, it had to be in groups – useless. My mother was off to the Cannes Film Festival for *L'Alsace*, so I had to board. One night I was woken by a friend who wanted me to go down to the garden to light fireworks. She said some boys I knew were there, but I was too cowardly. Soon the place was vibrating with fireworks. I heard the nuns' voices, then I drifted back to sleep.'

Next morning she was summoned by the Mother Superior and accused of starting it all: the boys they caught had known only her name. When her mother returned from Cannes, she invited the firework boys over and talked to them before H. was allowed to see them. A rumour started that they had broken into the convent and raped a nun. In Colmar Cathedral, Hermine showed me the very confessional where she had knelt, aged thirteen, trying to imagine her sins for the benefit of some clammy cleric. I drew back the musty curtains and flicked on an obnoxious little reading lamp – my contribution to enlightenment.

We had followed the old tram route to the outskirts of town, to her old house in the Rue de la Soie, a tree-lined avenue named after the synthetic material produced by the nearby factory managed in those days by her father. Standing on a dustbin, I located the window of the downstairs lavatory whose walls she had covered with Camembert labels, the same year I began my own collection of gramophone needle boxes. 'I would stand in there staring at myself in the mirror. I thought that if I stared at myself long enough the Virgin would appear out of my features . . .'

How well I understood those efforts at transfiguration, except that my own model had been my father. It would be another year before we both cut out the same photo of Brigitte Bardot advertising Perrier water; ten before we met.

I had caught glimpses of Hermine as she grew up; I was looking for a line going in the other direction – from the woman back to the child. The connection was merely rational until she showed me Colmar's greatest art treasure, the fifteenth-century *Vierge au Buisson de Roses* by Martin Schongauer. Instead of being dressed in the usual blue, the beautiful, red-lipped girl is wearing flowing scarlet robes whose transferred sexuality is almost palpable. She is surrounded by insects, birds and fruit; wild strawberries touch her foot. Hermine would pop into the Cathedral whenever she was passing and spend a few minutes gazing at this vision. I remembered the hours she had spent looking at certain paintings in the Royal Academy when we first met and I saw her now, standing in Colmar Cathedral in her illegal clothes, lines drawn down the backs of her legs for stockings. I looked at the ambiguous example expressed in the Virgin's worldly, perfect features and felt I knew what sort of understanding had passed between them.

[18.10.91]

In the Footsteps of *The Third Man*

'In the Footsteps of *The Third Man* – With Original Locations and Insights into the Vienna Sewer System – Bring your own Torch.' In 1948, Graham Greene was invited by the Viennese film mogul Alexander Korda to go to Vienna to write a quick thriller about the black market, before they destroyed all the ruins created by Allied bombing. Greene found a map of the city showing the sewers and noticed they ran across Sector boundaries. They didn't – our guide Dr Friederike Mayr takes pleasure in pointing out that Harry Lime could never have escaped into the Second District, as the old sewers cover only a small area of the city – but Greene thought they should and he was right. I notice that Dr Mayr's comments in English are shorter than the German, but never mind. We follow her into a urinous overspill tunnel giving onto the Danube.

Can this be the smell Orson Welles took exception to in 1948? He refused to film down here, so they 'perfumated' the walls and he agreed to one brief scene; all the shots of him splashing through water are of Otto Shurer, an unemployed butcher who used to hang around the set. The water, too, is a stand-in. The tunnel was dry then as now, so perfumed water had to be pumped in. Director Carol Reed wanted rats but real ones ran away and tame ones sat up on their hind legs and begged. Dr Mayr reveals these details in a knowing, contemptuous tone, as if unmasking the film for what it is – 'a fake', a favourite word of hers. We see the converging channels with hand-operated escape hatches, the ladders used by Harry Lime and the curved sewer architecture relished by Reed, who learnt his melodramatic cameracraft working as assistant to film director Edgar Wallace. (Can this be right?)

We seem to be off somewhere on the Underground, hopefully shedding children en route. The stately Josefplatz is the unlikely setting for the traffic accident that allegedly killed Lime, but perhaps there were cars here during the war. We stare at the window from which the old caretaker and his Nazi daughter witnessed the fake killing. Actor Paul Harbinger didn't know what was going on, or what he was saying, until he saw the German-speaking version of the film, purged of all Anglo-American class nuances, and, not surprisingly, a flop in Vienna when it came out. The Doctor explains that the Viennese had had enough of ruins and degradation in 1950. She reminds us that Austria was still on food stamps at the time. It was to protest at this that Harbinger took a week's food allowance to the film's press conference, upsetting only his family when he forgot to take it home again. An American in the crowd lodges his own complaint here: does the Doctor realize that the rest of Europe, including England, was also on rations? He is some kind of *Third Man* freak who would like to run his own walking tour, from a more radical viewpoint.

His presence further inhibits the Doctor, whose English bits are now even more cryptic. To hear her geographical quibbles you would think the film's numerous 'cheats' somehow impugned Vienna's authenticity, and by association, her own. The kiosk is in the wrong place; it doesn't lead to the sewers; when Harry and his shadow run along under those gothic windows, he couldn't possibly come out in the Heldenplatz, and so on.

The American unleashes a tide of Third-Maniana on me. Did I know that Greene himself speaks the intro on the British version, but not on the American, which is twelve minutes shorter, and, in his humble opinion, superior? Reluctantly, I accept his business card.

The much-reduced crowd has now reached the famous doorway where the cat rubs against Welles's shoe and a light falls across his face as the Harry Lime Theme begins, written, as everyone knows, by Anton Karas. I thought it was written by Larry Adler, but luckily say nothing, as Karas turns out to be a national folk hero. Reed and Greene found him playing the tune in an out-of-town wine garden and rejected the Vienna Philharmonic in his favour. He couldn't read music, so they sat him in front of the film and got him to improvise. When the record came out he opened a café called 'The Third Man' and played his annoying jingle an estimated 75,000 times until jealous, anti-Semitic or tired neighbours obliged him to retire – a millionaire.

The last insight of the tour is the grating where the dying Harry's fingers appear, but this too is not the actual grating, only the model for the real one, which had to be 'faked up' because the real one was too thick for Welles's fingers to be seen, although they aren't Welles's fingers, of course. I put my own fingers into the muddy holes and, sure enough, it is too thick. Dr Mayr says she will leave us on our own for the ride on the Big Wheel, which, as we know, was filmed at Elstree.

[1.11.91]

Roistering

In the wake of Bill Buford's study of international soccer hooliganism, it may be worth considering the related phenomenon of 'roistering', the original 'noisy celebration of life' from which the modern hybrid has descended. Roistering receives less attention than its mass culture derivatives of yobbery and lager loutishness, but it is still very much alive in certain parts of Wiltshire and Chelsea and may even be gaining in unpopularity. Although a pale reflection of its antique original, it is apparently funnier, sillier and less harmful than standard hooliganism, being based on nonsense rather than violence.

According to Angus Sixsmith, author of a semi-official work on the subject (*The Glossamery of Roistering Slang*. Bagwash Publications, 114 Bravington Road, London W9), a roisterer is one in whom 'the spirit of childhood lives on'. 'Goodwill', he protests, 'rather than aggression is what characterises the seasoned roisterer . . . Though sometimes contributing to knife-edge situations, he will always display a natural talent for avoiding confrontation and' – the cynic will smile here – 'would not do well in a brawl.' A random selection of roistering parlance will give some idea of the background to this thriving sub-culture.

The roistering arena is conceived as a *desert*, varying in the intensity of its sexual/alcoholic deprivation from the *Gobi*, through the *Kalahari*, to the *Sahara*, the idea being to *hurtle* (move) or *hose* (drink) your way from one *oasis* or *hoseria* to the next without reaching *Siberia*, a mental wasteland inhabited by those on whom the *portcullis* has fallen, a sudden blotting out of thought brought on by *over-refreshment*, which may leave the roisterer with some *gutterwork* to catch up on – *Royal Gutterwork* if he happens to be in Kensington or Chelsea. Signs of relief from the nomadic way of life include a *camel*, a woman of exceptional staying power who can lead him to an oasis; *a dated palm*, one who can provide only fleeting satisfaction; *wells* and *caravanserais*, which provide the kind of relief that has to be paid for. An *equatorial rain forest* is an oasis that turns out to be an unending stretch of lush vegetation, providing permanent assuagement from desert life, but which may be accompanied by certain side effects: *buffness* (as in envelopes), *mothballing* (unreasonable hoarding of money), *cloistering* (the reverse of healthy roistering) or *Ganges* (the condition of lingering in the mud of an oasis after the dates have dried up). A *mirage* may arise when a man *adged up* on sexual deprivation or alcohol poisoning makes a lunge at a *flicker* (girl) who is no longer there. *Gerrymandering* refers to his inability to tell whether it was Gerry or Amanda.

If the *roister* should indulge in a *boatrace* round too confined a *pitch*, or a *spoof* such as driving to London Airport stopping at green lights and shooting red ones, it is liable to *lose a rollock* (brush with the law). A *backburner* is a roisterer whose presence steadies the *roisterboat* at such times.

Central to the spirit of roistering is the concept of *building*, or *acceleration*, where the tempo of an outing is gradually increased to the point where a *crest* comes into view, if not a *snap*. This is achieved by techniques such as *hoovering* (collecting peoples' belongings), *chainwork* (linking hands across a busy street), *jumbo-work* (playing bagpipes on aeroplanes), and *sheepwork* (attaching a sheep's head to one's own). *Over-acceleration* occurs when one thing leads to another, dragging others down with it, to the point where an *avalanche* is set in motion, a state of affairs relished by some connoisseurs. It is now that a *snap* may be imminent. All roisterers are familiar with the sight of a scowling, quivering man who approaches, asking the eternal question, 'Why don't you grow up?'

While a *snap* may be the unwritten goal of some roisterers, for others it will always be *lassiework*, the rounding up of stray *flickers*, *ferrets*, *polecats* and *maidavailables* with intent to *ravish*, *roger*, *root*, or otherwise *merge with* on a temporary basis. If *over-refreshed*, the amorous roisterer may experience *trouser-calm*, or *marshmallow*, followed by *PRD* (post-roistal depression). *Trough-*

work will be called for. In his efforts to *fade and freshen*, or simply *boomerang* (return to the party), he may be seen on cold dawns anxiously addressing a taxi driver through a closed window, an activity known as *misting*. He will awaken back at the *low libido club* attended by the *weasels* and *badgers* of hangover, a day's *filth* (work) hanging over his head.

If the reader experiences no irritation at these childish locutions, hotly denying that they justify bad behaviour by dressing it in harmless metaphor, he may count himself, like me, a roisterer manqué. Many would-be hedonists, it seems, feeling themselves excluded by birth from football hooliganism, have found in the roistering fraternity (motto: 'The World Is My Roister') just what they have been looking for all their lives.

[15.11.91]

The Bright-eyed Mariner

Bruce Chatwin was in Wales on a flying visit to the set of *On the Black Hill*. He was just back from Africa, full of manic glee for the chaotic filming of another of his books, *The Viceroy of Ouidah*, whose star, the foul-mouthed Klaus Kinski, Chatwin was sad to report, had gone mad in the heat. Kinski: Do you live in England? Chatwin: Most of the time. Kinski: I don't even change planes in England.

According to Bruce, Kinski had taken over control of the film from Werner Herzog, positioning the cameras, doing the lighting and peering endlessly through the lens at his stand-in. The cameraman had made the mistake of shoving back when shoved out of the way by Kinski and the enraged Klaus had sunk his fangs into the man's arm. The cameraman returned to Germany for treatment and another one was sent for, a Czech. Kinski: Do you have toilet paper in your country? Cameraman: Yes, but not enough to wipe *your* arse.

Chatwin relished all this hugely and relayed it (repeatedly) to the

Black Hill crew, causing them to stop what they were doing and gather round. He was already ill by the time he came to Brecon in 1987, defiantly declaring it to be Chinese chicken pox, and talking, talking, talking to anyone who would listen, giggling at his own jokes, blue eyes gleaming out of his weather-beaten, angelic face. We were watching a Nativity Play done as a project for the film by the local primary school – much giggling and baa-ing of real sheep. 'Can you find us a room, sir? My wife's going to have a baby any minute.' Joseph's piping treble was incomprehensible, but Bruce was ecstatic. 'That's exactly as I took it down,' he said. 'The intonations are exact. You know, the whole story started from here, from seeing that Nativity, though of course the one I saw was more humble, almost insignificant.'

Chatwin first came to Wales when he was eight in 1946. 'Me and my father had to fetch our old car, a Lanchester, which had been sitting in my great uncle's barn since before the war. I saw the Black Mountains and I immediately wanted to go there. We spent the night on the hillside in the car and when we woke up we were surrounded by sheep and dew. I've never forgotten it.'

He next came to Wales from Marlborough with a youth club that was supposed to mix the classes. They went to a holiday camp and did walling and roofing. Later, he stayed at an abbey that used to belong to Walter Savage Landor. 'The place was owned by this Italian Contessa, who bought it from Landor. Eric Gill and David Jones used to stay with her. I remember her setting up a table in the cloister to receive rent from her tenants. It was like having a window straight into the world of Byron. Hardly anything has changed around here since my grandparents came on bicycling tours as teenagers in the 1870s. Even the clothes are the same. You can still get the double-fronted striped shirts in Hay-on-Wye. You have a gold stud for Sundays, a copper one for weekdays, which leaves a green mark. You have a silver watch chain, then, if all goes well, you have a gold one.'

When Chatwin began *On the Black Hill* in 1981, it was still possible to go out and find people who could talk about World War

I, but he couldn't have done it any later. Of nine WWI veterans he hunted up, seven were dead. 'I met one man with no arms and no legs, sitting by the fire being looked after by his sister. He was quite happy to talk, but when I questioned him about going over the top, he froze, as it all came back to him. He's dead now.'

Chatwin explained that, after the war, the raised hemlines of the 1920s had been too much for some Welsh people. One hill farmer on a rare visit to town had to turn back after what he saw: he felt physically sick, he said. It was this shock of light from another era that was to become the theme of Chatwin's book, the image of a century turning back in horror from what it was approaching. By the time he had written thirty pages describing this cataclysmic confrontation of men and women, represented by the nineteenth and twentieth centuries, he realized he was onto something more than just a short story.

He described his high-energy work methods as follows. First, he would find an 'informant' who was 'conscious' of a particular date. The informant would come up with some vague story and Bruce would go off to the *Hereford Times* or somewhere and pull out that date. He would then feed details of local news back to the informant – by now positively popping with the excitement of it all – who would then be able to produce a whole lot of further, more concrete information. If he needed a new chapter for the book, all he had to do was go fishing and pull one in.

'Fishing is an apt metaphor. Elizabeth Sifton, my editor at Viking, called me up and told me there was something missing at some point, a bridge passage of some kind. I was just going out to buy some cowslip wine for a party and the people in the pub were talking about this gigantic stuffed trout behind the bar, a "cannibal trout" they said it was. All I had to do was reel in.'

One hill farmer he hooked, talking about Kitchener's recruiting drive, remembered standing in line in Hereford in 1914 when the pompous English colonel, sizing up the new recruits, asked one of the farm lads, 'Well, boy, what would you do if the man next to you got shot?' The boy fiddled with his cap for a moment. 'Shut his eyes and take his watch.' Chatwin was taken over the farm by the man's grandson and found one of the first tractors to be used in this country, a Fordson, probably imported from America in 1914 as part of the war effort, buried up to its axles in earth and nettles. 'I said to the boy, do you realize what you've got here? It ought to be in a museum.' "Oh, don't worry about that," he said. "I'll soon get that going again." You see, he had no notion of time passing. He'd just start it up and carry on. It's like that around here.'

The recruiting scene and the tractor both turn up in the book. Chatwin couldn't finish it at first and put the first two-thirds aside to write *Ouidah*. It was then he heard about Yaddo, the American writer's colony, where, inevitably, he encountered the ultimate feminist sculptress, who knocked on his door one evening and invited him to view her 'vaginal iconography in sand and lacquer' – a case of the buttonholer holed. When he finished the book, he showed it to the Welsh farmer who had turned back in disgust at the sight of women's calves. ''Tis a good book,' said the man. ''Twere well writ.'

It was time for the Three Wise Men to come on, muttering inaudibly about gold, frankincense and myrrh. The camera swung round for a reaction shot and a crowd of local extras filed into the hall. All was as it should be and Bruce's face was a picture of satisfaction as he watched them doing their reacting. What did he feel, I asked, seeing his characters coming to life like this? He looked at me as if I were mad. 'Nothing, I feel nothing. It's all a lot of nonsense. There are people whose job is to make films and they need stories, that's all.'

I understood that the real story of the Black Hill was far away from that bustling film set, which he found enjoyably absurd. It was this which left him free to charm everyone in sight. He was there to have fun. I imagined him as a sort of alternative Ancient Mariner, indifferent to the wedding, but buttonholing the wedding-guests as they tried to go into the church, making them roar with laughter at his tumbling tales . . .

The Wedding-Guest sat on a stone:
He cannot choose but hear;
And thus spake on that ancient man,
The bright-eyed Mariner.

[29.11.91]

The Smile on the Face of Gioconda Belli

One of the most interesting Greville Press publications is Gioconda Belli's *Nicaragua Water Fire*. It consists of the title poem about her home country – 'my love my little raped girl / rising to her feet adjusting her skirt / stalking the murderer' – and 'New York', a contrasting diatribe against that city's 'unintelligible graffiti / signs of those who don't know what to say'. The work is remarkable for treating poetry's reduced battle lines (specificity, exclusivity) as if they didn't exist and going for the all-out assault: 'The peasant keeps Agrarian Reform titles in a wooden box / let the devils go round announcing the good news of forgiveness / to those who saw huts go up in flames.' Her decision to go ahead and put everything into a poem, regardless of the rules of good behaviour, make them hard to like in the way that one 'likes' the little book one keeps in the lavatory, but perhaps it is appropriate if the subject is a country. I wouldn't like to write a poem about 'England', but perhaps I should try.

Her Scotch Tape, shanty town approach to writing poems works well enough when she is speaking from inside her subject; in *Nicaragua Water Fire* she has earned the right to sweep it all up into a ball. But the poem about New York comes across as a collage of old clichés and paranoias, made even more corny by its disjointed syntax: 'country of mad enlightened poets painters / floods of light dance schools', although one would have to say the same about Ginsberg, who is partly responsible. Having visited both countries, I can confirm that 'tiny poor coffee-exporting countries drink watery

93

coffee / so that in New York we may go past shops / where coffee saturates the smell of the entire street'. But that glaring 'we' gives the lie to Belli's ambiguous status as a privileged travelling Nicaraguan. Where is she standing exactly? She gets into worse trouble when she identifies with 'Nicaragua my little girl' who 'goes off in planes to tell her story / talks till it's coming out of her ears / to newspapers in incomprehensible languages . . .' Her charm is that she doesn't give a damn.

Her friend Salman Rushdie has said that 'in Belli's kind of public love poetry she comes closer to expressing the passion of Nicaragua than anything I have yet heard'. His book about Nicaragua, *The Jaguar Smile*, takes its title from the limerick about the young girl from that country who 'smiled as she rode on a jaguar' (although I thought it was a tiger) and hints that it was Gioconda's gioconda smile – 'the girl on the jaguar looked like the Mona Lisa' – that gave him the idea: an ironical prophecy seeing that the Sandinistas were to be eaten up themselves a few years later.

Rushdie gave me her telephone number when I went to Central America in 1988. I was making a programme about the Pan-American Highway and Belli gave up an afternoon to be filmed driving me round Managua. The film crew called her the designer Sandinista, saying she looked as though she'd flown in from Paris for the Revolution. But she couldn't help having curly hair and being beautiful. 'I am a good driver', she told me, swinging the provocative 'action car' (a white convertible) through the depressing, quake-torn city. 'I used to drive for the *clandestinos*. I had to know how to calculate the lights so that we never stopped. Everyone drove in their rear view mirrors under Somoza.'

Belli had kept her job with an advertising agency as a cover. 'Nobody suspected me because I came from a bourgeois family and didn't look suspicious to a lot of people.' She was forced to flee and lived in Costa Rica for three years, 'dreaming of the day I wouldn't have to look at a newspaper and see people I loved dead on the front page'.

We were driving through scrubby fields that had been the busy streets of downtown Managua until the earthquake of 1972, when they were summarily bulldozed by Somoza. The occasional quake-proof relic of capitalism reared its head out of the wasteland – the Intercontinental Hotel with its 'dollar shops' and spies, the ruins of a Grundig showroom, the office block where Belli used to work in another lifetime. Then, down by the lake, the Plaza and the gutted cathedral, home to lovers, children, pigeons, trees and, in the old days, *subversivos*. A convoy of lorries entered the Plaza, full of sunburnt young Sandinistas home from the coffee front. With their bandanas and rifles they looked like Israeli *kibbutzniks*. 'This was the place to be on our day of Victory,' Gioconda said. 'I was in charge of bringing our Free Country newspaper into Nicaragua in this rattly old aeroplane. We hit a storm and the plane started leaking and I was trying to keep the papers dry, thinking we were going to crash on our day of triumph. Eventually we made it and there were our *campañeros* waiting on the airstrip with a truck, shouting "Patria Libre", so we called back "O Morir". All these people with radiant faces wanting to embrace us, they were crazy for the newspaper, raising their arms and touching us. I saw *compañeros* I hadn't seen for many years, who I thought had been killed and seeing them alive again, it was very romantic. They would take you and throw you in the air and embrace you. There was this mixture of elation and thinking you are still dreaming from tiredness and painful too because of the friends who were killed in the struggle, who would have been so happy. All this mixed emotion comes together so that you are laughing and crying and it was something I think you can only understand if you are there.'

We got out of the car so that Gioconda could be filmed reciting her victory-day poem: 'the deaths of Ricardo, Pedro, Carlos, / so many others they tore from our side, eyes they gouged / without ever blinding us to the day / which today breaks in our hands . . .' Prophetic speeded-up kitsch storm-clouds hurry over the cathedral in the finished film.

As part of a BBC film crew, I had thought I would be an exception to the rule that 'nobody passes through Nicaragua without something happening to him'. I realized later that I was wrong. I had met Gioconda Belli, she of the beautiful warlike smile. I had been driven round Managua by a poet who had driven cars for *clandestinos*. It occurred to me that her poetry had earned its right to inclusivity.

[20.12.91]

A Beige Plastic Gulag

I came home one night and found an Amstrad word processor sitting on my desk. It had been delivered to my house by Charles Shaar Murray, who was progressing to a Mackintosh for his life of John Lee Hooker and wanted me to have first pop at the one on which he had written his book about Jimi Hendrix, *Crosstown Traffic*. He only wanted £250 for it. He said it would revolutionize my life. He said it would play progressive guitar solos.

I remembered the year my wife brought a word processor on holiday with us to Brittany. By train, bus and foot, we transported the mass of hardware into our borrowed cottage and set it up on top of the fridge, the only place that had the right power point. The fridge had to be off while the computer was on, so my wife would sit typing away, her feet in the salad compartment, while a puddle of water formed round her chair. It looked like a bad murder-story scenario.

To justify the machine's easy dominance of our lives, she offered to put my growing list of wild flowers onto a floppy disc, a favour I was to regret when her own precious research into tightrope-walking was suddenly confiscated by the machine. Hanging on the phone to Paris, we pressed every button we could find. The only thing we could get to come up on the screen were sixty-five different lists of wild flowers, each with one more flower on it than the one before. It was then I understood why WP sufferers seem to stare wildly out into the night when they are working, like people under a curse.

I lost no time. I rounded up the various bits and pieces – keyboard, terminal, printer, other thing, the whole grisly gulag of beige plastic – and bundled them into a taxi. Charlie was dismayed when I turned up with his baby in the middle of the night. His study was now fully occupied by his new favourite and he was plainly in love. The Mac, he told me dreamily, could wake him up in the morning, cook him a three-course meal, cheer him up when he was feeling blue and kiss him goodnight when he went to bed – all in colour, with noises, jokes and cartoons. The last thing he wanted was a straight old Amstrad bringing him down. Why didn't I hang on to it for a month or two, get the feel of it, then, if I still didn't like it . . . but he was sure it would revolutionize my life.

I felt sorry for the Amstrad, but I had to say no. I explained that my problem wasn't just an allergy that could be cleared up by the gradual introduction of more and more technology into my life; what I had going for me was a full-blown neurosis, and, as he knew, a neurosis should never be challenged, only humoured. I would be more likely to exchange my Adler portable for a biro than to take one of those deadpan dinosaurs into my home. Besides, they were unclean, they spread diseases like VD, and caused impotence. The hygienic Adler, chaste yet virile, took the art of mechanical writing just as far as it could go before process started to impose its own louche values on the user, often without his knowledge. One more step down that road and it would cross the line dividing usefulness from hollow-eyed dependency. He'd be telling me next that there was a floppy disc that could correct grammar and spelling . . .

Charlie said there was. He himself had a disc that could check and correct facts, another that could tidy up his style. He had one that could cut or extend his work to order, by inserting or removing metaphors. He was thinking of sending off for a programme that could inject amusing one-liners into his copy, though he'd heard that these tended to date. I said that this might prove a worthwhile investment in his case, but what about people like me who had an old-fashioned attachment to paper and pen? And what about my own habit of cutting up my stuff with scissors and spreading the different bits out over my desk-top, so that I could see them all at

97

once and reorder them at will, wouldn't this be hard to reproduce in the confined area of a WP screen?

Charlie looked worried here. Strangely enough, he said, this was precisely his own method of working, but he had to admit that even the Big Mac couldn't display very many bits simultaneously, only a few; he had to remember the rest. I followed up my lead by pointing out what an incredible invention the pen was. As a technological breakthrough it would surely provoke a revolution in a computer-bound society. The golden triangle of head, hand and eye . . .

As he stacked the cartons of unwanted Amstrad in the corner of his study, Charlie was beginning to lose patience with me. If only people like me would take the trouble to enter the twentieth century, it would make the invasion of the body-snatchers so much easier. Believe him, he had my best interests at heart . . .

[10.1.92]

Short Pieces of Writing, which I Post

Ed Dorn, reading from his new book of poems, *Abhorrences*, at the South Bank Poly last week, said he didn't like the word 'poetry'; what he did were really essays. 'When we got rid of rhyme and metre it made the business of poetry harder, not easier. I consider poetry to be a long forgotten branch of science.' What he said seemed right and there were nodding heads all round, but when I came to wonder what my own poems really were, I had to conclude that they were letters: the old habit drummed into me when I went away to school: *Don't forget to write.*

It's after lunch on Sunday and the letter-writing period has come round again. What on earth is there to say? Mr Ray has put a few ideas on the board: results of the match, description of the floods, the Lecture on Roman Britain, dentists' appointments . . . I can't write about *that*.

'What rotten luck about not being able to come down', I wrote in 1952. 'But don't worry because Flower said I could go out with him, so we changed into his jeans and practised archery. I have started shooting and boxing. You'll really like Flower when you come down, but if you see him don't say anything about the gang, as we aren't sure about it yet. His father gave me a pound.'

Letters in those days were either begging letters not to have my hair cut too short – 'Can you write a letter putting VLT against my name for VERY LIGHT TRIM? I got an appalling cut again in spite of everything, short round the parting and the parting in the wrong place' – or thank-you letters, or letters promising I had written thank-you letters: dutiful, sloping, uphill affairs whose form is their content: 'Dear Mr Flower, Thank you so much for the pound.' (Pause for thought) 'It was so kind of you to give it to me.' Letters were to get letters back, emotional blackmail notes, veiled threats, agreements not to blub: 'I came 14th with 311. I wasn't looking forward to the fire escape practice but once my fingers left the ledge I quite enjoyed it. I'm sorry about my writing. I know it slopes backwards and is a sign of weakness.'

Reading these letters today, they don't seem so much unhappy as unnatural, like a new suit that still prickles. It's clear as day they were performances even then, with whirlpools of unspoken meaning. 'Darling Mummy and Daddy, I had a terrible week last week and on Friday night I felt as though I would never stop worrying. I made up a four-line dirge but it all seems so trivial now. *The day is done and failure hangs all around. / New worry's furrows live upon my brow, / And though tomorrow is another day / I cannot drive my dreams from dawn to dawn.*' When my guard comes down, feeling occasionally flickers: 'What do you think of Elvis Presley? I have listened to all his records and I think he's terrific.'

Letters from those days, wheedling, boasting, pleading, bragging, couched in that would-be swaggering language with the odd bad joke thrown in, seem all too aware, at the age of nine or ten, that writing was an attempt at transformation, like combing your hair into quiffs, or like the Knight putting on magical armour. They are blissfully unaware still of the paradox that it would be safer not to put on armour in the first place.

All my letters survive. None of my parents'. And yet the feeling of blue for me is still the feeling of blue envelopes propped on the shelf in break: perfect invisible margins from Him, lovely great loops from Her. How I wish I'd kept a few of those jolly, newsey, namey catalogues of ordinariness, designed to reassure, but always scented with that murdering trace of 'Moment Supreme', 'Fleurs de Rochailles', 'Joy', 'Amour Amour'. I used to keep the envelopes, but I let the letters slip from my fingers into the bin, even before I went outside to kick a ball around, or join the human radiator. 'I am sending the going out days for you to fill in', I wrote on one of those long ago Sunday afternoons. 'Can you write a letter saying when you are coming down? I don't know where it is, but apparently there is a map, or you could ask. If you write on Monday I'll get it on Tuesday and can use the envelope to smuggle the brawn out of the dining room. After supper on Tuesdays there is a big queue for the lavatories. Last week there was a blockage and all the brawn was found stuck together. When you come down can we go and see the model village?'

The letter is dated 1953, which means that by that year polythene bags hadn't made their triumphant debut in our particular backwater, rendering even my parents' sturdy dark blue envelopes redundant. I took their letters for granted then, yet part of me still waits for them, on the off-chance that they have filled in the going out days at long last. Poems are still short pieces of writing which I post. I suppose the idea is that if I write often enough the reply will be waiting for me in one of those blue envelopes, propped on the mantelpiece when I come out to play.

[24.1.92]

The Philosophy of Women, or An Essay on Self-Confidence

I received a call from 'Updates', organizers of English Literature conferences, asking me to give a forty-minute lecture on anything at all for £350. Would I like to think up a title and call them back?

Indeed I would. Fighting off the fear of public humiliation – I have never given a lecture – with the prospect of £350, I suggested the subject I was writing about at the time, letter-writing, adding 'In the Age of the Fax' to make it sound more academic.

After they'd hung up, I was left wondering if my rather thin article about letters, recycled from old poems, themselves recycled from even older letters, could in fact stand another recycling in the form of a lecture, never mind this subsequent rehash on the subject. A lecture sounded as though it had to have a point to it, or at least a theme. How low was I prepared to sink, I wondered, in order to avoid working?

I decided I was prepared to sink as low as trying to retrieve some of the hundreds of letters I had written to my first girlfriend from school. I still knew her, and I was sure she wouldn't mind my looking at them. After all, they had been my main occupation for years. They were all I did at school. While other boys were having masturbating races in class, I was taking notes for bi-weekly outpourings to my adored but vaguely remembered one on the other side of England. I remembered sending her, in a moment of intense displacement activity, a 'French letter', along with a copy of 'The Virgin Typist', painstakingly copied out from a crumbling manuscript that was going round the school. 'Eskimo Nell' was another of my billets-doux (it was a miracle I wasn't sacked). Had any heat from these slabs of porn transferred itself to my letters, I wondered, or had they been offered in a spirit of tired (but virginal) detachment?

I rang up and went round. I was dying to see this hoard of old thoughts, which, even if they didn't help my lecture, would give off some haunting lost innocence. 'I don't know why you keep on asking for unsuitable books', I read. 'How unsuitable do you mean? I always thought girls were more sexually educated than boys. Anyway I am not a connoisseur because they are always concocted and impossible.' After answering various enquiries about older, titled boys, I went on, 'I did a Sunday essay on Self-Confidence, but I managed to get well off the track onto the philosophy of women. I've done another on Revenge this week with lots of jealous lovers maddened by desire. Our biology teachers are Bugger Bolton and Sexy Morris. They are very keen on asexual reproduction.'

In the intervening years my ideas on the philosophy of women had long disappeared, likewise 'The Virgin Typist' manuscript. As I read on through my would-be cynical jottings, I realized that they were not love letters in content, so much as in form. Written furtively and too often, they were themselves a kind of lovemaking. As replacements for sex, it was natural that they should have become their own most urgent subject-matter. 'One person gets lots of letters from girls, never writes back and shows them to everyone. I just don't understand it.' 'Thanks so much for your letter, it was wonderful to hear from you. I think our letters must have crossed in the post, so I won't be able to make this very interesting.'

While other teenagers were 'seeing' each other to their hearts' content, we little monks were condemned only to 'hear from' our loved ones. 'I have no special news but just felt the need to write as it gives me a sense of perspective. Also the picture I have of you in my mind always seems to need a letter.' In fact, the picture I had of her in my mind was the one of Brigitte Bardot in my desk, but it is interesting that the picture needs a *letter* rather than a kiss. The two things had become mixed up in my mind and have remained so ever since: letters as currency, promissory notes, IOUs for love. Here was the dilation of sex becoming the dilation of writing before my eyes.

And here, thirty years later, was the object of my long-ago affection looking over my shoulder as I read. As far as I remembered, the letters had gone on for years, interrupted only by the occasional deflationary outing to Brighton in the holidays. Where were all the others? I asked. Were there only ten of them left?

It was a long story. A box of old letters had gone to Scotland with her when she first got married, then a few years later, when she and her husband started to drift apart, he'd been looking after the children one rainy afternoon and suggested they get out her old letters and use some of them to decorate an old screen, not just mine, lots of peoples'. She didn't know what had happened to the screen after the divorce. She said her husband had even prevented her from getting her bed back, by converting it into a four-poster.

I remembered so well coming home one holidays and, after the usual week of putting it off, calling her up. Following a brief exchange, she told me she was getting married. 'Don't be silly', I said. 'You've got your O-levels.' But it was true. Aged seventeen, she was engaged to an 'older man' of twenty-nine, a doctor of something. The three of us went on a jolly outing to Brighton of all places, where her debonair fiancé was arrested for holding up a cinema box office with a toy gun. The whole thing was beyond me.

Thus it was that my eager, defensive, concealing, revealing schoolboy love-letters reached their final destination in the appropriate form of a device for hiding behind, and, coincidentally, escaped a worse fate as the subject of my forthcoming lecture.

[21.2.92]

Blondin, Hero of Niagara

Not far from where I live in Islington stands the Business Design Centre – three unlovely English words which have a distinctly dated feel now that the matt-black 1980s are coming into perspective and ill-repute. I can't help thinking they should have stuck with the original name. Until recently, the old stained-glass window announcing 'Royal Agricultural Hall' was preserved over the entrance to the new subterranean car park. Now that too has gone, and the car park is called 'Car Park' in case anyone should be disappointed to find rows of BMWs down there instead of teams of marines dismantling field guns, Spanish bullfighters, mule and donkey shows, or the tightrope walker Blondin wheeling a lion through the foggy air.

Of course, 'the Aggie' was facing in the opposite direction in Blondin's day. The horrible fake façade which now elbows a view between two buildings on Upper Street was the back of the building in the 1890s. Crowds in those days would have drawn up on Liverpool Road, now graced only by a new Sainsbury's. The Business Design Centre has the grandest back door in London, albeit sealed.

Blondin himself drove there from his home in Ealing every day towards the end of his life. He had a room in the Hall, where, on a bitterly cold night in 1897, a reporter from Cassell's *Family Magazine* was granted audience. 'In he came from the performance simply dripping with perspiration', wrote the awestruck man. 'No word was spoken. An attendant first attacked him and pulled the clothes right off him, another began to towel him, then they both towelled him, and, as they did so, he too got a towel with which he kept rubbing his face and neck. Then he began to speak. "Bicycle no good tonight. Too much fog up there. No rope to see."'

Blind in one eye, diabetic and subject to fits of giddiness which made it hard for him to walk across a room, Blondin joked that he was going to have his house fitted up with tightropes to move about on, 'or I shall have my brains dashed out one day'. He couldn't see at all in sunshine, he said, so it was no hardship for him to walk blindfold. 'The sack, though it appears to add to the blindfolding, is really a guide to me. By hanging evenly all round me it tells me that I am perpendicular. What else is there to tell me?'

A recently married man, Blondin boasted that he had worked every week that year, besides getting married. 'I was on the rope again after a honeymoon of only twenty-four hours.' The reporter had to conclude that he was only human, however. 'Having eaten the food brought with him from home and had a good drink from a selzer siphon, he lay down on a couch, was warmly covered and fell asleep.' In two hours he had to perform again, then drive himself back to Ealing, presumably in an open carriage. Within months of the interview and five days short of his seventy-third birthday, The Lord of the Hempen Realm, Knight of the Fearless Foot, Emperor of All Manilla, would be dead.

Blondin's career was long and glorious, culminating in his walk across Niagara Falls in 1859 and his residency three years later at the Crystal Palace, where he pulled crowds of over 80,000 and was paid £100 for every ascent. With the proceeds of these triumphs, the Frenchman settled in England. He built a fine house near Ealing, which he named Niagara House, and spent the rest of his life there, raising trotting ponies and black-and-tan terriers and doing all his own plumbing and carpentry as well as continuing on the wire. 'It is because I do so much that I have no accident', he told a reporter. 'I know everything safe. That gives me confidence.' In his multi-talented determination, he resembles our latter-day Blondin, Philippe Petit, the wire-walker of Notre Dame and the World Trade Center, who played him in a recent documentary.

Niagara House has long disappeared, but Blondin Avenue and Niagara Avenue still commemorate the great funambulist, who is buried nearby in Kensal Green Cemetery.

My wife, Hermine Demoriane, who is also French, was once a tightrope walker herself, and last Sunday we took champagne and flowers to Kensal Green to toast the great man on the anniversary of his death. He is buried in some style, with not one but two wives, his second having died soon after him. (Both are named on the gravestone.) An angel with an anchor presides over a small pavilion, while a lifelike marble relief in a verdigris-stained frame shows the purposeful features of 'Jean-François Gravelet Blondin, Hero of Niagara'.

We felt happy and heroic ourselves last Sunday as a dozen or so friends joined us in a graveside party. On the way home, past the tombs of William Thackeray, Anthony Trollope, Sydney Smith, Thomas Hood, Leigh Hunt, Wilkie Collins and Winthrop Mackworth Praed, I wanted to see again the beautiful stone hat and gloves thrown down on a broken column at the foot of the magnificent Egyptian mausoleum of Andrew Ducrow, proprietor of hippo-dromes in Blondin's day, 'whose death deprived the arts of an eminent professor and liberal patron'. Since I was there two years ago, vandals have been with bolt-cutters and all that remains of that poetical finishing touch are two pathetic bronze rivets. Luckily, I have a photograph, if anyone happens to have seen it for sale.

[13.3.92]

Why Don't I Work?

I received a remarkable document called a 'Party Wall Award', the result of a survey I had to have done before the owners of the house next door could 'commence work' gutting it and throwing it into the street. The purpose of a Party Wall Award (which you don't have to pay for) is to establish the condition of your property so that you can't claim damages afterwards. It's one of those things like toothache, which you don't ask for, but have to receive anyway.

In my case, it's a highly disturbing document, full of gratuitous running innuendos about the general decrepitude of my home, and, by extension, my life. My living quarters are 'deemed to be in a poor state of repair'. The word 'damp' occurs fourteen times, the word 'crack' twenty-seven. There are numerous references to 'deflections', 'indentations', 'separations', 'penetrations'. Paintwork is said to be 'loose', lining paper 'wrinkled', plaster 'unkeyed' with 'many areas of porosity' and 'numerous blown nail heads'. Grudgingly, the survey admits that the floor 'appears sound', although 'a full inspection was prevented by the occupants' belongings'.

Perhaps I should apologize for this? I remembered that a man had been round my house a few weeks earlier, whispering disparagingly into a tape recorder. I didn't realize that he had also been taking photos: nasty, dispassionate snapshots in the Dirty Realism tradition, showing not the colourful paintwork, but the areas of damp, not the interesting pictures, but the cracks between the pictures. There was a shot of my bulging back wall taken from the garden which purported to show me at my desk, smoking, although I gave up years ago. How did the survey know that I would soon be taking it up again? What annoyed me most of all was how good the pictures were. I couldn't stop looking at them, but why?

A few weeks later, I saw a young builder waiting to be let into the house next door and asked him if he'd like a coffee. He looked at me strangely. Now every time I go out, picking my way over cement boards and between skips, I wonder what the workmen are thinking. I worry about my walk. My wife is away at the moment, living in Paris, so I do all the shopping and cooking. Why don't I work? Am I on the dole, or just rich? If I am on the dole, why do I talk like this and wear a suede jacket? One day, I looked out of the bathroom window and saw the workmen sitting round an open manhole, eating their lunch. They were laughing and pointing at things floating past below them. I'm sure one of them looked at my window.

All day long, the cement-mixer turns, like a great brain in turmoil. My brain. Now and then someone comes along and tips the contents into an old bath, from where it is shovelled into a barrow and wheeled out of sight. The banging, knocking, shouting, sawing and drilling goes on all day, like the tapping of one's conscience, although the workmen do go home early, enabling one to 'commence work' oneself at about five.

A notice from Gulliver Timber Treatments, Infestation and Damp Proofing Specialists advises me that they will shortly be commencing work on the house: 'You may notice that our operatives wear protective equipment. DO NOT BE ALARMED. Once installed, the treatments should present no hazard to the environment.' A DANGER notice on the front door warns builders against eating, drinking, sleeping or smoking on the site. 'Do not store foodstuffs in treated areas. Fish and caged birds should not be reinstalled in treated areas.' I sit in front of the television with tears rolling down my face from fumes seeping through the walls.

I sometimes feel as though it is my own house which is being gutted, or at least treated for sloth infestation. Coated with a thick layer of dust from the work next door, my things have an air of lingering on after my death. It is only a matter of time before it is all chucked out and a firm such as Gulliver is brought in to perform long overdue remedial treatment.

One Sunday, when all was quiet, I climbed over the garden wall and got into the house through the hole where the extension is going to be. There was nothing left inside. Floors, walls, fireplaces, cupboards, shutters, partitions, everything had gone. Unsurprisingly, the house seemed more spacious than mine, and I realized that my own place had been getting smaller for years with the accumulation of possessions. Perhaps it was time to take part in the community project of a skip.

I stood where the desk is in my house and looked out on the familiar gardens from a slightly different angle. The view was better than mine. You could see the Church of St Mary's and a new catalpa tree. I thought of the bleakly unrecognizable photographs of my house included in the Party Wall Award: the scene of some unspecified crime, photographed by Home Office pathologists. I remembered how interesting they were, like the photographs of William Eggleston. It occurred to me that the potential of a camera, like that of a pen, is limited only by the preconceptions of the person wielding it: get rid of the Self in the equation and the possibilities are endless.

[10.4.92]

Yevgeny Yevtushenko and the Cold War

The poet Yevgeny Yevtushenko came to our house once. He was strikingly handsome, with a sharp haircut, silver shark-skin suit and hand-painted tie which made my parents' pleasant sitting room look like a faded photograph in the winter sunlight. It was 1962 and he was Russia's Angry Young Poet, the James Dean of the Cold War, cast by the Press as anything from stalking-horse of the Soviet government to anti-communist rebel. Most people at the time thought of him as the latter, but over the years they seem to have changed their minds. All I knew about him then was that he could fill stadiums with fans.

He's wearing the same shiny suit in the photograph on the inside cover of the Penguin that was due to come out later that year, translated by Peter Levi and Robin Milner-Gulland. Robin was the son of a local headmaster my parents knew and the whole family came over for drinks one Sunday lunchtime, bringing Yevtushenko and his wife Galia, who spoke a little Italian. Ghenia was greatly interested to see the house of our landlord, the then Prime Minister Harold Macmillan, across the fields. He wanted to go over there immediately, before lunch, in order to recite a poem to him that would clear up everything between our two countries and put an end to the Cold War. Somebody rang up and fixed it for the next day. Apparently the two dandies sat there talking about clothes.

I was eighteen and had just had my first poems in a magazine. I was terrified someone would tell Yevtushenko this and that he would ask me something. Sure enough, it came out and he demanded a recital on the spot, never dreaming how impossible this would be among the pink gins and cardigans of a Sussex Sunday lunchtime. He insisted, however, so we had to go into another room where I read out a poem about picking up girls being like writing a poem. Robin translated, while Ghenia stood there smoking. I don't know how it came out, but his comment has stayed with me. It was fine, he said, I was not to worry, all poets should be half man and half woman. Obviously it had gained something in translation.

It was the year after that, 1963, that President Kennedy landed in his helicopter a few yards from our house. The place had been swarming with detectives for weeks. We leaned over the fence and cheered and President Kennedy waved to us. By that time Yevtushenko had been summoned back to Russia following the Cuban Missile Crisis, his youthful break-out curtailed for several years, his star waning. The New York School poet Frank O'Hara wrote in an angry, insult-laden poem 'Answer to Voznesensky and Evtushenko' (who had been touring and wowing America): 'We are tired of your tiresome imitations of Mayakovsky / we are tired of your dreary tourist ideas of our Negro selves . . . how many sheets have you stained with your semen / Oh Tartars . . . I consider myself to be black and you not even part . . .' Becoming stuff? Obviously these two wild boys on the make in America were too much for the Assistant Curator of Painting and Sculpture at the Museum of Modern Art and the cosy coterie that had gathered round the abstract expressionists. They had cracked a new kind of dribble-poetry in the manner of Jackson Pollock and they were pleased as Punch about it. These Russians were old hat. Specifically, 'Maya-kovsky's hat worn by a horse.'

They were right about Mayakovsky, but then Yevtushenko was never an avant-gardist like O'Hara, he was a pop star whose books sold by the lorry-load. He could even write a bit. Did O'Hara know that Yevtushenko was a famous dancer in his Siberian village? Had he read his beautiful sad poem about dancing at wartime weddings? I suppose it all depends on whether you accept the idea of Yevtushenko as a cynical Party *apparatchik* (i.e., a fraud) or as a young man out to conquer the world like anyone else. Like O'Hara, maybe. The fact is he was a Siberian peasant and Siberians consider themselves to be bigger, tougher and *freer* than ordinary Russians.

I'm not pretending that dear disgraceful dandified Yevtushenko is a better poet than O'Hara, it's just that I prefer him, and I love his poems 'On A Bicycle' and 'Weddings': 'She weeping / and her friends weeping. I frightened / don't feel like dancing, but you can't not dance.' What I marvel at when I read an O'Hara poem, or any New York School poem, is the incredibly high marks they seem to award themselves just for picking up their pens. It's as if they have been set down in front of the finger paints by adoring mothers who can hardly wait to frame their little darlings' doodles. The spoilt-childishness of it all is invariably justified as an artistic reflection of the spoilt child that was America in the 1950s and 1960s, when everything American was bigger and better, but this doesn't make it any easier for outsiders to keep the polite smile of approval pinned to their faces.

Anyway, it's too late now; the graphs of their reputations crossed long ago. Yevtushenko's always going down, while O'Hara's goes on rising unstoppably, a licence to every creative writing student to dash off and write his poem about what he did in his lunch hour. O'Hara is safely dead, killed when a beach buggy reversed into him on the resort of Fire Island, while Yevtushenko is a big wheel in the Russian Writers' Union and living in some style in the old house of his friend Boris Pasternak. He recently made a film about what he was doing on the day of Stalin's funeral.

[24.4.92]

Un Petit Silex Sympa

I have joined my wife on a dig in a wood beside a reservoir in the Creuse district of the Massif Central, a strange, depopulated part of France with green hills, heavy skies and lukewarm rain. The town of Eguzon is conservative and uncommercialized in the extreme. 'Vacances en Creuse', the saying goes, 'Vacances creuse (hollow)'. We shall see.

It is raining beside the reservoir as dig boss Denis Vialou gives us a rundown of the area twenty thousand years ago. The weather was bad then too. It was like the Steppes here in winter. Stone Age 'Solutreans' came in Spring bringing silex (flint) from 120 kilometers away (the nearest source). There were twenty or more different kinds, all used for different things, suggesting a flint economy in the area. The Solutreans would sit on this ledge overlooking what was once the Creuse Valley, chipping away and keeping watch on the game moving about below. The narrow bottleneck in the valley would have been perfect for trapping deer and horses.

In 1926 the world's first hydro-electric dam was built here, converting the valley into a reservoir. The raised water level, lapping the site of the Solutrean camp, unearthed hundreds of flint tools, which were chanced upon by a schoolmaster called Rigaud. For the last ten years Denis Vialou has brought a dozen or so prehistory enthusiasts from the Institut de Paléontologie in Paris – of whom my wife is one – to work on the little lakeside site for a month. Hours: 8.30–6.00. Accommodation by dormitory in a nearby run-down chateau, so we are in a hotel, thank God. The site looks like the abandoned excavations for a small house. Rudimentary scaffolding holds up a polythene cover on which the rain patters. The dig is divided into thirty-five square metres, each square divided into four quarters, each numbered quarter having its own spiral-bound exercise book in which the date, level, description and finder of every flake of flint found within its borders is recorded. The notebooks are kept in a big leather satchel which is guarded like the ark of the covenant. It alone remains dry.

Most digs have strings going everywhere, but Vialou likes the 'carroyage' to be 'discrète'. For him, if not for his workers, the site is alive, responsive, vulnerable, a body, his by right of inheritance, which he reluctantly allows us to tamper with. He tells us with some satisfaction that there is '*très très peu* de matériel archéologique' in the area. Clearly the rewards are to be of a spiritual kind. 'Il faut rentrer dans la *dynamique* des différents niveaux', he assures us, although for some of us engaged in this creeping, bending, silent, thankless brushwork the word 'dynamic' comes as a shock.

In truth the dig is misnamed; it is more of a caress, feathers rather than spades being the tools of the trade. The last time I took this much interest in a piece of earth was in 1969, discovering the universe in a grain of LSD. This time I am less ecstatic but no less damp. The earth too is damp, which does not make it easier to sieve.

Within an hour of starting work I think I have discovered a section of Romanesque relief, which turns out to be the imprint of my trainer. Later, I unearth what looks like a mud-clogged arrowhead, but isn't. 'C'est juste une pierre', I say, throwing it back and getting to my feet for an unearned rest. There is a long silence. 'Juste une pierre', says Vialou sarcastically. '*Juste une pierre* . . . Is that what the Solutreans said when they discovered silex: "C'est juste une pierre"?' Having been told to leave everything where we find it, marked with a coloured drawing pin, my wife asks if we are supposed to bury them again. This too is greeted with an ironical silence, then a threat to bury her in the barren C3 to which she has already been condemned for light-heartedness. Vialou himself has found what he calls 'un petit silex sympa' – a near perfect flint needle which I suspect he brought from home.

A potter friend supplied us before leaving home with a wonderfully realistic prehistoric goddess statuette which we were going to pretend to dig up, but the hierarchical atmosphere on the dig is such that anything so frivolous would be considered *extremely unfunny*. Nobody talks except Vialou, who offers rounded monologues on anything from bananas to the Tower of London, gesturing elegantly in my direction when the latter is mentioned, but not hesitating long enough for me to insert so much as a comma. The dig is never mentioned, except as a dig. According to the archaeologist's coda, ideas do not exist until the dig itself provides them, hence Vialou's quaint expression 'from the dig's point of view . . .'

From my wife's point of view this is sad, since the lack of bones or ashes on the site provides circumstantial evidence that these hunters took all their meat home to their loved ones for cooking rather than cooking it and eating it on the spot, the central tenet of Chris Knight's revolutionary book *Blood Relations*, which inspired her to take Vialou's course in the first place. She is given no opportunity to mention this. When the first day's findings are passed round for inspection, she asks humorously if she can keep a couple of arrowheads for earrings. Vialou says nothing, refusing even to acknowledge the joke, leaving Hermine to take the blame for her own lack of taste. It might seem easy enough to pocket the odd flint on a dig, but the spirit of competition is so fierce among the diggers, all striving to come up with 'un petit silex sympa', that if one finds so much as a toe-nail of flint one is so excited one tends to run around like a five-year-old, showing it to everyone.

After a day and a half spent relating to the sticky, cold earth with no noticeable response, I feel I have experienced archaeology at first hand and come to my own conclusion that it is not for me. I am stiff, cold, bored and tired. I keep hallucinating 'un petit café sympa' waiting for me back at the Café des Sports in Eguzon, maybe even a Croque Monsieur. Before another sparse and rainy picnic by the reservoir, I say I have an article to finish and make my joyous exit, foolishly promising to return at teatime with a cake.

I dash back to the hotel just in time for the *Menu du Jour*. I have a sleep, then buy a gâteau breton and leave once more for the dig, only to discover that there are no less than seven roads leading out of Eguzon, none of which looks familiar. I am pretty confident at first and set out briskly in what I assume to be the direction of the reservoir, recognizing nothing. By six o'clock, I have tried three of the roads without success, returning to base each time with renewed blisters and despair. While the diggers are searching for evidence of prehistoric man, I am searching for evidence of the diggers. Once I get within sight of the reservoir and hear the cuckoo which I know to be in the region of the dig, but have to give up when I realize that the diggers will have gone home by now. It seems that I am not supposed to find the dig, perhaps so that I do not suddenly fall on my knees again and start feathering the reddish mud for toe-nails.

[29.5.92]

Hay-on-Wye

'Squantum' is a Massachusetts native American word for a pleasure party, but I am not sure how much pleasure was involved in the version thrown recently as part of the Hay-on-Wye Festival of Literature. As a participant, my own feelings were more akin to those aroused by a coming-out party. Coming out as an ignorant fool.

All the poets attending the festival were commissioned to write a poem on the same theme. To ensure a fair start, the theme of the poem was to be revealed only on our arrival in Hay. The 'Squantums' were the various public progress reports we were required to give during the course of the weekend, showing our initial approach to the subject, the work methods we intended to adopt and our subsequent falterings into 'verse'. 'The poets will discuss their progress with each other and the audience in a series of open workshops', said the brochure; the finished poems to be read out on Sunday evening.

When Mick Imlah was first asked to take part in the Squantum, he accepted immediately, saying he had a poem which could be adapted to more or less anything. The joke was smiled at thinly by the organizers. I am sure the thought had gone through all our minds that if we took all our notebooks and old drafts of failed poems to Hay, we would probably be able to come up with something which would at least allow us to collect our £150. We might even get a poem out of it. With the shortness of writing time available as an alibi for literary inadequacy we were surely laughing all the way to Hereford?

We laughed on the other side of our faces when the subject was unveiled to us after dinner on the first evening. By the time it had been passed down the table to me, it sounded rather like the not unpromising 'Pantyhose', or possibly the word for one of those big lorries. When the nervous gaiety had died down, we were each left alone – very alone – with the horrifying 'Pentecost'. I think most of us realized it was something to do with religion, but how were we supposed to rig up that vital element of personal experience over the subject when none of us had been listening when it was explained to us in Divinity? We would find out.

On Saturday morning at eleven came the first of the public humiliation workshops in which we were to reveal our thinking to one another and the world. It seemed that none of us had done much overnight except grab some sleep and a shower. What to say? Never was panic better served by the soothing nonsense of words and the knowledge that we still had a day and a half to stiffen our resolve and comport ourselves like Englishmen.

All Saturday I roamed the bookshops (there are twenty-six of them) in search of inspiration. I bought Lytton Strachey's *Land-*

marks in French Literature (the property of Bristol Grammar School) and Edmund Blunden's British Council pamphlet, *Keats* (nearly everything underlined in red). By the end of the afternoon, I felt as though I had returned to 'Go' without writing any poetry and without collecting £150. Then, ten minutes before we were due on stage again, I found something called *The Handbook of Christian Terminology* and noted with relief that 'Pentecost' figured prominently in the index. I was saved.

At the Squantum that evening, I said I had changed my tactics completely, I had decided to concentrate on the theme of 'the quest'. From listening to the other poets' conversations, I had gathered that the word 'Pentecost' was associated not only with the Tower of Babel and talking in tongues, but with fire, doves, weddings, animal sacrifice, personal transfiguration, the bringing in of the harvest, the giving of the law on Mount Sinai and the gift of the Holy Spirit to the disciples. I had decided that my own interpretation of the word would involve a quest for its true meaning.

I described my afternoon's search through the bookshops of Hay and read out selected passages from Strachey and Blunden: clues, perhaps, to the style my poem would be written in. I described my growing sense of despair at the wilderness of possibilities stretching ahead of me, my relief at finding *The Handbook of Christian Terminology* just in time. I quoted from the *Handbook*:

> On the day of Pentecost, as they waited in prayerful expectancy, the Disciples felt themselves to be changed men, clear of purpose and animated by the very spiritual vitality which they had seen expressed as fully as was possible within and through a human personality when they had 'been with Jesus and learnt of Him'.

According to the *Handbook*, this was the fulfilment of Our Lord's promise of the Comforter. In a very real sense, it was the gift of an ending for my poem. Now all I needed was a beginning and a middle.

Sunday was long and hot, and somehow I couldn't settle to my work. By the final meeting that evening, the presentation of the finished poems, I hadn't had time to enlarge very much on my rather ambitious ground-plan. There was something about my room which seemed to preclude the possibility of creative thought. In desperation, I enumerated the blockages I was encountering: 'If only there were a table', I began,

If only there were a chair.
If only I'd brought my cassette recorder with me.
If only it weren't so hot.
If only there weren't so many other writers wandering about . . .

I went on like this for a while, adding in mitigation that I had chosen to take the word 'Pentecost' not so much as a theme for my poem as its title. This would, I hoped, cast a sort of glow of meaning over it, although I didn't feel it had totally succeeded.

Strangely, it went down well with the punters, who seemed to think it was a fairly typical example of my work and that, even though it obviously wasn't finished yet, it might even turn out to be one of my best. They liked the repetition, and they liked the honesty. They identified all too well with my difficulty. They even persuaded me that I had been making a lot of unnecessary fuss over the subject of Pentecost. All you had to do, they seemed to be saying, was put down what you were feeling and leave it at that. As usual, the answer to my problem had been staring me in the face all the time.

[12.6.92]

Did the Manager Notice My Age?

15 June. Off to Portugal on my East German MZ 250, 'the worker's bike', bags of Euro-credibility, but the factory has just gone bankrupt, which makes me feel rather lonely.

I should be crouched in the fo'c'sle, stubbly with goodness, smoking Old Galleon, but I am sitting in the no-smoking lounge of the Plymouth–Santander ferry waiting to hear if I have got a bunk.

People with cabins stroll about the deck in clean shorts. 'I think we'll just pop down and tidy up before dinner', says a young husband. I watch the sun setting over Brittany, feeling excited and nervous in the growing heat and adventure. This shirt will be filthy soon. I will smell. Risk awaits. An announcement that there is a bunk for a 'Mr Huge' turns out to be for someone else, so I kip down on my 'Swagman' saddlebags.

16 June. Burgos — vistas of cool courtyards and shade through archways, overhanging medieval box windows, propriety and sobriety in the garden avenues beside the genteel river where an old soldier scowls at my unsightly gear. One disadvantage of a bike is that you can't lock up your baggage while you look for a hotel. Or I can't.

Watching a bullfight in the TV room of the youth hostel. Missed the hostel meal because I forgot to put my watch forward, so I am sharing a bowl of tiny snails with a German, who teaches me how to extract them with my teeth. The first two bars of the Harry Lime theme endlessly repeated on a video game. In the dormitory I find some child porn stuck in the springs of the bunk above me and wonder if the others know it's there. Shall I say something? Did the manager notice my age? The police cadet next to me sobs in his sleep. The athlete above curses and gets up to close the window I have just opened. I open it again and he closes it. Thunder and lightning the whole stifling night.

17 June. Woken by Queen at full blast on the hostel PA. My breakfast companion hit a wall on a motorbike and hasn't worked since. His arm was hanging from a thin piece of ham fat, which he holds up on his fork. There was a hole this big in his groin. He was twenty-two on a 750, I am fifty on a 250. Perhaps the odds are in favour of me holding on to my arms. Also my groin.

Outside Burgos now with a San Miguel beer and a roll-up, the map of Spain so big I daren't unfold the lower half. I'm shifting across it slower than the hour hand of my watch (50 m.p.h.). I think of the Queen Mary passenger asking 'When does this place reach America?' Motorbike travel is sitting waiting for places to reach you. You cling to the handlebars, the wind of time battering you in the face.

Mosquitoes and swallows in the shimmering siesta heat of the square at Alaejos, the only sound a woman talking on the open-air phone, then the ubiquitous Harry Lime theme from a video game in a café, where I lay out the Old Virginia on a table and try to map-read, watched by silent old men. Cigarettes are the close companions of foreigners: something normal to do with your hands. Suddenly the rain comes down like a clown's bucket of water and we all run indoors and begin talking: extreme bonhomie and sociable San Miguels.

Difficulty keeping my eyes open when they're screwed up in the heat. Nearly dropped off just now, which could be nasty. Coffee not beer from now on.

Straight through to Salamanca, the big drops starting again as the Moorish cathedral looms. I see an American going into a *hostal* and duck in after him. We dump our things and hit the Plaza Mayor — pale pink sandstone, paved and traffic-less, cafés and cake shops under cool cloisters, students paseo-ing. Benny is a black Canadian farmer and masseur from a village in Alberta, here to run the bulls at Pamplona before his multiple sclerosis finally trips him up. He is also keen to run the girls. We exchange perversions as the beers line up. Benny says he likes to make girls bark like dogs, which seems quite a good idea. My own experience of doing it listening to a Spanish Linguaphone tape seems very effete and Old World by comparison.

Joy, Pete and Ruth at the next-door table invite us to American Night at the Bar Cuba: balloons, flags and streamers, a veritable victory celebration over the concept of 'abroad'. We teach the girls to twist, but they aren't interested in barking.

18 June. Light on, helmet off, moving at a snail's pace across the map, which I have tied to the handlebars with an old scarf. I notice I have started pair-bonding with the bike. The gears now all have distinct personalities. Four is courageous, businesslike. Five is temperamental, artistic, occasionally inspired.

Seville. How many times have I waited exhausted at the desk of some Hotel Central while some old war hero copperplates my middle name, spelt wrong, 'Morgalk', on to one of those slips of paper? Very slowly, he shows me a room without a window. The Hotel Central. Miles from anywhere.

19 June. Burgos seemed to specialize in pharmacies – ancient chapels to Chemistry, with panelling and painted ceilings, cupids and no shampoo. Salamanca was pastry shops and frantic displacement activity. Seville is a Martini ad with scooters and balconies and royal palms, high heels and steep shadows up alleyways, tales of scooter crimes. I wrote the first line of a short story: 'He went upstairs and entered her room without knocking.' A German woman in the hotel is interested in dancing Flamenco Sevillana, but there is no room to give me a demonstration. Tapas: a bowl of tiny snails, which I extract with my teeth, Harry Lime in the background, the first two bars only.

I find Seville extremely difficult. The Museo de Bellas Artes is closed for reconstruction. The Great Tower closes while I am up it. A man lets me out and I spill blinking into the dazzling, deserted street. I take a nap on one of the mosaic benches in the Murillo Gardens and wake to find a beggar making cigarette noises in my ear. I don't have any, so I get up and walk away, cross to have been woken. He follows, muttering. 'Lend me money, lend me money.' He has drawn a knife. I head towards a busy road, only to find it is a cul-de-sac of wire netting. By now he is poking my bottom with the knife. I can feel its point through my money folded in my back pocket, just enough to get me to Portugal tomorrow. I walk faster, edging out of the trap. When I look round, he has fallen back. I feel the flimsy gooseflesh between my ribs that might so easily have provided his revenge on society. Beautiful Seville oranges lie where they have fallen under the trees.

20 June. The joys of being alive and off again are undiluted. The joys of taking the ferry at Vila Real, standing in the prow with my motorbike and hearing Portuguese spoken again, are tempered by

the bike conking out a hundred miles from home. 'Hitler's motor-cyclette!' sneers the stationmaster at Conceicao (Consequences) as we heave it on to a goods train for Albufeira in the Algarve. 'Why not you don't get some real proper Honda motorcyclette?' He revs imaginary handlebars. The first two bars of the Harry Lime Theme drift down the track from a café.

[7.8.92]

The Untamed Fashion Assembly

My wife has just got back from Latvia with a wicked expression on her face and scratchmarks down her cheek. She has been on a group expedition to 'The Untamed Fashion Assembly' in Riga, where the artist Andrew Logan presented his mirror-jewellery in a dance-parade choreographed by Lynn Seymour. Hermine was supposed to sing and perform with Christine and Jennifer Binnie, who call themselves 'The Neo-Naturist Cabaret'. Also included on the trip was a woman called Potting Shed, some Australian fashion students and Burnel Penhaul, otherwise known as Miss Gail Force-Wind, winner of the Alternative Miss World title for 1991.

Sponsored by the Latvian Shipping Company, 'Untamed Fashion' had originally planned to send a ship up the Thames to collect the performers from Andrew Logan's house near London Bridge. This fell through and a coach was sent instead. On arrival in Latvia, they were deposited at their hotel in the beach resort of Jurmala and told they had twenty minutes to get back on the coach to go to the opening celebrations in Riga.

From now on, the schedule was hectic. Logan, Lynn Seymour and her assistant Potting Shed ('Don't call me "Potty"') had two days to audition and rehearse fifty non-dancing fashion models in a would-be Busby Berkeley routine to be choreographed by Lynn. The models were supposed to come on wearing Logan's jewellery and holding aloft gigantic aluminium hammers and sickles which he had brought with him from London. Sensing humiliation, they went on strike. If they were going to have to dance they wanted more money. (They were making 45p a day.) They were given a small rise and told they would get the sack if they didn't perform properly.

Believing that something was badly wrong with the presentation, Hermine took Andrew aside and pointed out that it was a bit tactless glorifying the symbols of their host country's long subjugation when twenty people had been killed by the Russians as recently as last August. The touchingly pro-Western 'Untamed Fashion Assembly' was itself a reaffirmation of their new-found liberty: didn't he see that his celebrating of Soviet insignia was an insult to their struggles? Andrew replied that he was an artist and that this was what he did. It had gone down well in Moscow a few years ago, why not here? Hermine said that mocking the flag on its home ground was one thing, parading it in an ex-colony was another. Andrew would hear nothing of her protests, so she resolved to try and save him from himself by making her own impromptu contribution to the show.

Gaining access to the backstage area on the night of the perform-ance was no problem for Hermine, as she was due to perform her own 'Litany of Baltic Goddesses' later in the programme. After the models had been made up, she got the make-up artist to make her up the same, donned her dress of the Latvian flag and added an improvised travesty of Latvia's folkloric oak-leaf headgear. Then she waited.

Lynn Seymour's choreography asked for the models to skip through the audience wielding the glittering hammers and sickles above their heads, before mounting the catwalk and continuing their dance on stage. But lo and behold, Hermine is there ahead of them! She appears in the spotlight holding a telephone, which she has brought from her hotel room, miming the glad tidings of Latvia's liberation to wildly inflated orchestral trumpetings. As the models approach the catwalk, bearing the symbols of their enslavement, Hermine comes forward and gaily relieves them of their burdens, which they are only too happy to surrender. She chucks them in a pile at the front of the stage. Now, holding one of the giant sickles above her head, she prances round the stage in mock imitation of the dance, an inane smile on her lips. The TV cameras follow her every move. She is the spirit of the New Latvia.

Meanwhile, the horrified progenitors of the performance were sitting in the audience, powerless to halt its metamorphosis into the Hermine Demoriane Show. At the very least she had saved them from committing a breach of good manners; at best she had created something memorable out of something mediocre, the only 'untamed' thing in the entire 'Untamed Fashion Show'.

One by one they came backstage to castigate her. 'Dreadful', said Logan's second in command Michael Davies. 'Dreadful', said his secretary Scarlett. 'You've done it now, Hermine', said Andrew. 'Twenty years of friendship up in smoke. See you in another life.' In vain she tried to reason that she had saved the day for them; they only forbade her to appear on stage in her own act. Suddenly Lynn Seymour hit the dressing-room, threatened to kill her and came at her with nails flying (hence the scratchmarks). Hermine retired hurt to her hotel room and lay awake the entire stifling night, terrified to open her window lest Lynn attack via their adjoining balcony.

The following day, Andrew Logan came to tell Hermine that she would have to find her own way home, that he never wanted to see her again. She tried to apologize to Lynn, to no avail. For the rest of the visit she stayed in her room, ministered to by the Neo-Naturists and the Alternative Miss World. When she told them later that her husband was writing a piece about the adventure, Burnel Penhaul said, 'What a good idea, and thank goodness it won't be *biased* in any way.'

[21.8.92]

Return from St Petersburg

Readers have expressed anxiety about the fate of my wife Hermine, marooned in Latvia at the end of my last report. As part of artist-jeweller Andrew Logan's contribution to 'The Untamed Fashion Assembly' in Riga, she had attempted to redeem his and Lynn

Seymour's dance celebration of the hammer and sickle by suddenly appearing on stage dressed in the Latvian flag, relieving the sulkily skipping Latvian maidens of their mirror-encrusted Soviet insignia and dumping them in a heap at the end of the catwalk. The gesture was appreciated locally, but this only inflamed the creators of the piece. She was rewarded by a violent attack from choreographer Lynn and the news from Andrew Logan that she would have to find her own way home. Her ticket for the group excursion to St Petersburg was cancelled and £50 thrown at her as journey money. With an unused Russian visa in her passport, she was not about to pass up the trip without a fight. Unfortunately, a fight is what it came to.

She persuaded the Untamed press office to give her a new ticket to St Petersburg, but when she got to Riga station, discovered it was for the wrong day. She bribed the guard, who gave her his cabin for the overnight trip. She then had to remain invisible until St Petersburg, where friends put her up and showed her the sights. Among these was the John Lennon Temple, in a tiny fifth-floor flat in Pushkin Square, run by a Russian Beatles fan who had been illegally worshipping John Lennon since the 1960s, narrowly escaping prison for his beliefs. Lennon memorabilia crowded every wall, occasionally yielding space to the prophet Elvis. Hermine's escort, an art teacher from Liverpool, claimed to know Paul McCartney and promised to get him interested in the construction of a John Lennon Temple, complete with lake, two globular structures and a tower, of which there were plentiful sketches. Six hours of scratched Beatles records later, Hermine, never a Beatles fan, was more interested in getting something to eat.

Taxis in St Petersburg seem to be a whole medieval underworld – ancient sedans that career all over the road to avoid the craters and break down miles from anywhere, demanding double what you agreed. If you mention dollars, they want them all. The only place open at one in the morning was a German pub which seemed to have the same policy: you could pay their very Western prices in whatever currency you liked, so long as it wasn't Russian. For two frankfurters Hermine had to hand over a ten-pound note and got about four pounds of worthless roubles back.

The next day she was taken to meet Russia's most famous pop star – 'Boris something' – a one-time protégé of the Eurythmics, whose concert that night she had to promise not to sabotage. After the concert – nine musicians in biblical-style robes playing pleasant rock ballads to seated fans – she was taken to Boris's flat. He lives in somewhat reduced circumstances due to his ill-fated venture in the West, but his swashbuckling 1960s overview remains unreconstructed. The men sat around a single lamp drinking quantities of gin and talking English for her benefit, while Boris's wife took care of the children. 'They seemed quite surprised when I opened my mouth . . .'

It so happened that in another part of St Petersburg that night, a well-meaning Russian video-maker was showing the Logan contingent a video of the Untamed Fashion performance. Intended as oil on troubled waters, it had the opposite effect, sending the offended parties into fresh paroxysms of rage. Hermine heard of this next day and became even more frightened of bumping into the Logan–Seymour axis at St Petersburg station. A Russian friend made her a paper mask to wear, which disguised nothing, but appealed to her sense of cloak and dagger. Back in Riga, she stowed away on the coach to London optimistically disguised in a headscarf.

Logan lieutenants Michael Davies and Scarlett soon spotted her, grabbed her many bags and began throwing them on to the pavement. 'We gave you £50 to get home. You're not coming with us. Phone your husband. Get yourself repatriated.' They were pulling and pushing her off the coach when two members of the Neo-Naturist Cabaret and a massive bloke in leather who won Andrew Logan's Alternative Miss World title in 1991 came to her rescue and overpowered her attackers. 'You don't touch her, she's our friend.' 'In that case', said Michael Davies, 'you can all stay behind.'

At this point, it looked as though half the touring party were to be marooned moneyless a thousand miles from home. Luckily, the prospect seemed to alarm Andrew, and he relented. 'It seems we are no longer a group', he said. 'You lot get in the front and stay there. We'll go in the back.' In this way, a kind of apartheid was maintained, with Hermine staying on the bus for two days, ministered to by her guardian angels bearing the odd sandwich.

So it was that she arrived home with that bad child expression on her face and those triumphant scratchmarks down her cheek. If ever there was a backstage musical comedy come to life, this was it – and in a musical comedy country. It may be too optimistic to expect all the characters to live happily ever after, but when one of the Neo-Naturists went round to collect her things from Logan's studio the next day, Michael Davies greeted her as if nothing had happened. 'Darling, how lovely to see you . . .'

[11.9.92]

Breton Afternoons

In the 1970s and 1980s, I used to visit a village in Brittany called Kercanic. It was five minutes from a wide, deserted beach, half an hour from the painters' paradise of Pont Aven, where a plaque on one of the hotels commemorates the stay of Ernest Dowson. His poem 'Breton Afternoon' describes a mood I remember well: 'The world fades into a dream and a spell is cast on me.'

Kercanic had a few tarted-up *chaumières* and the inevitable television personality, but the trails of manure down the one road proclaimed the sovereignty of the original inhabitants, who spoke Breton. One got one's 'Bonjour, monsieur' only if one said it first.

The one local we did see a lot of was Marie, the eighty-year-old widow of a fisherman, who sold vegetables out of an earth-floored shed behind her house. The daily visit down a wooded path and across a field, bearing empty cider bottles, egg boxes and crusts for her chickens, was part of each day's time-honoured routine, the dream within the dream. We would stand in the doorway, peering into the dark interior, trying to make out the old wardrobe, the piles of wooden boxes, the mountain of potatoes, the cauldron of beetroot, the curtain behind which she kept the cider. Was that a staircase leading into the house? Bouquets of parsley lay on the blue-and-white oilcloth where she weighed out the courgettes or green beans. The tomatoes, she said, would ripen if we kept them in a brown paper bag. One year, I helped her old friend Albert get in the potato harvest, a task he performed drunk, but which almost killed me.

Marie was a talker, a gossip, a fraternizer with 'americains' (anyone not Breton). She was never seen outside her garden, yet the village lived in her conversation as vividly as that in *Under Milk Wood*. *Mauvais gens* stalked her imagination. Her stern, egocentric pronouncements, spoken with a wealth of knowing looks and facial contortions, became our folklore: 'Je ne dis rien. C'est comme ça parce que ce n'est pas autrement.'

It was Marie who kept the key for the owners of our *chaumière*. At the end of the holidays, we would be invited into her immaculate kitchen to drink a glass of home-brewed calvados, for which she held the village licence. We waited while she shuffled off into the unused front room where the 'eau de vie' was kept: a glimpse of brass, a plaster swan, a veiled television. She would stand at the kitchen table, holding forth, leaning across to ladle the fierce liquor into our reeling glasses. If we were lucky, she allowed us to buy a bottle. Then we would carry it home to England and lapse into Marie-ese whenever we had a drop: 'Qu'est ce que vous me demandez? C'est comme ça parce que ce n'est pas autrement. Je ne dis rien. Mais je n'y pense pas moins.' We wrote, but she didn't answer.

We went back this year, fearful of change. A few telephone poles had disappeared. A retired English couple had arrived. A rich Swiss woman had bought the big house and erected four Monopoly boxes for her four children in the orchard next to our *chaumière*. Marie was still alive, but she had ceased trading, alas. It was sad to see the green door of the outhouse padlocked, the potato field abandoned, the chickens gone. The gaudy flower garden that was never as good as the year before was still ablaze, but we noticed that Marie was limping now. She didn't seem particularly surprised or pleased to see us after five years, but invited us indoors for the inevitable *coup*.

Since we were last there, her old helpmate Albert had had his right hand amputated due to gangrene, hence her retirement from the vegetable business. Despised during his working life, the drunken Albert had become a saint in Marie's mythology. 'On a coupé le main', she said, drawing a finger across her wrist as if she were crossing herself. Knowing her hatred of mushrooms, I said we had been reduced to eating cèpes stolen from the Swiss woman's garden. 'Ach! Vous aimez ça?' said Marie, her features contorted with disgust. 'Marie n'aime pas ça.' We heard later that the sainted Albert had given his life's savings of £34,000 in cash to a young woman who wouldn't even visit him in hospital. In reality, it was Marie's arthritis that brought an end to her working life. Boxes of pills were piled on the sideboard. Paracetomol. Good for everything, she said.

Kercanic was always as much a mood as an actual place, and therefore hard to recapture by merely going back there. It was a way of life best symbolized by a stone fountain we once found buried in undergrowth half a mile from the village, which Marie said she used to fetch water from during the war. This time we couldn't find it and guessed it had been uprooted to decorate someone's front garden.

Thinking to avoid the final, killing drink, the eyelid-propping, the difficult route home, we went early one morning to say goodbye to Marie. It was no use. Trying to stop her shuffling off to fetch the jar of calvados from the front room was like trying to stop the march of time. We sat and drank and listened. 'Marie a dit.'

[23.10.92]

A Writing Course in the Dordogne

I have arrived a day early at this deserted farmhouse in the Dordogne where I am due to run a writing course. Pencils, pencil-sharpeners, rubbers and writing pads have been laid out on the dining table like grave-gifts. The course has been so widely advertised, and so often postponed for lack of applicants, that most people think I have been doing it for years and must be an authority on the area, not to mention writing courses. I must say the countryside more than lives up to the brochure; the question is, will I? These rolling valleys and woods have had a million years to become 'magical'; I have until tomorrow morning to become 'a stimulating and experienced writer who will help you explore your writing skills and yourself'.

The first thing I explore is the empty house, determined to bag the best room, only to find yellow labels stuck on all the doors, telling everyone who they are sharing with. I am in a nice little room under the stairs, alone. I check the pillows. Dunlopillo. The zip-up cushions in the sitting-room have proper stuffing, so I quickly change them over. The cushions look somewhat bloated, but no one will notice.

With no television, books or radio, time passes slowly waiting for the writers to descend on this pleasant hillside. Distant voices carry across the valley. Bright orange slugs feast in the overgrown orchard. I feel like a country-house murderer waiting for my cast of victims to arrive. As each would-be poet fails to satisfy, so I will bump them off in the name of literature. Then eat them. I make myself a meal of hand-picked cèpe mushrooms, then lie awake all night setting people writing exercises. Describe your own bottom so accurately that anyone seeing it for the first time would instantly recognize it. Did I say 'bottom'?

'I suppose it's a nice holiday for you', says the first arrival in what may or may not be a trick question. I say 'yes', knowing the next question will be how I 'structure' my courses. Within half an hour of our gathering for tea, one of the ladies, by way of self-introduction, has expressed extreme racialist views; murmurs of outrage have gone round. I try to put it off as jet lag, and indeed it turns out to have been a bizarre form of shyness.

The first evening, we have self-talk: how you got interested in writing, what you want to write, what you expect to get out of the course, what you think of it so far (a joke). Antonia says she thinks it is too early to judge, but she will let me know.

There seem to be five ladies of a certain age and one young electrician who is writing an experimental novel about creeping about in the air-conditioning of a feminist craft workshop, which sounds good. Of the others, one has had a novel published locally, another writes poems, stories, novels, television plays, and stories for children about Jeannie and Johnnie, another is married to a very old man, and a fourth is interested in Richmal Crompton. By far our most exotic bird is the headmistress of an English girls' school in Buenos Aires, who claims to have won a rock'n'roll contest because she was wearing red knickers. Every year she has come to England to visit Gabbitas and Thring, the ancient teaching agency of *Decline and Fall* fame, where she picks out someone she likes and takes them back to Argentina with her. One of the directors sits in on the interviews and attempts to close the deal by saying how splendid Argentina is, with lots of gauchos and gins and tonics, until she has to ask him to stop. It sounds like the white slave trade, I say, and she laughs.

Day two or three. It's extraordinary how quickly one gets used to luxury, good food and being deferred to all the time. Every morning, a charming chap called Gavin arrives with fresh croissants, fields people's problems, and removes with a giant vacuum cleaner any leaf that has dared fall into the swimming pool during the night. After breakfast we do a few light warm-up exercises. My love / hate / fear is like . . . (remove the abstraction). Write six true and six untrue things about an animal. Invent a plausible name. Write your own blurb. Once the 'structured' side of the day is out of the way, the table is cleared for lunch and it's downhill all the way.

Day four. John the electrician has failed to mend the cooker – a serious down-note as the cook is an invaluable co-star in this production and has stolen all the notices so far. During the power failure which follows, a hornet becomes trapped in Angela's bouffant hair, and she goes understandably mad for a while. At last it escapes. Then Jill gets my copy of *Hello*, climbs on a chair, and flattens the insect against a beam, falling heavily as she does so. Everyone has seen the bruise except John and myself.

'I was looking at your motorbike this morning', says Jackie. 'It's rather more . . . insubstantial than I imagined. It's only about one up from a mobilette, isn't it?' 'Two up perhaps.' Later, Antonia, a practising psychotherapist, says she believes there is something 'insubstantial' about my own make-up, but she withdraws into the voguish 'ungrounded' when pressed and claims it is what makes me 'artistic'. I don't mind for myself, but resent the suggestion that my bike is light on its feet.

Last day. I have brought photostats with me of, among other things, Louis MacNeice's 'Soap Suds', and after we have looked at this in speechless admiration for a few minutes I get them to do their own list-poem, starting off 'And these were the joys of that house . . .' A mistake. The ladies all manage nostalgic inventories, but John takes the opportunity to make his point about the course by writing succinct notes about some vomitous dump near Birmingham with nailed down lino etc. My toes curl as I pass out the usual compliments.

Last readings. Angela's Just William story, about us. Jackie's sex poem – 'My four-letter word went ding-a-ling-a-ling' – and her TV mini-series about castration. John's brilliantly animated 'Sentence' which won't leave him alone. After it, he lets on that he knows more about body-piercing than he is letting on. Tongues, nipples, navels, foreskins, eyelids, are all common, he says. A 'Prince Albert' is the vertical piercing of the penis, from top to bottom, as worn by the Consort himself. 'I sometimes feel frightened of where my writing might go if I keep on with it', he tells me. Why do I get the feeling that he is talking about something else?

Farewells and photographs as the taxi arrives next morning. I have decided to stay on an extra day in the house to wind down and pick mushrooms. From my window I can see a few white plastic chairs placed here and there in writerly seclusion, or still huddling in pairs where I was helping someone with a poem. The weather has turned. Autumn is in the air. Apples thud to the ground with every gust. In the night, the lime tree has let fall hundreds of little floating contraptions which parade gradually around the swimming pool in great irregular crowds. Later, they too will be harvested when Gavin arrives with his giant vacuum cleaner.

[6.11.92]

Brighton Rock

There is only one good reason for ever leaving London, and that is to go to Brighton. Until recently, I had never had a serious reason for going there – unless you count living there for a year when I was seven, or going to Brighton Technical College – and the reader may feel that the present occasion was no exception: a poetry reading at the Sussex Motor Yacht Club.

The American poet Eva Salzman, organizer of the Brighton Poetry Festival, had agreed to put me up, organized publicity in the *Evening Argus* and arranged for me to supplement the £100 fee by doing a workshop the night before.

When you meet the usual haunted-looking individuals who organize readings – men with eyes red from crying, women with garlands in their hair – they have either just taken over from someone who committed suicide, or are trying to pass the job on to someone whose sanity is still intact. They are poets themselves, whose work has stopped since they took on the job, whose partner has left, whose love of poetry is on the rocks. They sound kind on the phone, but there is a misunderstanding about the hour / day / month / year the reading was supposed to take place, or the station has two entrances and they were at the other one.

Eva isn't like that. She is there at the station when I arrive, and instead of leading me through dark streets to a branch library where thirteen people watch hypnotized as I lay out my things for the last rites, she invites me to her place for something to eat. On the way, I mention the reporter from the *Evening Argus*, who told me about a brilliant new poet living in Brighton, Don Paterson. Was there any chance of meeting him? 'Every chance', says Eva. 'I live with him.'

Don and Eva met at Colin Falck's poetry group in Camden Town.

132

Their eyes met across the photocopies: he a fast-talking Scot, she an even faster talking New Yorker, both writing poetry, both now bringing a touch of un-English professionalism to the Brighton scene. Her first book, *The English Earthquake*, came out from Bloodaxe last year; his first, *Nil Nil*, is published by Faber in the spring. So far so good. 'We've had success in about equal measure up till now', says Eva cautiously, as we repair to the Caxton Arms for the workshop. Sheets of paper are passed round, and I do my utmost to understand what is written on them.

Next morning, it is Indian summer in Brighton, and I have a day to kill in my second favourite town before my reading at the Motor Yacht Club: a near-perfect state of affairs. As I head down Queen's Road past the Clock Tower, the smell of the sea grows stronger, mixed with that of tar, old ropes and frying fish. Suddenly there are the two piers, to right and left, still bravely stepping out for France, still wisely thinking better of it.

What is it about Brighton that causes that lift in the blood? Perhaps I am prejudiced. When I was seven, I went out with Wendy Hannington, daughter of the local department store owner, and we passed ecstatic hours making multi-coloured bus ticket concertinas. Her initials being the opposite to mine was a bond between us, but I also loved Miss Flower, who taught me to skate backwards at the Brighton Skating Rink, now replaced by a shocking municipal bunker. Later, my first dates would be undergone in the Bamboo coffee bar next door, or the Continental in North Street. Then it was on to the pier for tentative embraces in the ghost train or that old red speedboat which plied between the piers, canvas up to our necks, spray in our faces, which look like those of children in the early, smudged photo-booth portraits.

I buy an *Evening Argus* and find a large, blurred photo of me taken in the jungles of Panama, alongside a local-boy-returns type of story. What's this? 'Hugo Williams has everything, brains, beauty, fame . . .' This Fiachra Gibbons is setting me up. 'He's not so much the thinking woman's crumpet as her canapé.' Thanks, Fiachra. I find a café in the North Lanes and begin my villanelle: 'In spite – or

133

because of? – our good looks / we are writing better and better books . . .' Hooks, cooks, crooks, chooks . . . this should keep me busy.

The day passes quickly, cruising the old haunts, our house on the Steine where we switched out the lights if we saw the landlord's car, the Lorelei café where I met Keith Richards: 'We don't know all the people who say they know us, if you know what I mean.'

Don's copy for the brochure of the Autumn Season of the Brighton Poets recalls those self-conscious days, which seem likely to stay with me now: 'Hugo Williams, the man who elevated hair-combing to an act of religious and paranoid intensity, makes a rare Brighton appearance. Bring a hanky.' It is touching to see Don and Eva lugging great cardboard boxes of poetry books into the venue, putting on some jazz, lowering the lighting in this splendid domed room. Apart from two prints of boats, the Sussex Motor Yacht Club has long forgotten whatever connection it once had with motor yachting – luckily, because it is two miles from the Marina – and settled into a nice old drinking club with a faint air of subterfuge: very Patrick Hamilton. I duck into the historic marble urinals on the first of several hair-checks.

If ever there was a form of therapy guaranteed to regress a patient to the good old days when he was suspended in warm fluid inside his mother, it is the poetry reading. After it, I am dragged kicking and screaming from the stage and taken back to the house for dinner. Later (almost too late), we make plans to form a rock band of poets to be called 'Brighton Rock', with Don on guitar, myself on words, and Sean O'Brien on drums. It is the end to a perfect day. Now all we need is someone who can play bass and someone to manage us, always supposing the group itself, or our memory of it, survives our hangovers.

[20.11.92]

134

Margaret Vyner and the Perfumes of Jean Patou

1925. Paris passes from high Anglophilia to unbridled Negromania. The Charleston is born. Women bob their hair, smoke cigarettes, embark on love affairs. The couturier Jean Patou creates three new scents to evoke the three great moments of love: 'Amour Amour', 'Que Sais-Je?', 'Adieu Sagesse'. On the other side of the world, in Winona, Sydney, a skinny eleven-year-old girl called Margaret Vyner walks through a plate glass window and amazes everyone by escaping unhurt.

1927. Lindbergh crosses the Atlantic. The Surrealist Gallery opens in Paris. From a boutique on the beach at Deauville, Jean Patou launches 'le sportswear'. He dresses tennis star Suzanne Lenglen. The suntanned look is *à la mode* and Patou is the first to introduce suntan oil to the world. It is called 'Chaldée'. In Australia, outdoor girl Margaret Vyner enters Ascham School for Girls, where the uniform is a disappointing beige, like everyone's permanently tanned skin.

1929. Diaghilev dies. Black Friday on Wall Street. For Paris society it is the high summer of ostentation and elegant extravagance. This last wave of desperate optimism inspires Patou's homage in perfume to a generation: 'Moment Suprême'. A gawky fifteen, Margaret Vyner is attending the dancing classes of Alexei Dolinoff, who came to Australia with Pavlova and also teaches Robert Helpmann. Her only despair is that she has grown too tall to be a ballet dancer.

1930. Gandhi comes to Europe. Picasso is awarded the Carnegie Prize. René Clair shoots the first talkie on the roofs of Paris. In the salons of Patou's *hôtel particulier* in the Rue St Florentin, a cocktail bar has been opened for the benefit of customers. In recognition of the new decade's sophistication, he has mixed his 'Cocktail' range of scents, bright and fresh as an aperitif. In Sydney, the skinny sixteen-year-old is starting to be toasted.

1933. The Bauhaus closes its doors. Pierre Bonnard paints *Le*

Grand Nu au Miroir. In America, conserves of pickled rattlesnake go on sale. In Paris, Patou's 'Divine Folie' captures the mood of the moment as one mad craze follows another into oblivion. Margaret Vyner is touring Australia and New Zealand as a chorus girl in the musical comedy *Flora Dora*. *Her* divine folly is a plan to run away to Europe.

1934. Miss Vyner arrives in Paris with no money, no French and no contacts. She attends a Jean Patou dress show for fun and is instantly offered a modelling job by the vigilant couturier. He takes her to dinner in the Bois de Boulogne and then on to the lesbian night-club Le Monocle, where the virginal Australian orders her usual glass of milk.

1935. The liner SS *Normandie* breaks the record for the Atlantic crossing: four days, two hours, twelve minutes. Later the same year, Patou launches his own version of 'Normandie': a spell blended of the sea and the voyage, bound with that special sense of bewildered luxury. Margaret Vyner is photographed in nautical mood at the party to launch the fragrance on board the SS *Normandie* at Cherbourg.

1936. 19 June: total eclipse of the sun. Sacha Guitry introduces 'Le Mot de Cambronne' to polite society (General Cambronne is reputed to have uttered 'Merde' when asked to surrender at Waterloo), while the French government introduces paid holidays to the people. 'Why does the air smell so sweet when I wake in the morning', Paul Poiret asks Patou. 'What is that subtle flavour of dawn, as if the whole garden has poured into my room?' 'It is the fragrance that has just been created by Patou', replies Patou. 'And it is called "Vacances".' Margaret Vyner tours his Collection to Lyon, Dijon, Deauville, Biarritz and Cannes. Then flies to Croydon Airport for the next stage of her adventure.

1938. Matisse paints *Le Jardin d'Hiver*. Le Corbusier draws up his plans for the urbanization of Buenos Aires. The skies look threatening over Europe. Rumours of war are mixed with dreams of escape. In this loaded atmosphere, Patou-Prospero summons up his 'Colony' — a scent evocative of sun-ripened fruit and beautiful

Creole women in blue-plumed head-dresses. In London, our colonial friend has wangled herself the part of someone's girlfriend in a Broadway-bound Freddy Lonsdale play, *Once is Enough*, in order to meet its leading man, Hugh Williams. The first evening on board the SS *Washington*, he sends a note to her table, 'Champagne better than milk. Why don't you join me?' She is soon weaned.

1939. Auden and Isherwood leave England for America. Hugh Williams and Margaret Vyner pawn his mother's mink for a last pre-war holiday on Capri. On 3 September she is sitting in a basket rehearsing Terence Rattigan's *French Without Tears* when she hears the news that war has been declared. The party is over.

1946. Sinatra fever. René Simon opens his acting school in Paris. Death of Gertrude Stein and actor Raimu. Jean Patou's new scent, 'L'Heure Attendue', celebrates the longed-for Liberation with an access of joy for the rebirth of his beloved Paris. On the Left Bank, a new world is stammering into existence. It is the epic poem known as St Germain des Prés. On the other side of the Channel, I never go anywhere without my mother's empty Patou scent bottle in the shape of a crown.

[4.12.92]

Hair Trouble

My heart leapt in sympathy with the gentleman in the news recently who has been going round setting fire to all the hairdressing salons where he has had bad haircuts. I had my first bad haircut at Thomas's in Eton when I was four. I was frightened of the big revolving brushes whirring over my head, but the real danger lay elsewhere. The barber was one of those old-fashioned ones who make lots of little snips in the air all the time. His snipping scissors flashed and fluttered round my head, then suddenly he snipped the top of my ear. Blood flowed on to the towel. Screams and apologies filled the air. Cotton wool was applied. My impression of hairdressers was established.

It happened that Thomas's was no stranger to pain. As well as dangerous haircuts, they sold canes to the Eton boys, straight 'house canes', knobbly 'school canes', bent-handled 'Pop canes', all displayed with pride in the shop window alongside the 'Rules of Pop' and other regalia. The association of haircuts with pain continued when, years later, I was sent to Thomas's by the head of my house to buy a cane with which to be beaten. Recently, I looked in the window and was disappointed to find the instruments of torture had been replaced by tropical fish-keeping equipment and cacti.

Hairdressers may look as though they know what they're doing, pulling your hair up between their fingers and cutting it off at strange angles, but often, I believe, they are completely out of their depth in three dimensions, relying on primitive weapons such as the thinning scissors to get them out of trouble. Remember spray? 'Any spray, sir?' God knows what was in that old chrome bottle with its orange rubber pump. Essence of Barbershop? Savour of Gents? The adhesive wetness was a last-ditch camouflage for incompetence, which dried later to reveal the ridges, valleys and tussocks of the battlefield, if not actual areas of baldness. The final flourish of the hand-mirror was surely sadistic, the gloating flag of a victorious general.

I think one realized early on that words were uniquely important at the start of a haircut, and also uniquely impotent. After all, what is 'short'? What is 'long'? What is a 'trim'? What does 'over' mean in the phrase 'over the ears'? What does 'layering' really mean? Is 'reshaping' different from 'restyling'? Is 'grading' the same as 'graduating'? I have come to the conclusion that it is better to say nothing at all to a hairdresser, for fear of being misunderstood. Most barbers have one haircut they can do, and if they suspect you are asking for something different, they panic. Scissors snip frantically for too long in the same place. The more graphic your descriptions become, the more wildly they are misinterpreted. A simple request for more off the back suddenly results in a fringe at the front. Conversation dries up as you both realize that something has gone wrong, and the poor man tries to even out what he has done by taking

138

more off the other side. In the end, someone else's haircut starts to appear on your head, which you have to go home with. When you say, 'No, shave it off and we'll start again next year', your suggestion is treated as humorous and you have to pay the usual £18.

The great thing in the 1950s and early 1960s was to have a haircut which looked the same after as before. Over the years, most people found a hairdresser who was prepared to leave their hair virtually untouched, and it was this which led eventually to the long-haired styles of the 1960s, when people with long hair had two choices: let it grow even longer, or find a women's hairdresser who took men. This was when pleasure was first added to pain in the subconscious of hairdressing. Not only were there girls all round you, looking at themselves in mirrors, but female hairdressers leant their pelvises against your shoulder and said what nice hair you had. The sensation of surrendering to an alien world was increased by having to lean backwards instead of forwards to have your hair washed, exposing one's vulnerable adolescent adam's apple to the whims of unpredictable femininity.

It was a relief when Gary Craze opened Sweeney's in Beauchamp Place, the first official long-hair hairdresser in London, but the problem was now how to stop people trained in women's salons from 'layering' your hair. To the new hairdresser, trained in long-haired techniques, the word 'layering' was synonymous with cutting. What else was there? 'You don't want your hair layered?' 'No.' 'Well, what *do* you want?' As always, it was hard to say, without risking a revenge job. If they didn't know already, how could you tell them, using words?

With Sweeney's, Gary Craze changed utterly the image of the old hairdressing salon. From now on, they would look like the reading room of a gentleman's club: dim lighting, brass fittings, smoked mirrors in walnut frames, dark basins, slate work surfaces, the effect completed by middle-class chaps asking you if you'd like a coffee. This new idea of the hairdresser's as a coffee bar lasted twenty years, and can still be found in certain provincial establishments.

Having started at Thomas's and Trumper's, over the years I have gone gradually downmarket in search of the elusive good haircut: Harrods, Simpson's, Meekers, Austin Reed's, Bush House, Scissors, Rough Cut, Zoo, Overhead Worker's, Dave's. For a short time, I went to the flat of a haircutting drug-dealer in South London who carried on his twin callings with a joint in one hand and a pair of scissors in the other, often confusing them and occasionally burning one's ear. Instead of the old 'Will there be anything else, Sir?' or the later 'D'you want another coffee, Hugo?', a joint would pass back and forth between us, and at the end of the haircut, if he remembered to get there, he would say, 'By the way, your shopping's on the table.' In this way, the two sides of his business worked in harmony, the blurred effect of one ameliorating the blurred effect of the other, sometimes for weeks on end.

Perhaps high-street salons should follow his example and offer a general anaesthetic alongside the old cut and blow-dry, with euthanasia as an optional extra if anything went badly wrong.

[18.12.92]

Out and About in Women's Clothing

A new fashion magazine had decided to have a social column featuring the dozen or so glamorous Danish girls who modelled most of the clothes. The idea was that these girls should become famous in their own right, with interesting night-lives and love-lives, to be recorded in photographs and captions, which would make their clothes more interesting commercially and help generate advertising. The editor asked me to edit this column, and I agreed.

What I didn't realize was that these Danish girls were nothing more socially charismatic than the finalists of a modelling competition organized in Copenhagen by a Danish photographer who worked for the magazine and wanted to have some of his country-women on hand for carnal as well as photographic duties.

One evening, I was at the flat talking to Cindy and Rut about their imaginary affair with Rupert Everett, when Rut suggested that I put on one of her dresses, then we could all go out and see *Shanghai Express* dressed as Marlene Dietrich and on to a nightclub she knew about. She showed me a copy of a Danish magazine in which she featured as a mermaid, naked from the waist up, advertising junk jewellery, and gave me to understand that she would like me more if I did as she suggested, or rather, that she wouldn't like me at all if I refused.

The two began taking dresses out of their cupboard and holding them up against me for size. They found a black sheath that almost fitted, then a fur jacket, long gloves and a pillbox hat with veil. Rut applied foundation cream, mascara and lipstick, and I was gradually transformed into a drag version of myself. What I was frightened of was going out into the street. Though all three of us were dressed as women, myself for the first time, I noticed that it was still me who had to find a taxi. I did my best, but if you don't wear a petticoat with a tight evening dress, the material gets caught between your legs, slowing down your movements and attracting people's attention. I was suffering severe trouser withdrawal, but I thought that perhaps I was having a good time.

When the three of us reached the Electric Cinema, where *Shanghai Express* was supposed to be playing, we discovered that some other film was showing that evening, which the girls had seen before. 'What shall we do now?' they asked, holding their heads on one side. My first instinct was to jump back in the taxi and return to where my own dear clothes were waiting, but Cindy and Rut's first instinct was to parade up and down Portobello Road, swinging their arms up and down and blowing smoke in people's faces. I had trouble keeping up with them. As rearguard to their progress, I was vulnerable to comments and harassment from the Saturday night crowds, who weren't taken in for a moment by my costume. The words 'It's a man' dogged me as I followed my dubious copy towards a nightclub called *Déjà Vu*, where Rupert Everett was said to hang out.

We were too early for the club, so I suggested we drop in on a friend of mine who lived nearby. He wasn't in, but I knew how to climb around the service well and break in through the bathroom window. I let the girls in through the front door, found some drinks and tried to act as if everything was going according to plan. By this time, the girls had started speaking Danish. Suddenly one of them said she had to get some cigarettes, the other one said she felt like an ice-cream.

When the girls had gone, I found a copy of *Harpers & Queen* and started reading Jennifer's Diary to see if I could get some ideas for my column. I read the magazine very slowly, not wanting to look up until I heard the doorbell ring. About an hour later, when I had read it from cover to cover, I had to face the fact that Cindy and Rut weren't coming back for me and that I was marooned in a strange flat in a long evening dress, a fur jacket and a pillbox hat with veil. I doubted I could get any mileage out of it for my social column, but I felt I had learned a valuable lesson: that girls seldom make passes at men who wear dresses.

[1.1.93]

Paris at Its Perfect Greedy Smug Best

Christmas in Paris. We favour the coach because it is like the Dover Stagecoach, untouched by Progress or Duty Free. We sit on the deck of the packet with our thermos flask and sandwiches, watching the coast of France getting closer at the right speed. At La Villette, we take our luggage out of the back of the coach, not off a roulette wheel of other possibilities, as in airports.

Paris is at its perfect greedy smug best in the season of conspicuous consumption and self-congratulation, though not perhaps for the melancholy fool playing 'J'attendrai' on a suitcase full of wine-glasses on the Pont Saint-Louis, or the lonely Ethiopian selling wind-up birds in the Tuileries Gardens. Oscar, a black pig in a red harness, snorts among the Christmas trees outside Le Pied de Cochon where Oscar Wilde once begged.

Midnight Mass at Saint-Eustache in Les Halles, famed for

142

hundreds of years for its music. Mozart's mother is buried here. She died on Mozart's second, failed trip to Paris, when he was twenty, and was buried here because it was cheap and near. The church is packed. *Le grand orgue* booms. People come and go, lighting candles. A duet for soprano and cornet, followed by a woman reading a translation of Martin Luther King's 'I have a dream' speech, which comes as a bit of a shock and doesn't really work because there is no way of saying 'I have a dream' in French; it has to be 'J'ai rêvé que . . .' We creep around, pressing the time switches in the side chapels to see the great paintings, one by Rubens in his Caravaggio phase. The crib is very small and plain, as there has been a spate of arson attacks on them in recent years. Last year, a giraffe was stolen by a *clochard* and sold to a bar.

How many marrons glacés will there be in the big box we open on Christmas morning? Thirty? Forty? Fifty? There are eighteen, each one set apart from its neighbour, as if it were afraid of catching something.

Christmas lunch with my 101-year-old French grandfather-in-law, who will ask me if I have got a car yet. Electronic problems. First with the entry-code to his block, which has been changed, then with his deaf-aid, which emits screeches of feedback whenever anyone speaks, finally with the foot-bell, which I know his cook detests, but which I am ordered repeatedly to press. I only pretend to press it, and she comes anyway. We eat and shout, inhibited by screechback. After the meal, we go into *le grand salon* for coffee. The flat creaks with every step.

Boxing Day. My favourite thing on weekend afternoons in Paris is to go up to the flea market at the Porte de Clignancourt and hear the gypsy jazz guitarists, les Manouches, playing in the dingy Aux Chopes des Puces where Django Reinhardt used to play. They sit under yellowing photographs of the master and take it in turns to play lead on 'Sweet Georgia Brown', 'Blue Moon', 'All of Me', 'Lady Be Good' . . . their guitars worn thin as old bone knives, whittling away at the tunes as effortlessly as if they were speaking. You put some coins in a basket as you go out.

Sunday. Back to Saint-Eustache for the *visite* – the free conducted tour by a genuine Loden-wearing intellectual, who asks: 'How much time have you got, because this is the most interesting and beautiful church in Paris?' His commentary is a cultural history of Europe since the Renaissance, of which this church is an expression, standing at the point where horizontal classical forms take over from vertical Gothic ones. I take in the round arches of the gallery, but the overall effect is still Gothic, still Northern. This is because all the white and gold of this showcase of light and art was stripped out during the Revolution, the statues smashed, the bronze melted down for cannon. A carved Baroque screen showing St Agnes (whose church once stood here) was saved only because someone found her aristocratic crown and baton symbol and thought it was the baton of Revolution. She was given a Phrygian bonnet to wear, and her putti were given *tricolors* to wave in her face. The greatest of the church's treasures, a white marble statue of Jean-Baptiste Colbert, Louis XIV's finance minister, by Antoine Coysevox, was rescued by Alexandre Lenoir and put in his new museum, now the Beaux-Arts. It was later returned to the church, but placed in a new, humbler position, so that instead of gazing piously at the Virgin, the gorgeously arrayed finance minister now regards the doorway, where beggars congregate.

Our guide reminds us that there is to be a concert by the organist Pierre Guillou in a few minutes, but his mind seems to be on other things when he suggests, 'Vous pouvez rester pour la cuisine . . .' We all laugh. The voice of Guillou comes over the loudspeaker like a tired DJ. He plays some 'variations' on Christmas themes which sound remarkably like Jimmy Smith.

Monday. We are giving a mulled wine and mince pie party in our borrowed flat, but we have only brought twelve mince pies from England. Marks and Spencer, the only place you can buy mince pies in Paris, is packed with Parisians turning up their noses at all the overpackaged sugary products, which I may say do look strangely repulsive here. As I linger shamefacedly near the mince pie island, wondering whether to buy the deep-filled or Luxury mince pies with cherries and Grand Marnier, I hear a young woman dismissing them as 'horribles petites tartes pleines de confiture et de sucre'. Stung by this, I tell her that they are not full of *confiture*. I show her the pack: 'Aux Fruits Secs et Epices'. When I get home, I see that they contain sugar, soya, dextrose, vinegar, colouring and E127.

[15.1.93]

Laurence Olivier Knew My Father

When I was born, my father received a telegram from Laurence Olivier saying I should be called Torquemada: 'I think he'll be to life as is the osprey to the fish, who takes it by sovereignty of nature.' A few years earlier, he had named his own son Tarquin, a somewhat milder kick up the pants. Tarquin must be fifty-six by now. We have never met, but our lives have shadowed one another from time to time, first at Eton, then travelling in Asia and writing travel books, more recently in writing about our actor fathers. Tarquin's *My Father Laurence Olivier* came out at the end of last year, a hopelessly touching account by a son who barely saw his father but adored him from afar and treasured every scrap of conversation, every fragment of correspondence. I suppose we are not the first sons of actors to pick up our pens and try to write ourselves a part in it all.

Our fathers first met in 1928, juveniles whose careers were at about the same level, although my father claimed to have seen Olivier, aged about eleven, playing Kate in his school production of *The Taming of the Shrew*, his hair cut straight across his forehead in a prototype of his Henry V hairstyle. A few years later, my father had a success in a play written by his own stepfather, Mordaunt Shairp, *The Green Bay Tree*, the first modern play about homosexuality, and Olivier played his part when it went to New York. They were both up for the part of Stanhope in *Journey's End*, which unfortunately went to Olivier. In 1938 they were both in Hollywood making *Wuthering Heights* — two married men, now separated, with beautiful new girlfriends on their arms, one of whom had just got the

145

part of Scarlett O'Hara in *Gone With The Wind*. My mother remembers a happy, madcap time, mostly spent dodging the press. The two didn't meet again until 1944 when, according to Olivier, my father suggested it might not be a bad idea to make a film of Henry V, although his idea was to do it in battledress.

Olivier was knighted soon after Tarquin went to Eton in 1948, and made one of his rare visits to the school to celebrate. They had a bottle of champagne in Tarquin's room and foolishly left the bottle in his waste-paper basket. His housemaster, E. P. Hedley, heard about it and nearly got him sacked on a point of school law that should have been bent for the occasion. Tarquin assumed that Hedley disapproved of his father's knighthood, probably rightly; I went to the same house at Eton and had a similar experience of the man.

My father always said he chose Hedley's house because he had met him in a nightclub during the war and thought any man out dancing with an attractive wife couldn't be all schoolmaster. Hedley must have left his sense of life's gaiety behind in that nightclub, because by the time I arrived in 1955 he had turned into 'Deadly Hedley', a Christian of the bloody-minded variety, whose heavy frame and brick-red scowl always filled me with foreboding.

Hedley was thoroughly suspicious of theatrical people's morals, although his attitude may have had something to do with my father's bankruptcy. He had read about it in the newspaper, assumed I was no longer coming to Eton, and calmly taken me off his house-list. When my father turned up to make arrangements for my arrival, Hedley was speechless with embarrassment, but had no choice but to put me back on again. It wasn't an auspicious beginning.

Like Tarquin, I went travelling in Asia for two years in the early 1960s. When I came home, dreading the writing job I saw looming, I found Tarquin's *Eye of the Day* waiting on my table. Inside, my father had written: 'His father may be a better actor than I am. May you be a better writer than he is.' We know from Tarquin's later book about his father that Olivier refused to read *Eye of the Day* on the grounds that he was too busy.

It was about this time that the two men found themselves at St Thomas's Hospital together with prostate problems, cancer in Olivier's case. They used to visit each other's room, carrying their catheters and what looked like bottles of claret. Olivier made an extraordinary recovery and went on to some of his greatest successes at the National, including *Othello*. My father's health declined, and four years later, in 1969, he was dead, an old man at sixty-five.

Olivier was marvellous. He summoned our entire clan to his office on the South Bank and asked us all to write to him with our own contributions for his eulogy. These he blended with his own memories into a memorable send-off, which he delivered at the Memorial Service at St Martin's-in-the-Fields. We all have a copy of it on tape, and there is one bit I am particularly fond of. He is recalling the shooting of *Wuthering Heights*, in which my father played the dissolute Hindley: 'One day, I, as the menial underdog, had to hold my hands clasped together so that the cruel master could have his mud-covered boot photographed as it squelched into the hands that were helping him on to his horse. It took four men to hold the horse's feet, two men to hold his head and one on the other side to hold Hindley on, in case his progress did not stop in the middle of the horse's back. Our friend was a great sportsman, you understand, but not quite in that sense. When we got back to our dressing rooms afterwards, I offered him a drink and he thanked me whole-heartedly, saying, "I've been in the saddle all day".'

[29.1.93]

Bob Castle and the Lock of Shelley's Hair

I went down to Bournemouth last week to see my friend Bob Castle. He had promised to take me round the Shelley Museum, which he was once involved with; also to show me the Shelley family tomb, 'the Tomb of Talents', where Shelley's heart lies enshrined in a silver casket.

Bob is sixty-seven, a wide-eyed, diffident figure in trainers and raincoat, his curly hair, worn long under a John Lennon cap, giving him a wasted, boyish air. He is a poet, who long ago ceased writing poetry – 'when I realized my limitations' – and has instead dedicated his life to the love of poetry, notably that of Tony Harrison, whose work he has published in limited editions. All his life he has lived at home, looking after his widowed mother, who went blind towards the end of her life.

He met me at the station and took me to lunch at the Miramar Hotel, a crumbling, country-club-like place, where, he assured me, J. R. R. Tolkien used to spend his summers. He had booked a window table in the empty dining room, but was dismayed to find the sea shrouded in mist for this much anticipated occasion. He sat with his back to the view and apologized twice for its absence, as if I needed something other to look at than his friendly face. As we talked about his life, the mist slowly parted, like a veil lifting on an older, gentler world, also a harsher one.

Bob retired recently as night watchman at the nearby Russell-Cotes Museum. He was originally technical assistant at the museum, with responsibility for hanging exhibitions, until eye trouble obliged him to seek night work. 'They called it Security, but I call it night watchman.' He still suffers from constant pain in his eyes, and was highly gratified to learn that Tony Harrison's work-room remains permanently darkened, because his own living room has three layers of curtains against the light.

Bob began his working life in 1940 at the age of fourteen as a van boy with the Sunray Laundry. 'I used to sit on the tailboard, which would never be allowed nowadays, then run inside with the laundry. I used to deliver to this hotel, as a matter of fact.' His father, a cabinet maker in a furniture store, died when he was two, leaving his mother to bring up three children by charring for a different household every day of the week. 'We discovered his boss hadn't been paying his stamps, so we were penniless. You don't want to be poor in a rich town . . .' A crowning sadness was the death of his sister Violet, aged seventeen.

As soon as he was eighteen, Bob volunteered for the Navy and found himself in the magazine of the battleship *George V*, passing up shells for the bombardment of some Greek islands. Later, he took part in an armed landing on the Arakan coast of Burma, where low-flying Japanese aircraft 'made life difficult for a while'. He came home and took up a position, vacated by the death of a relative, as storeman in the motor repair shop of the Branksome Carriage Works. From there he moved to the Russell-Cotes in 1971.

After lunch, we walked along the front to the Museum, where Bob had to pick up a packet left for him by the Keeper, containing a video of Tony Harrison's play *The Blasphemers' Banquet*, which he'd missed the beginning of. We had time for a quick look round before the light failed.

Once the sumptuous home of Sir Merton and Lady Russell-Cotes, now 'A Living Record of the Life and Travels of an Extraordinary Family', the museum is stuffed with prestigious paraphernalia and kitsch, including a naked butterfly fairy and other period porn. A sentimental picture of a beautiful exhausted maidservant in an attic drew from Bob the comment: 'Overworked and underpaid'. In 'The Irving Room', we saw the skull used by Henry Irving in *Hamlet*. Sir Merton liked to cultivate the famous, and Irving got free digs at the family's Royal Bath Hotel next door, in return for little favours such as turning on the fountain in the hotel grounds, the iron turn-key being duly preserved in the museum. When I asked Bob if he had been able to sleep during his twelve-hour shifts as night watchman he told me no, and his hand went up instinctively to find one of the old clocking devices he had had to turn on his rounds, now gone.

Next stop was St Peter's Church, where the white Shelley tomb stands out on a tree-backed rise. The remains of William Godwin, Mary Wollstonecraft and their daughter Mary Shelley were transferred here from the Church of St Pancras in London when the railway was built through it in 1851. By a strange chance, it was Thomas Hardy, then a young architect working for the railway, who accompanied them to Bournemouth. Shelley's heart, saved by Byron from the beach cremation at Viareggio, was brought back to

England by his son, who kept the shrivelled object at Boscombe Manor for fifty years before interring it here with the other 'persons of notoriety', as they were known.

A short bus ride and we were at the Shelley home in Boscombe, now an art school in a suburb of Bournemouth. Among the exhibits in the two tiny 'Shelley Rooms' is a waxen effigy of an ecclesiastic, which was the doll of Byron's abandoned daughter Allegra. There was also a lock of Shelley's hair. Bob remembered going up to London on behalf of the museum's founder, Mary Brown, in order to collect the hair from Shelley's descendant, Lord Abinger. 'What happened?' I asked. 'Nothing much. I rang the bell, went up the stairs and he let me have the hair.' 'Did he offer you a drink?' 'No. But when I got back to Bournemouth I lifted up the cardboard, thinking there might be a letter hidden underneath, and there was this big hank of much fairer hair, which must have been cut off when Shelley went to Eton.' 'Did you keep it yourself?' I asked. 'No, I couldn't really.'

Over tea at the Golden Egg in Boscombe High Street, I tried to turn the conversation away from Shelley towards Bob's own writing life. Had he ever published any poems? He admitted with some embarrassment that he had once had four poems in the little magazine *Envoi*, although he wouldn't say in which decade. 'I wasn't educated, you see.' I asked him how he had first got interested in poetry. Was it through Shelley? 'No, tell the truth I can't read him. It was really jazz that got me interested in culture. My brother and I used to cut out the advertisements for films and stick them in a book, and from there we got interested in jazz. We had this record, *When Buddha Smiles* by Coleman Hawkins. Then one day I was looking at *Poetry Chicago* and I came across a poem about King Oliver. I couldn't believe there was anyone writing a poem about jazz . . . and of course it was Larkin.' When I told him I had had a similar experience with Thom Gunn's 'Elvis Presley', we were back on safer ground, and for the rest of my short visit the names of writers passed back and forth between us like fabulous jewels. 'Did you know Verlaine used to teach in Bournemouth?' he enthused. 'Yes, not far from here. St Aloysius's School for Boys, 24 Surrey Road. Would you like to go there?'

[oooo]

Glucovision

Winter evenings = TV-watching = guilty feelings = heavy feet on the way up to bed. How did they do it? How did the great depressive TV empire colonize our free time? How did we succumb to something so . . . harmless?

TV is like white sugar. It used to be good for us. Our mothers gave us spoonfuls of it to keep us going, 'give us energy'. We ate sugar sandwiches. Now we have got false teeth. 'What's on next?' 'Oh, I think there's something good on after the news.' Like innocent tribal people, we queue at the Mission for our nightly fix. How wonderful, we think, that there are four different flavours. In our naivety we imagine we are free to choose between them. We aren't, of course. It is we who are being chosen. The TV companies draw lots for us. Like shepherds at sheep-dog trials, they decide how many of us they want in the pen and blow the whistle accordingly. They are helped by the way we seem to associate television with entertainment, just because it has a rectangular screen and happens in the evening. Over the years, TV has been brilliant at mimicking entertainment values in order to breach our immune systems. Nowadays we are all telebetics, our bloodstreams seething with glucovision.

It won't be long before only the lack of television is noticeable: a thinning of the atmosphere, a sense of loss, a feeling of panic. When every known form of diversion has been piped into the home like running water, only its forcible removal, by doctors or policemen, will be practicable. When that happens, crime will be punished by TV licence endorsement, rehabilitation programmes and the ulti-mate deterrent, conversation.

'TV is a medium of fantasy', says Jim Fowles, Professor of Humanities at the University of Houston, Texas. 'Its purpose is to

151

remove mental debris from the minds of viewers. Like all fantasy material, it does not put things into our brains, but takes them out. It gets rid of the tension and anxiety accumulated during the working day. It is not meant to impart information.'

His researches show that watching television is replacing not only conversation and social life, but sleep as well. The average viewer sleeps less than the non-viewer. It seems that TV's effect on us is similar to that of dreams. And the reason sex and violence are so pervasive on TV is that they are so prevalent in the subconscious. 'The real world offers few chances for the release of aggression', says the Freudian Fowles, 'while TV is an ever-open vicarious outlet.'

Just as, in Freud's day, dream fantasies were scorned as trivial or grotesque, TV shows today are disdained by an élite who want television to be an intellectual force. According to Fowles, when members of this élite declare that they do not watch TV entertainment, they are lying. In fact, there is only a 1 per cent difference between the viewing habits of the best and the least educated. Even this gap is closing. What hope can there be?

There is always the 'off' button. But in my experience, the off button is a strangely unappealing alternative, very different from the 'on' button, which works almost automatically by comparison, just like opening your eyes. Switching off in the middle of an average evening's entertainment can be an unpleasant shock to the system, leaving one feeling cold and confused, in need of a cup of tea. Not work but the toad television squats on our lives. It is a fact that some people can hardly bring themselves to turn the sound down a little when the family comes round at Christmas, or when the prodigal is brought home by the police. The Officers and the boy's family stand round facing the television. Gaps open in the conversation as they wait for the outcome of a car chase.

No, the on-off choice is only an illusion of choice; either way, the box sits there, accumulating power, like some queer Pinteresque house guest with only two moods, both strangely disquieting. In vain, we switch back and forth in search of some lost peace, unaware that it is both further away and closer than we think.

I note that the snappily titled EXIT organization for quickie euthanasia deals has had to change its name to something less New Wave, but the advice it offers still involves sleeping-pills and plastic bags, which, if wielded wrongly, can result in brain damage and life. While TV represents a possible compromise measure for EXIT members, is there any reason why it should be performing this function for the rest of us? If there were an organization dedicated to helping four- and five-hour men like myself to pull the plug on their flickering life-support systems, I for one would join. It could be called OFF and the kit could include a brick for going cold turkey.

[26.2.93]

The Remarkable Recording Briefcase

I saw an advertisement in a giveaway magazine for surveillance and counter-surveillance equipment, including something called 'The Remarkable Recording Briefcase', which I thought might be the answer to the problem of how to write more.

I sent off for the catalogue and was favourably impressed by a picture of the usual squared-off, executive-type case with brass combination locks. 'The Recording Briefcase is built with discretion in mind', ran the copy. 'There is no visual evidence, either internally or externally of its electronic capability. Open or closed, even locked and unattended, the Recording Briefcase will monitor conversations with the utmost discretion.' Surveillance equipment, I learnt, was usually employed in a 'need to know' capacity; the beauty of the Recording Briefcase was its 'need to prove' facility, a need I wholeheartedly shared. Excited by this, I sent off the money immediately.

The first time I went out with the briefcase, it attracted more attention than I had hoped, first from people on the train, then from the Australian relatives I was with. They couldn't take their eyes off it. Did all executive briefcases have recording facilities, I wondered? Or was it something about the way I held it, poised on my knee?

There seemed to be no opportunity to set the thing in motion, but after they had gone, I did manage to record myself ordering tea and later to record one of the 'Sounds of the Seventies' programmes on BBC2. The next day, I took it along to the Royal Society of Literature to record a talk by Alan Ayckbourn, all achieved with complete (but unwarranted) 'discretion'.

At about this time, I received two letters. The first was from an organization in Manchester offering me the chance to start an exciting new life by attending a seminar on the subject of international intelligence. I was given to understand that my name had been selected following the interest I had shown in electronic surveillance equipment. Might I be interested in travelling and making considerable sums of money?

It so happened that an exciting new life was not exactly what I was looking for, but I have to admit my heart leapt at the thought of becoming a spy. I called a number in Manchester and spoke to the convener. He seemed plausible, but when I pressed him on the format and subject-matter of the seminar, I had the impression he was more interested in the surveillance equipment than in the uses to which it could be put. He kept talking about telephone and wiring analysers, VDU and computer screeners, automatic switches, hand-held detectors and counter-surveillance receivers, until I got the idea he had some sort of concession on the stuff. At first, I thought he was trying to unload some of it in my direction. Then I realized he was offering me the chance to learn how to organize sales opportunities of my own. He wasn't interested in recruiting agents for foreign travel with a little light fact-finding thrown in; what he had in mind were cosy Tupperware parties for people interested in being deceitful electronically. People like me, in fact. This was pyramid sales for voyeurs. I said I'd think about it.

About the same time, I received another letter. 'Dear Sir', it began, 'I am 33 years old private detective from Bulgaria, a small European country. Here there was 45 years communist dictatorship and the entrepreneurs didn't prosper but the attendants to the authorities. In 1989, the dictatorship fell and I established private detective agency.

With great difficulty I succeeded in auction for installation of video and remote control cables and security systems in Nigeria. I got huge loans of USD320,000 for incorporation of our company there. One of my officers was constrained to travel to Nigeria so to pay the state security deposit. But on the first day of her stay she was abducted by Mohammed Alao, robbed and violated and menaced with killing. The partners of M. Alao – all black negro-Moslem high corrupted govt. officers – forged the document and we couldn't get our money back. I have lost my flat and USD 280,000. I have no way to repay my lenders, my only chance is to shoot myself. My deadline expires in 23 days. While finishing arrangements for my earthly cares, I decided to write you this letter. If you are able to save my life, here is my account number. [He gave details of an account at Citibank, New York.] You are my last bright heavenly gleam in the immense deadly black world. Yours gratefully, Vladimir Russev.'

Where had he got my name from? How did he know I might be sympathetic to the plight of a bankrupt private detective? Were the two letters connected? The moral of the story seems to be that people who send off for remarkable recording briefcases in the belief that they will transform their lives artistically or materially are well known to be amongst the world's most easily conned. I wrote back to Vladimir giving him the pyramid salesman's address in Manchester. If they didn't know each other already, they do now.

[26.3.93]

The Jerusalem Poetry Festival

Every decade or so, I seem to go to Israel for one reason or another: First in 1963, by accident, because I didn't realize Jerusalem was in two different countries, picked the wrong one and had to go through the Mandelbaum Gate to get to the Arab sector; this time on purpose, to attend the Jerusalem Poetry Festival, not as a poet, but as a guest who might write something. I suppose this is the 'might'.

Israel has changed greatly since 1963, when it was a great big holiday camp with everyone holding hands and laughing. There was no Coke and no television. Now the gallant little David has become a materialistic Goliath, and the smiles have become frowns of anxiety as schoolchildren are slashed in their classrooms by Palestinians, or another Arab boy is shot by terrifying American Jewish 'settlers'. Russian pimps are at large in Tel Aviv. In the game of musical countries, the Palestinians have become the Jews.

Salman Masalha, the Palestinian poet, issued a statement during the festival saying that the Israeli poets were living in ivory towers and had not even been to the window to see the fire. His poetry was heavily symbolical in the way of committed poetry. It was all very Sixties. Personally, I admired organizer Eyal Megged's determination to keep it apolitical. Since the situation is acknowledged to be insoluble, why fan the flames with bad poetry? Of course, Megged's stance was taken as political by some elements, who wanted to know why committed poets like Nathan Zach and Mahomet Darwish were not invited.

The London Poetry Festival was never like this, but the Jerusalem Festival is indirectly descended from it. In 1969, Martin Mooij was in London from Holland to hear Auden, Hughes and Poppa in one of Eric Walter White's South Bank events and decided to do one of his own the following year in Rotterdam. The Jerusalem Festival was modelled on his achievement, and he was in Jerusalem this year as an adviser. 'Our intention was to do ours in the London way,' he told me, 'but people didn't come, so we had to do the foyer thing'. It is this 'foyer thing', loosely interpreted as bar and cabaret for the punters and various fringe benefits such as free meals and sightseeing tours for the poets, that has set the mould for all subsequent jamborees. No money changes hands, but everything is magically taken care of by a crew of volunteers, interpreters and translators who dash about being indispensable, attempting to introduce China to Ireland, Israel to Malawi, etc., sometimes with more success than they had hoped.

For the readings too, the idea is to pair each foreign poet with an Israeli poet, often one who has translated the other's work into

Hebrew. It is a noble plan, but six such pairings every evening – making twelve readings in all – can prove too much if you only understand one of them. The Greek poet Katerina Anghelaki-Rooke maintained that she could tell a good poem even if she didn't speak a word of the language, but when pressed on this skill, seemed to suggest that it all depended on whether she fancied the poet or not. It was a form of literary appraisal which struck a familiar note, and many of the poets were so busy trying to apply it in the festival bar that they missed other poets reading their works on stage.

For other reasons, I missed Philippe Jaccottet from Switzerland and Shuntaro Tanikawa from Japan, but caught Pulitzer prize-winner James Tate's laidback surrealism and Ma Gao Min's seemingly consonant-free communications. I enjoyed watching the Chinese poet stroking his own non-existent beard in sympathy with his translator's long and luxuriant one. His main poem, translated in the brochure, a series of lamentations on being twenty-eight, began every line with that figure, a sound in Chinese which hovered somewhere between 'argy-bargy' and 'artsy-fartsy'. It seemed, for some reason, to produce levity in Western listeners and became the catch-phrase of the festival.

The Byzantine-profiled Nina Cassian, Romania's answer to Edith Sitwell, provided another. Reflecting on the reserved seats in tube trains, she asked people to give up their seat to one suffering from 'Pride, loneliness and art', which seemed to include everyone. She was accompanied by the dreaded 'Poetry Theatre of Tbilisi', who were reported to have brought the flu with them in their brown monks' robes.

Another notable profile, English performance poet Joolz, caught the bug, but came boldly to the microphone and peeling off her cardigan revealed an upper torso covered with beautiful tattoos, some of them in half-tone, which I hadn't seen before. She appeared with David Avidan, a respected but chaotic 'Nobel nominate', who did everything in his power to upstage her reading, dropping things, kicking others, tearing up bits of paper, even applying a breath freshener. 'Why do you have tattoos?' he asked suddenly. 'Ah, you've finally noticed,' said Joolz, brandishing long decorated arms, 'All Jerusalem has been talking about them.' 'But why?' persisted Avidan. 'Because it is the earliest form of art known to mankind,' responded Joolz. Invited to dinner by a mildly religious woman doctor, she scandalized her hostess by asking to say a prayer to the Goddess after Jewish grace – and was hotly refused.

Organizer Eyal Megged provided an interesting opposition between the middle-class Joolz's downwardly-mobile, New Age/rock 'n' roll approach to performance poetry and Simon Armitage, who has travelled rapidly in the opposite direction in recent years. (The *Sunday Times* Young Writer of the Year Award awaited his return to England.) There may have been many more such contrasts among the Israeli poets chosen by Megged, but these remained inaccessible to me. Armitage seemed the most interesting of the English-speaking poets because of his unaffected eye-on-the-ball concentration. 'Poem', his anthem to fickle human nature – 'Here's how they rated him when they looked back. / Sometimes he did this, sometimes he did that.' – was the most quoted poem of the festival, seemingly applying to everything that took place.

It didn't sound good, apparently, in the Hebrew of ace translator Amir Oz with whom he shared the stage. This may have been because Hebrew, a comparatively new spoken language, lacks the layers of colloquial tradition available to English and is better suited to meditational poetry. It is wrong to judge the sounds of a language one does not speak, but even some of the Israeli poets seemed to find Hebrew unpronounceable at times. On the plus side, at least there is no phrase for 'Have a nice day' in Hebrew.

[9.4.93]

A One-Minute Tour of Israel

'So it's goodbye for the time being, this has been a one-minute tour of Switzerland . . .' Lying in my bath in the five-star Hotel Laromme in Jerusalem, watching CNN via an arrangement of mirrors, I think of the air-lock leading into the humid covered-for-winter hotel swimming pool – 'It's quite dangerous to open the second door before the first door is closed behind you' – and how there is, mercifully, an air-lock between the visitor and everything that happens in this country. It seems only natural to be sitting in tropical air-conditioning drinking orange juice and reading the *Jerusalem Post* (slipped under my door each morning) about the latest slashings and reprisals a few miles away. '4,000 people demonstrate outside the home of Prime Minister Yitzak Rabin to protest the deteriorating internal security situation.'

No problem with security up here. All I have to do is dial seven and speak to the house detective. (Clients are advised to leave their valuables with him.) I can see the Old City from my window, but it might as well be a hundred miles away. My only hazard is the gross Jewish New Yorker fund-raiser who haunts the breakfast buffet. He buttonholed me yesterday and explained in about a million words how the fate of the world depends on how well it treats (i.e., becomes) greater Israel. 'We Jews are just teachers. Did you know the entire Bible is based on the figure seven?' I told him I was a poet attending the Jerusalem International Poetry Festival, and he fell back in fear.

There is another air-lock – two sets of doors and a heavy curtain – between the Festival Bar and the auditorium where the poetry readings take place each evening. These doors translate noise into silence, jollity into sobriety, holidays into term time. The air-lock is guarded by a severe gentleman in a trilby who discourages late-comers and early-leavers, which includes nearly everyone sooner or later, for that is poetry in there. I approach him as a happy, slightly drunk human being and am reluctantly translated into the long, dark, silent, selfless incomprehension of poetry. The hall is packed.

We have a free day, so I go looking for the location of the old Mandelbaum Gate that used to be the ultimate air-lock between two worlds. For two decades, 1948–67, it was the only crossing point between Israel and Jordan. To walk down that bombed-out street, observed by bedouin soldiers, one's two passports getting nervously mixed up in one's pocket, was to walk a hundred years back in time. It had been the beginning of a great adventure for me, but no one seems to know where it is any more. Now, like the tomb of Christ, for which there seem to be nineteen contenders, the Gate has been smeared back into time; the eternal palimpsest of Jerusalem offers a different reading.

Nowadays, Arab Jerusalem has withdrawn into the Old City, and even there the flavour is fading as the Jewish Quarter spreads its restored look like a sort of creeping Torremolinos. We were advised by our hosts not to go into the Old City, but everyone did. With armed guards in every alleyway, some of them with long beards and T-shirts, there was no real danger for tourists, but Israelis resent the fact that while their restaurants and bars are safe for Arabs, the Old City is a powder keg under their noses. The atmosphere is not helped by the fact that there are Orthodox types in there drawing up plans for the Third Temple to be built on a site – the Dome of the Rock – currently occupied by the Great Mosque.

Spring and Passover vacation have begun, and all the poets are heading north in a bumpy coach for a spot of tourism and a reading at Kibbutz Kfar Blum on the River Jordan. After the Church of the Feeding of the Five Thousand, we picnic on Mount Gilboa where Israelis come on the first weekend of Passover to witness the short blue life of the wild iris. We witness couples sitting here and there on the hillside gazing raptly at their chosen plants. Then we visit the archaeological site where they filmed *Jesus Christ Superstar*.

The kibbutz is more like a country club than a work farm, with restaurant, pool and television. After dinner, we walk through eucalyptus to a theatre in a field, where the stage alone is big enough to hold the reading and its sizeable audience. The Chilean dissident and editor, Serge Pey, stamps slowly across the stage holding a great staff from which he reads the names of many relatives burnt by Inquisitions ancient and modern. The staff becomes a bull-roarer and finally, as it whirls interminably round and round his head, a full-borer. Peter Florence, director of the Hay-on-Wye Literary Festival, makes a striking contribution by reading, with some feeling, the highly appropriate 'Strange Meeting' by Wilfred Owen. Later, we go to a disco on a neighbouring kibbutz. Syria is five miles away.

A trip to the Dead Sea and Masada with Paul Durcan and Simon and Alison Armitage. By comparison with the fulsome explanations of our Israeli guide on the trip north, the comments of our Arab guide, Jamal, are cryptic in the extreme: 'Administered territories (West Bank) . . . Israeli settlements (invariably on hilltops) . . . World's oldest inhabited town (Jericho, 6,000 years) . . . You want souvenirs?' When Paul asks what the red flowers are beside the road he replies, 'You see, they are just flowers really, for this is spring now.' Some of his phlegmatic Arab nature rubs off on us, and when he asks if we want to stop for a photo with the big 'Sea Level' sign, we don't even have to confer: 'Straight on, Jamal.'

As we bob about in the Dead Sea, shoulders and knees well clear of the bitter water, I think of my hotel swimming-pool, its air-lock and orange juice and pampered atmosphere, a hundred years away from the Intifada and any possible danger, and how, if you stick with the tour, obey the instructions on the air-lock doors and steer well clear of any 'administered territories', it is possible to bob about in a country without ever really being there at all, let alone touching bottom, although Paul did get a nasty flick of salt in one eye. 'So it's goodbye for the time being, this has been a one-minute tour of Israel.'

[23.4.93]

Mordaunt Shairp and *The Green Bay Tree*

I inherited a laundry-basket of old notebooks and plays by a man I never knew but whose strange Christian name I have on my passport. Mordaunt Shairp, my step-grandfather, author of (arguably) the first modern gay play, *The Green Bay Tree*, was by far the most talented member of our family, but unfortunately no blood relation. My real grandfather, an 1890s' dandy, died of consumption in 1904, the year my father was born, leaving only a few pale poems and some deeply felt letters to his tailor. A few years later, my grandmother met and married Shairp in circumstances which have become a family legend, but which I now see are tinged with ambiguity.

He was a teacher at University College School in Hampstead, where my father was a pupil. One day my father brought an excuse-note signed 'H. Williams', and Shairp asked if it was his father's writing. 'No', said my father, 'my father's dead. It's my mother's.' Shairp took pity on the boy and wrote a note asking if he could take him to the zoo. My granny said no, not unless he came to tea first.

At tea, it emerged that Shairp had nowhere to work where he lived, and my grandmother said she had a spare room he could work in during the day. This all seemed proper enough until she came home late one night – she was a Gallery First Nighter and took her son to see all the new plays – and found the young man still there. She was rather shocked, but perhaps not displeased. The next thing that happened was that Shairp turned up on Jersey, where they were on holiday, at which point the situation seems to have become more romantic. She started teasing him by staying in the water much longer than he could stand, obliging him to stay with her. She was a large, powerful woman in the Edwardian dowager mould, and Shairp was very tall and thin and turned completely blue trying to keep up with her.

One day, the three of them were sitting having tea when my father came up with the obvious: 'Hadn't you two better get married?' And so it was. Shairp – 'Sandy' – moved in and my persuasive granny began the process of turning this mild schoolmaster into a successful playwright (a thing my mother did for my father thirty years later). He was twenty-eight. She was forty-six.

Stephen Spender was at UCS at the time and remembers that Sandy was always writing playlets for the boys to act in. There was one about Keats, he told me, in which the poet starts coughing and looks in his handkerchief and suddenly realizes he has TB. I wondered whether this was written before or after the author met and married a consumptive's widow. Was he already using material from his own life, before his commercial début? Spender remembers a buoyant, sympathetic, rather moody figure in the Leslie Howard tradition. 'He had rather charming affectations. He used to stand by the window of our classroom saying whimsical things like, "I wonder where all the litter comes from on Hampstead Heath . . ." '. This was heady stuff to the 'effete set' to which Spender belonged. Did he think he was gay? 'Oh yes, we all assumed he was gay. We thought his getting married was something to do with your father and that *The Green Bay Tree* was semi-autobiographical. I know Forster and J. R. Ackerley thought it was a gay play.'

I was fascinated to learn that a certain sector of London life also assumed that my father was gay. When Spender told me that Shairp had been 'completely hooked on psychoanalysis', I started to see through a mist the origins of a whole range of phobias and prejudices which had been knocking about in my childhood. Not that my father didn't worship his sweet and gentle literary step-father. He became an actor because of his influence; he probably stopped me becoming one from the same influence. He may even have become a playwright in later life in imitation of Shairp.

The Green Bay Tree wasn't the first of Shairp's London successes. That was a piece called *The Offence*, about a sensitive boy who breaks a porcelain bowl and is severely whipped by his father, a punishment which haunts and alters the course of his life. 'We meet the boy again twenty years later', recounted *The Times*, 'a happily married novelist, but the victim of repressed fear that clouds his outlook, thwarts his talents and freezes his affections.' It seems pretty clear that Shairp's affections had been frozen until he met the ebullient widow with the handsome little boy.

The Green Bay Tree itself discusses a more sophisticated sort of offence. A middle-aged bachelor falls in love with the 'voice' of a choirboy in Wales and buys the boy from his drunken father for £500. He brings him up to a life drenched in pleasure, but when the boy falls in love with a sensible girl, cuts off his allowance. A battle ensues for the boy's 'soul' (sexuality) which the unfortunate girl loses when the boy's real father, a reformed man, turns up and shoots the sybarite dead. The boy now steps straight into his protector's decadent suede shoes.

As if this were not enough to cause Spender, Ackerley and Co. to draw conclusions and construct equations, the part of the young man was played by my father, by then a coming juvenile lead. There may be a shadow of truth to the idea that the part represented him, but it seems more likely to me now that the boy was Shairp himself, torn between his modest calling as a schoolmaster and the soft, unnatural (because he was gay) married life. In fact, the more I think about it, the more I see the wolf under the old lady's bonnet: the wicked sybarite was none other than my granny.

If the play was autobiographical, it was also tragically prophetic. It was 1933. The talkies were booming. Shairp was a hot property, and Hollywood beckoned. He and my granny upped sticks and moved to Santa Monica, where, of course, Sandy went into artistic decline. The people at Paramount, instead of getting him to write the screenplay of *The Green Bay Tree*, passed him the odd medical story – *The Men in White*, with Clark Gable, was one of them – in the mistaken belief that his doctorate was a medical one. The pair came home to England in 1938, having gained a set of stuffed models of Walt Disney's Snow White and the Seven Dwarfs and lost a promising career. Sandy went into hospital for a minor operation, caught pneumonia, and died aged fifty-two.

I thought about him recently when I saw an article in Nicholas de Jongh's book, *Not in Front of the Audience*, in which he accuses *The Green Bay Tree* of pretending to be about luxury and diabolism when it is really about homosexuality. One can see his point, but one might as well jeer at Rembrandt for his poor grasp of cubism. The fact is, homosexuality was an unacceptable subject for the stage in the 1920s; it was considered evil, so Shairp cleverly chose the metaphor of evil to discuss an unacceptable subject. What de Jongh doesn't seem to know is that the play's true content was abundantly clear to contemporary audiences. 'Not for years have I observed such an outbreak of horrified protestation at any play', wrote the

Sunday Referee. 'The association between the man and his adopted son is such as to fill normal-minded people with abhorrence', wailed the *Evening Standard.* 'Only Shairp's tactful handling of a very unsavoury theme can have got this play past the censor', said *The Times.* Or, as James Agate put it: 'Perhaps one cannot expect a playwright to go the whole hog when too obvious a hint of the cochon might suppress the animal altogether.'

[14.5.93]

'Ted Hughes'

At the inauguration of Bernard Stone's new bookshop in Great Queen Street, I met a young Australian poet who told me she had been picked up on a tube train by someone calling himself 'Ted Hughes'. He'd caught her eye and come and sat next to her, saying 'So where do you come from?' I asked if she thought it was the poet laureate, and she said she wasn't sure, but she thought it was. At any rate, he didn't deny being a poet, and she hadn't liked to ask if he was the 'real' Ted Hughes in case he was. I asked if he talked with a Northern intonation, and she said yes. I found a photo of the young Hughes in one of the archives, and she said it looked like him, but she couldn't be sure. He was powerful, with a big nose, but his hair was completely white. She'd thought it was Hughes because she'd been on her way to a poetry reading in Brixton and assumed he was going there too, but he wasn't. He said he lived in a flat nearby and invited her to call on him some time. Thinking that he was indeed the famous poet, she went round to see him the next day.

The flat was anonymous-to-bleak with only a few old books of a non-Ted Hughes type. One of the things that made her think he might still be the poet was that he said he was a vet and that he used to live in Devon when he was married, although he was now divorced. With so many animal poems by Hughes, this seemed plausible. More surreally, he claimed to have been in 'Buda' (short for Budapest) recently with the Queen, at which she remembered the

laureate had East European connections and thought it not impossible that he had escorted Her Majesty on a little known official visit.
When she tried to show him some of her own poetry, he peered at it
dully, laid it aside and seemed more interested in steering her
towards the bedroom.

She said that she had to get along to her job making sandwiches,
and he said she didn't have to work, she could live in his flat and he
would look after her, adding 'People who walk with me for a while
are always successful.' She declined, but she didn't want to be too
nasty as she still thought he could be the great man. Instead, she
asked to see some of his own poetry. He said he would show her
some the next time she came to see him.

Sure enough, he had them ready – two sheets of hand-lined paper
filled with childlike script. I asked to see them, and she produced
what looked like an average entry in a poetry competition, except
that they were all signed 'Ted Hughes'. When I saw these, it crossed
my mind that they might indeed belong to Ted Hughes, because it
was likely he had a store of such things left over from one of his
adjudicating jobs, which he was using as scrap. All he would have to
do was sign some anonymous entry in the same hand. The first read
as follows,

> A tree of life, a river of love,
> A longboat full of dreams
> Your book of life I love to read
> Framed with golden beams
> Your pictures are my stories
> A countryside companion
> Of woodland walks and wild flowers
> A bookshop full of knowledge
> Travel to far off shores
> Surrendering in a warming sun
> Togetherness in the Theatre
> Humorous laughter in the home
> Poetry in the garden

When sitting all alone
If togetherness is the essence of love
Then sharing is fulfillment.

It was signed 'Think beautiful, with love Ted Hughes'. The other poem was if anything worse, a soggy thing called 'Woman in a Graveyard' which she was terrified might be about Sylvia Plath. As she handed them back to him, it was her turn to smile weakly. Could this be a cynical try-on, or was it the pathetic effort of an imposter? I said the only way to find out was to take some Ted Hughes books along for him to sign. I gave her my copies and arranged to meet her in the bookshop in a few days.

As soon as she produced the books, she told me, he became very agitated, got up and started walking around the flat 'looking for a pen', although there were plenty on the table. Finally, he settled to the task, looked in the first book and noted that it was dedicated 'To Sylvia'. 'This must be an old one,' he commented. Then, seeming to write with some difficulty with his left hand, slowly wrote in the flyleaf 'To someone who loves poetry, T. Hughes'. He asked if she liked *Crow*, and when she said she did, wrote in that one 'Love is Life, Life is Love, T. Hughes'. As I took back my prized first editions of Hughes, now inscribed, I wondered if they were more or less valuable than they had been.

We decided to ask Bernard Stone what he thought. It certainly wasn't Ted's writing, he said, and produced a card he had just received from Hughes enclosing a marvellous unpublished early poem by Sylvia Plath, 'Image of a Pigeon', soon to be published in his broadsheet series. The writing was the familiar Hughes scrawl. He produced more photographs of the poet, but she still seemed uncertain, possibly unwilling to accept the betrayal. How tall was he? Shorter than me, she said, which seemed wrong.

Bernard suggested ringing the imposter, and somewhat reluctantly she yielded up the number. 'Hello. Is that Ted Hughes?' said Bernard. 'I'm a bookseller in Covent Garden. I found a message on my desk to ring you. Oh. And . . . you're not a poet? Oh. All right.

Goodbye.' He confirmed that it was not Hughes he had spoken to, and that seemed to be the end of the matter. Instead of being relieved to have the truth at last, the victim of the subterfuge seemed vaguely depressed. She had already told me that she was homesick. Now it seemed she had come half-way round the world to meet a dirty old man pretending to be a famous poet. She could have done that without ever leaving home. But then again, perhaps not.

It may not be illegal to be called Ted Hughes and to fail to correct people when they take you for a famous namesake, but this character had gone a step beyond that when he put his name to someone else's books. Clearly this wasn't the laureate using his left hand to protect his public persona but a member of the public doing so to protect his private one, possibly from the law.

A plot for a particularly unpleasant feminist detective story came to mind, one in which the true identity of 'Ted Hughes' would remain in doubt until the very last moment. I realized for the first time that the young Australian had been part of such a plot and that she may even have been in danger.

[28.5.93]

Mr Ray Was Our Homosexual

There it all stands, exactly as you remember it: the roller under the beech tree, the cricket pavilion, the tally board with 'LAST WICKET FELL AT . . .' Can this really be the same drive where you were put to find 'the most interesting stone'? I wonder if mine's still here, with a hole in it. I wonder if Scott's is still here, the one with the face on it, which won the Mars bar? I must be walking through the ghost of Mr Darwell-Smith, jingling the change in his pocket and going 'Heh-heh-heh', as he talks to my mother about the unpaid bill.

For the first time in my life, I knock at the Headmaster's Entrance, knowing it to be wrong. The smell of cabbages and lino is like lifting a curtain. Only the sight-angles have changed. I'm floating up near the ceiling, seeing myself in grey flannel shorts.

'Williams, Hugo . . .', muses the Head as he looks me up in the dream-annals to prove I am grown up, sitting here with him on 'the private side' having coffee in 1993. '1950–1955 . . . well before my time, I'm afraid. You passed your Common Entrance, I see, after that the trail goes dead. What have you been doing?' His pen is poised over my file, ready to bring my career smartly up to date. I tell him that I am a writer and he adjusts his guard. 'It must have been very different in your day', he tells me. 'More severe, hierarchical. When I took over, a lot of old boys simply weren't interested in sending their sons here, after what they'd been through. We had a hard time at first, persuading people we'd changed.' I am sitting on one of my hands and spilling my coffee with the other, but the Headmaster assures me that it is much more relaxed here now, boys can go home for the weekends if they want to. I am about to ask permission to do so when he picks up the phone and asks Mr Lee to come down.

'Not the Mr Lee who was here in my day?'

'The same. He's getting married later this year.'

Mr Lee is showing me the new Science Block and the theatre, and I am looking at the suit of armour, the stags' heads. Work stops in the science lab as we put our heads round the door. I am the boy at the back putting something away in his pocket. A man half my age is taking a watch to pieces. He blushes when Mr Lee tells me it is his hobby. I see the same ropes are hanging from the ceiling of the gym that I climbed so easily thirty years ago, their ends still frayed. They have a hobbies room now, with dinosaurs strewn about. Here is the milk table where I stood drinking my quarter bottle through a straw. There's the low sink where I washed the bottle out afterwards. If it weren't for Mr Lee, I would go and smell the wall where I stood for punishment, staring at the butterfly-wing Madonna. I would run my finger along the groove that was once at eye-level. That was where I ran my Sunbeam Talbot, making a car noise, pretending to have fun.

Our tour continues over polished lino, pocked with stud marks: pointed ones for summer, round ones for winter. Over there's the Nurse's Office where the Lost and Found is. Are those my football boots on top? That's a whole point lost for my set, named after Field Marshal Earl Haig. When I scored my first goal, the whistle blew for off-side, and I lost interest in football and took up squash, which meant losing to Mr Ray, who hugged you afterwards.

Mr Ray was our homosexual. He was our Natural History master, there to encourage our interest in seeing insects half-heartedly confined in matchboxes or transfixed with a casual pin. The 'bug hut' behind the squash court was his unnatural habitat. We wouldn't have dreamed of reporting him for what he did because we realized that it made him not a master any more – and we were proved right. One day he didn't turn up for Natural History, and the Headmaster explained that he had had to leave because he'd been hurt in the war. It was the nearest he could get to a rational explanation. I imagined Mr Ray sprawled in hospital, transfixed by a bayonet and labelled 'Raybug'. We were put to look for the most interesting stone out on the drive to take our minds off things.

Mr Lee escorts me to the cricket field, now half life-size. Here's the pavilion where I'm standing in the team photograph with the sun in my eyes. Cut grass would have been lying in the outfield covering the trap of nostalgia I would one day fall into. Today perhaps. My bat is a Gradidge Imperial Driver, four-star. I lay it on the table in the pavilion for the ritual blessing of linseed oil from Mr Darwell-Smith. One dollop, like the ritual dollop of brilliantine on the tops of our heads for Father's Match. Do they still keep pads in this locker? Yes, here they are, all higgledy-piggledy, marked with people's names in biro inside the knee. I wonder does that one belong to Timpson's son? Timpson's father was a professional cricketer, so Timpson already had pubic hair and could make his sperm shoot across the bathroom. I connected this in my mind with his advanced bowling technique, which made him grind his teeth and turn white. I remember the vicious expression on his face as he showed us the different finger grips for off-breaks and in-swingers. He'd take hold of his penis in two fingers and a thumb, the way he took hold of a new ball.

I have a map I made of my dormitory, aged nine, showing positions of beds, chairs and shelves. It hasn't changed, except the ceiling has been lowered, masking the beams we swung from or strung people up to. Teddy bears, comic annuals and blue anoraks have replaced the military precision of Bible, photograph and hairbrush. We used to get so bored up here we made ourselves faint by holding our breath. We made our face go red. We sucked chains of love-bites up our arms. We made our arms go up by pressing our wrists against the wall. We made false tits out of handkerchiefs. We made slings called 'bonkers' which held a squash ball or a conker. Sex and violence. If I concentrate, I can remember how to construct these artefacts and my world shrinks to that tight animal existence, reading the *Eagle* with my back to the wall and a twelve-inch ruler in my lap. Didn't we sign our names in blood on the back of the dorm mirror? One boy cut his wrist and they thought he had committed suicide. I look on the back of the mirror, but nothing remains. I wonder are teddy bears compulsory in the new prep schools. They certainly seem to be in my old dormitory.

Was I unhappy here? You don't know how to be. Experience and feeling were hived off from one another on arrival, like Hugo and Williams, term and holiday, past and present. Feeling was sublimated in possessions and rank. You concentrated not on going back to school but on your new suit, laid out like a wedding-gown.

I think of the last few minutes of holiday, having tea in the Berkeley Hotel, before the taxi ride to Euston Station, the beginning of the end. Why did the taxi come so soon? The traffic fell away from us as if we were royalty. The Euston Arch and railway station were demolished after I stopped going there, but not in my mind.

Remember porters? You had to have one before you could go anywhere in the 1950s, but they weren't easy to find. 'Quick, darling, run and find a porter while I get your ticket.' I run around meaninglessly for a while, but when I get back there is one standing there saying, 'Which platform, Madam?' No platform! Go away! We don't want you. We aren't going anywhere. *We're going home.*

[11.6.93]

171

Afternoons in the Sack

The literary tears and bloodshed on a recent Arvon Foundation course at Totleigh Barton were nothing compared to the literal bloodshed on the train going down there. I was sitting reading and wondering why we were waiting so long at Reading, when I became aware of something terrible having happened up the other end of the compartment. One minute there was laughter and shouting, the next there was silence and a man in surgical gloves pushing through a crowd of staring people.

It seemed a young man in a wedding party had cut himself trying to open a bottle of beer with a penknife. The knife had slipped, and he had opened up his forearm from wrist to elbow. The little old lady who described this to me expressed wide-eyed amazement at the size of the wound, how much blood there had been and how far it had shot across the compartment. She had escaped with only a spot on her sleeve, but was in shock at what she had seen and the fact that the young man had said he was HIV-positive. 'The pressure builds up in the veins when they have AIDS', she told me with the authority of the eyewitness. 'It gets like a hose pipe. They're having difficulty moving him. He's already had to have his leg taken off.' At first, I thought she was telling me the unfortunate man had had to have his leg removed in order to get him out from behind the table, but as she went on I realized the amputation had been another inevitable result of being HIV. 'He was trying to get drunk', she said. 'He was the best man.' This too seemed entirely logical.

By now, one could see a heavily bandaged arm being held in the air above the back of a seat. Medics arrived with a wheelchair. Others came with mops and began sponging down the windows and ceiling. Tapes were put up. Helped by his friends, the best man was wheeled away down the platform. The bride herself had to stay on the train in order to be in time for her wedding in Exeter.

After we had been waiting over an hour at Reading, an announcement came over the PA which must have aroused more curiosity than it satisfied. 'We apologize for the delay at Reading, due to an accident. Cleaning staff have had to be sent for.' A further announcement requested all passengers for Exeter to call at Passenger Reception on arrival, without saying why. My companion looked alarmed at this and said she hoped it wasn't for a blood test, because her pregnant daughter was meeting her off the train. I said I expected it was for people who had missed their bus connections. Perhaps we would be given vouchers for taxis. My guess turned out to be as wild as hers. At Passenger Reception we were offered bus timetables.

Creative-writing courses tend to develop themes. Everyone has been to Afghanistan or had a sexual experience with a ghost. I feared that after the event on the train the entire week would be bathed in blood, but apart from the unscheduled appearance of Ted Hughes at Christopher Reid's mid-week guest reading, and the fact that our bus driver had only one eye, the week was uneventful.

At the pre-reading drinks, Hughes wondered whether he would enjoy teaching a course at Arvon. I can't see it, somehow. As a creative-writing tutor, one is a sort of dancing girl, proficient in tap and other corny routines, moving among tables with a flower behind one's ear, available for more intimate sessions later. The students book you for half-hour assignations in the 'goose house' or the barn: heart-to-hearts over cigarettes and coffee. The half-hour is soon over, and another petitioner can be seen lingering in the background with a cup of coffee and some papers stuffed into a Collected Larkin. 'Hello! How are *you* getting on?' And so it goes on all day.

For the smooth running of these hectic afternoons-in-the-sack, it is essential to be able to gauge the particular desires of each individual punter as soon as he or she walks through the door: something to do with a look in their eye or the way they handle their manuscripts. Is that precious bundle sacred? Or up for grabs? Is he or she here for the country air? Or something more bracing? Correctional treatment or infantile regression? Fantasy games or full intercourse? Sometimes it is hard to say, because they don't know themselves. One has to tread carefully on these dreams. Many of the punters have never done it before and don't want to do it now, thank you very much. No way! You know you're in trouble when a gleaming ton of computer print-out is handed over with the request to 'tell me honestly what you think, that's what I'm here for'. 'Be brutally frank' is usually a plea for mercy. Generally speaking, 'My stuff's crap' is the only possible good sign, and even that is usually true. So how is one to distinguish the shrinking violets from more red-blooded customers? Is it one's duty, on occasions, to go against their wishes? The answer is in the individual skill of the dancing girl, and not easily put into words.

One remembers the failures more than the successes. I think of the crestfallen craftsman who had thought his poems were 'timeless' until I pointed out, probably sadistically, ways in which he might 'work' on them; the American who had hoped for a more inspirational experience; the woman who reacted to my criticism by asking for a vote to be taken on her work. I find that as soon as a writer goes on the defensive about his or her poems – 'But that's what actually happened' – I go into a sulk. This is my own particular dysfunction.

Inevitably, there are disappointed faces on leaving day, addresses not being taken etc. But as I look back over the week, I can't help remembering most clearly the young man on the train, relaxed and intoxicated as he disappeared down the platform, holding his bandaged arm in the air; more powerfully still, that of the bride-to-be, sitting alone on the train in her blood-splattered dress and looking resigned as she was carried away towards her new life.

[25.6.93]

Some Block

How to make the pen touch the paper? Sometimes I feel like taking a hammer to it, whamming it through the paper and into my desk and leaving it there for people to find after I have disappeared to Africa. I need a nudge, a little 'don't care' potion.

Portobello Road. A black man and a white girl. Man: 'Need any sensomilia?' Me: 'What's sensomilia?' Man: 'Don't you know what sensomilia is, man?' 'No.' Man: 'That's your choicest weed, man. Just the flower-heads of the female plant. Blow your head off for you.' Me: 'How much?' Man: 'This is cheap. We got it off the police. Only £20.' Me: 'I've only got £15 on me.' Man: 'OK. Give it here, then.' Me: 'Only when you give me the stuff.' Man: 'Look, I have to get it off a bloke in the pub. She'll stay here with you, OK?'

The girl is a pretty blonde teenager who smiles at me sweetly and even shrugs slightly. From a great distance, I see myself handing over the money and the man disappearing into the pub. All the girl has to do now is keep me happy for five minutes while her partner leaves by the other door. She is shy, but frank. Mimicking my accent, she confides: 'I don't usually do this. I've done some modelling. My father's in LA. Do you know Keith Surprise? He works for him.' For some reason, I am reassured by her connection to someone I have never heard of, and we discuss different parts of London for five minutes until I realize this is a variation on the classic con-girl routine, except that I am left with a sort of hostage that I can't possibly hold on to. After ten long minutes, she starts apologizing and explaining that she doesn't really know the bloke that well. We look into each other's eyes like cheating lovers, then she runs off into her life, having ruined my evening.

I know all this is wrong. I know it is erroneous to associate hypnotic drugs, even remotely, with the possibility of writing anything sensible, yet I can't help also feeling that a little lowering of my resistance to the void might at least get me started. I could write something completely stupid, perhaps, then start again tomorrow morning.

Someone's brother knows someone in Bethnal Green. I go round to an office being used as a squat by mostly Scottish beggars and fly-posters, one of whom, a hyperactive redhead called Greg, says we can go on my motorbike to a place he knows about in Homerton. We set off, and it soon becomes clear that Greg is one of those people who can't ride pillion. Every move I make he corrects for me, flinging us off balance. Alarmingly, he also shouts at people as we career down the middle of the road, going north. At least he seems to know the way.

We arrive at some terrorized tower block in some indeterminate part of London and take a lift like a meat-safe to a dark hallway seething with armed and menacing Africans and Jamaicans who seem to be guarding a full-length iron grille door which eventually opens to admit us whites. At the end of a long corridor is a dimly-lit, concrete room with twenty or so mostly white Rastas lying about. Wimbledon is coming through weakly from another world, the sound turned down in favour of some numbing techno-thrash. One twitchily excitable youth has a toy gun which seems to fire real bullets into a wardrobe.

To pass the time (the dealer isn't here), Greg commences rave-dancing among the pizza boxes, a tactic which arouses no comment or notice. Rather, the interest is in me, as my large eyes take in what is probably a crack house. Time passes like treacle as I carefully unpick the lining of my crash helmet.

A scuffle outside the grille door and a white Rasta appears in the room, holding a dagger. He laughs hysterically when he hears how little we want to buy, then hacks a little piece off a block the size of a hassock and weighs it on a handscale. We pay, or rather I pay, and try not to leave too jerkily.

On the way back, the one-way system quickly flummoxes Greg, and he ceases to give me directions. Instead, he appears to be singing. I have illegal substances in my pocket, and my passenger is lurching from side to side on a carefree youthful high. At some traffic lights, he talks to a girl in a taxi and actually manages to get her name and address. A police car seems to be checking my tax disc.

Where are we now? After several wobbly miles, I notice the streets have filled up with Orthodox Jews out walking their children in their Sabbath finery. I stop and ask one magnificent patriarch the way back to the West End. He lifts a prophetic arm and points back the way we have come. (It is a one-way street.) 'How far?' I ask. 'About a hundred miles,' he tells me with a smile.

Is it worth it, when dope can give you such a headache? The wild goose chase north (or south or east or west) is and was and always will be an excursion back in time to when things were more excitable than they are now and a glow came off the page if one buffed it sufficiently.

I mentioned this to a woman I met recently who worked in a New Age health store and she told me she had some drops for my problem – one of the Australian bush flower remedies, called 'Turkey Bush'. Three drops under the tongue, she said, and I would experience something like the breaking of a dam, creatively speaking. She suggested I begin writing a soap opera for radio. I gave her £6.50 (a 'discount') fully expecting to hear nothing more from her, but a few days later, a little bottle arrived, smelling of brandy. 'Negative condition', ran the brochure, 'creative block, disbelief in your own creative ability. Positive outcome: inspired creativity, creative expression, renewed artistic confidence.'

The bottle sits on my desk as I write. I've been meaning to try it for some days now, but for some reason or other it has remained unopened. It isn't that I don't believe in the drops, it's just that I don't like to try them until I have got something decent to write. I wonder, are there any drops I could take for my condition.

[9.7.93]

Letter from a Foreign Country

A narrow, sandy country near a cliff, where the people live under brightly-coloured shades with a single roof-beam and poor quality flooring. They are poor because unemployment is high – the only occupation involves being hurled into the sky on a piece of roofing material – so they spend most of their time lying down. There is no purpose to their lives, but they always seem to enjoy themselves, laughing and waving their arms about and talking nonsense to one another, which they pretend to understand. When they become tired of doing nothing, they go into one of their little hospitals for a blood transfusion and come out looking more relaxed.

177

The children are not nearly so satisfied with their lives and build models of the way they would prefer to live, without their parents, in towers with battlements and moats. When the sea comes in and the walls crumble, the parents are happy and laugh because they knew it would happen. Although people often try to kill themselves by rushing into the sea, the suicide rate is low; only the children sometimes want to be buried alive in the sand. Happily, racist violence is non-existent because the white people rub themselves with dye until they are indistinguishable from the dark ones. They examine one another's skin carefully, and when they find something interesting they squeeze it.

Half the population of this country have two short front arms, like stumps, which they don't use. The stumps are kept in coloured slings, which come off unexpectedly, making everyone happy. Sometimes they are left uncovered all day, to heal. The ones without stumps use them as targets for eye-practice and every day they score hundreds of bull's-eyes, which are marked on the stumps. At first, the ones with stumps are embarrassed by this. They blush all over, but then eventually the blush peels off and they don't seem to mind any more. The stumpless ones have balls, which they hit back and forth as hard as they can, getting in everyone's way (big ones aren't allowed) or they strut around pretending to admire the way the waves go in and out, which is not that interesting.

It seems the two different sorts of people have some sort of business going on between them, but I have not been able to find out what this is yet. It may have something to do with the piece of cloth they wear between their legs, which probably indicates their credit-worthiness, or serves as an advertisement for their product, what-ever that is. The way they go about it is like Pelmanism. Everyone lies face down, and when it is your turn you go over to someone and they have to turn over. Then, if you are a pair, you can have them. But first you have to run into the sea and try to kill yourself, don't ask me why; what these people are really doing is anyone's guess. Most of the time they are screwing up their eyes and glancing around as if they don't know themselves.

Their lives are very short, but they don't seem to mind about this. Towards the end of their lives they become very excited because the sea comes in and they have to move their homes very close together, almost touching, the way they prefer it. Then they laugh and shout even more and become even more happy, examining each other's skin with utmost interest etc.

Later, when they cannot see each other any more, they fold up their homes and go away to die in another country nearby, full of tombs, where they bury themselves alive in big soft envelopes, left open at one end. Some people are very excited about being buried alive, especially the pairs, but the small ones cry and suffer terribly, because they are not ready to die yet. When two people are buried together, sometimes they change their minds about dying and do all different kinds of things to try and escape. When this happens, one of them has to hold the other down until they become completely desperate not to die, shouting out 'No, no, no' or 'Yes, yes yes', as if they cannot make up their minds what they want, or calling each other's name, even though they are in the same tomb. Finally, they become completely exasperated with the other person who is holding them back and suddenly decide to give up their lives and lie still. Then one of them puts out the light.

Next morning they seem to be perfectly all right again, except that they look older and move more slowly. As usual, they set out for their narrow, sandy country carrying their roofing and flooring equipment, as well as hundreds of other things they need, such as big models of prehistoric animals.

[30.7.93]

The Last Summer in Albufeira

It looks like being my last summer in this cool, tall house overlooking the beach in Albufeira in the Algarve. It is too big for my mother now and she's trying to sell it and move home. As she waits for a better offer from some canny chap in Sweden, time is imperceptibly running out and yet everything goes on as usual. All the pictures and books have gone home already and there is a gap on the shelf where the gramophone used to play old musicals all day long. The cabinet that used to be beside my bed as a child, can it really be on its way back to me after all these years? The dear old place has an air of leftover life to live, but our routine remains unchanged: early morning swim (for me), work in the morning, drive to a different beach in the afternoon, out to dinner, perhaps a video.

Today, for the first time that I can remember, the red flag is flying on the beach below the house, meaning no bathing. A sort of bright spray is in the air, making the beach look as if it is in Asia. Overnight the weather has changed from blue to white, due to a hot, dark wind from Morocco, known as the 'Levant'. This stirs up the people as well as the sea and is sometimes taken in mitigation if a case of violence comes to court. Today it feels like some sort of ill wind, clouding the future, picking clean the past. I wonder if I will still be coming to this place after my mother has left. Will I stay at the Villa Recifé, drink strong little *bicas* and write poems about being happy which don't make it back to England? Will I have my own beach-bed and *toldo* and tip the beach-boys? Am I that old man with a poodle? Notices saying 'Zona Perigolosa' have appeared on the beach, alongside 'No Ball Games'. Instead of lying down, the people are standing, watching the turbulent sandy sea that has thrown up all kinds of dead fish.

By the time I come up from the beach, Albertina has arrived with the *Daily Mail* and bread for breakfast. She puts on her apron, goes upstairs to the living room to get her instructions, goes downstairs, takes off her apron and goes out clutching the empty packet of whatever it is my mother wants from the mini-market.

Over the years my mother's breakfast-cum-writing table has shifted gradually rightwards for some reason, so that this year it is parked almost completely across the stairs to the bedrooms, making it difficult for 'Albert' or me to mount. With one hand on my mother's shoulder and the other holding a cup of coffee, I lever myself past her on my way to the room I use to write in. In a minute there will be a knock on the door and Albert will come in, dragging the heavy chair she needs to reach the washing line on the terrace, accessible only through my room. She is four feet tall, partially blind and permanently in mourning. My mother hasn't told her she is leaving yet.

All morning the characteristic short sharp warning whistle from the beach-boys drifts up to us, punctuating the crash of the waves and children's cries. At about three or four, despite the malevolent wind, we drive to our favourite beach, one unprotected by beach-boys or flags, so that I can swim. Over beach-bar sardines, we watch surfers trying to struggle out behind the breakers, sometimes taking half an hour for a five-second run and a dumping. A Portuguese teenager gets into trouble and a friend of my mother's has to swim out to rescue him. He takes the boy further out, then brings him ashore in the next bay. They reappear exhausted and heroic, but the parents hardly look up. The mother remains seated under her umbrella, the father continues picking up dead fish and putting them in a bucket. No words are offered. Smiling with a secret pride, my mother says that the Portuguese are strange.

Today is the feast of São Joao. Loud fireworks go off all day long, frightening my mother's cat, which runs up the curtains and sits on top of the pelmet, hissing at the saint. The Albufeira marching band goes past, led by the traditional drunk. It pushes disapprovingly under the umbrellas of Bizarro, the British bar next door. We lean out of two windows with our wine glasses, talking, my mother exchanging greetings with her neighbour Graciette. Children run up and down the *esplanada* in the exciting, swift-filled hour before dark. Some of them are making a dog have rides on a trike. Later they will build bonfires in the street and there will be cries and laughs as they jump through the flames in this pagan hangover that has come down to São Joao.

Most of the holiday-makers have come up off the beach by now, leaving it to the young footballers and their admirers. They pass beneath our window, lugging their Lilos and other equipment, offering their sunburnt shoulders to our inspection. We watch the sea turning indigo, the lights coming on round the church pergola, the fishing boats setting out. Hard to believe we will not be watching this time next year.

[13.8.93]

Telephone, Stomach and Moustache

I blame Mr Shaw. One day he explained blank verse to his fourteen-year-olds and got us to write some on a biblical theme. I did 'The Heavenly City' out of Revelations:

> My heart is old and full of wondering dreams.
> I was a bird and in the sky I flew,
> Till through a mystic haze of love I saw
> A city glistening like a star of hope . . .

It seemed like a piece of cake and I was amazed that everyone made such a fuss about it. Was that the fatal turning of my head? If only it had been singing or engineering. The only interesting thing about the poem to me now is the choice of the first person.

I never really liked doing poetry at school because they only gave us old things to learn, as if they were trying to inoculate us. 'The Glories of our blood and State / Are shadows not substantial things' moved me in a vague sort of way, but I always heard 'The Glories of our bloody school . . .' My favourite poem was de la Mare's 'Tartary': 'If I were Lord of Tartary / Myself and me alone, / My bed should be of ivory, / Of beaten gold my throne.' I was fifteen before I discovered that poetry was still being written.

My first interest in words was largely adjectival, a way of scraping an extra mark by adding richness behind the master's back, a little cream and sugar. 'Don't be arch', I found written on an English essay in which I had referred to the hour of night in which 'the birds die their small deaths'. It was a compliment in that he assumed I knew what it meant. But did he? My only knowledge of the word still relates to that early lapse, although I see now that the word is

182

supposed to mean 'innocently roguish'; I thought it meant coy. When he asked for a definition of the word 'cliché', nobody knew (we were the bottom stream), but someone put up his hand and suggested 'amble shabbily'. 'That's not a cliché', said the master, rather put out, 'it sounds more like poetry.' I must have been struck by this, because I wrote under the desk, 'I amble shabbily through downhill leaves / While air in waves cuts cool precision', my very first attempt at plagiarism.

It was round about this time that David Cecil came down to Eton to give a talk on poetry and told us, in apparent seriousness, that there were three words you couldn't use in poetry: telephone, stomach and moustache. 'Tennyson tried to get round the last one', he said, 'by writing "The knightly growth that graced his upper lip" – k-n-i-g-h-t-l-y, not n-i-g-h-t-l-y.' I believed him absolutely and decided never to use any of those words in my work.

I was coming to realize that writing, if used cunningly, could get one out of trouble. 'Explain the importance of the Treaty of Utrecht'. If I was lucky I had a fact, a date and a name at my disposal and I learnt to deploy these limited resources across two sides of paper. I have been doing the same ever since, but what I have never been able to accept is that it would have been easier and quicker in the long run to learn about the Treaty of Utrecht.

One Christmas, my half-sister Prue found favour at home by making an anthology of poems as a present for my father. The slim notebook seemed never to be out of his hands, so I decided to attract his attention by making him one myself. I bought the blank book and set about copying in the poems. Omar Khayaam, Arthur Waley, Rupert Brook (*sic*), G. K. Chesterton, John Keats, Sir Richard Lovelace. Pretty soon I had included nearly everyone and still the anthology was only a quarter full. With Christmas looming, I had to ask my sister for ideas and she started sending me poems at school. She seemed to have made the extraordinary discovery that some poets were still alive. Gradually it dawned on me that poetry was a contemporary thing, like rock 'n' roll, and that it always had been. Half-way through the anthology the names of John Wain, Laurie

Lee, Stephen Spender, Dorothy Parker, Robert Graves and Alun Lewis start appearing, still interleaved with those of W. E. Henley (my father's favourite) and John Masefield (my mother's). Thumbing the old book today, the excitement is palpable. The strenuously sloping handwriting, straining so hard to be my father's, is so obviously still mine today, the enterprise so grand and youthful and full of copying mistakes.

One day I was browsing in the County Library in search of more John Wain ('I hope to feel some pity when it comes') when I came across *New Lines*, the Movement anthology, which became my Bible. Thom Gunn, I discovered, had written a poem about Elvis Presley. My head turned again. I bought a leather jacket.

When I think of my own first fumblings into Gunnish pastiche, it is always at school, always at night, always instead of work. In the holidays there was no time and no need for poetry. Separation was what produced words and sometimes, with their help, I could get back into the holidays. Nothing has changed.

When a poem of mine appeared in a school magazine, my housemaster looked at the floor (he wore spats), then arranged for me to visit the chaplain. The chaplain said if I was desperate he knew Louis MacNeice. I can't have been because I never met him.

[3.9.93]

Stavros Melissinos, the Poet Sandal-maker of Athens

I might as well have rubbed my forefinger at one of the hundreds of sponges in the sponge emporium in the Athens flea market as try to communicate to the proprietor that I was looking for a pumice stone. Stepping back into the stripey light of the tourist-tacky alleyway, I saw the word 'POET' written in giant letters on a revolving pole outside a sandal shop, with 'Stavros Melissinos – Poet Sandal-maker' written over the door. Yellowing framed press cuttings showed Jackie Onassis, Rudolph Nureyev and the Beatles posing sandal-shod with a smiling, Zorbaesque character, whose older, still smiling face was just discernible hovering in the dark interior. If I went in, would I be able to escape without buying a pair of sandals and/or a book of poems?

Half an hour later, I had laid down the makings of a lifelong friendship with Stavros, had bought two books of his poetry (one in Greek) and was even wearing a pair of open-toed sandals, my first since I was ten. His sandals, Stavros told me, were like his poetry, influenced by Greek mythology and based on the footwear of Plato and Pericles.

Since he started writing poems in the Army in 1953, for friends writing home to their girlfriends, Melissinos has published ten highly popular books and been much translated. His trilingual *Athenian Rubaiyat* is now in its eighth edition. He has been the subject of attention by the BBC and various American networks. Yet he still works seven days a week making sandals.

He told me he had translated into modern Greek some unpublished poems of C. P. Cavafy and showed me his 'bilingual' edition which a professor of glossology at Athens University uses to discuss the problems of Greek ancient and modern. Confused by the idea of translating Cavafy into Greek, I asked what he meant. It seems that Greek, like Arabic, is a sort of double language, with two sets of unrelated words for nearly every basic concept, the result of their nineteenth-century identity crisis following liberation from the Turks, one used in everyday life, the other in education, bureaucracy and newspapers. Cavafy's poems employ an idiosyncratic mixture of 'Katharevoussa' (cleansed and stilted formal Greek) and the demotic form. What Stavros had done was convert this amalgam into his own more colloquial style.

A week later, another chance enquiry showed me the other side of the Greek language coin. I was wandering around Delphi trying to locate the ancient path up Mount Parnassus known as Kaki Scala, the evil stairway, where murderers were taken to be thrown over a cliff. The path leads to a cave where the Oracle would go every

November to hold orgies for the god Pan. It was supposed to be marked with yellow diamonds, but it wasn't easy to find the start, and I had to ask its whereabouts in a large house. This turned out to have been the house of the late poet Angelos Sikelianos and his American wife Eva Palmer; it is now the Museum of the Delphic Festival.

For a few years in the late 1920s, the Sikelianos organized this would-be revival of 'The Delphic spirit', believing that 'the principles which had shaped classical civilization had been neglected and misconstrued and that if they were re-examined they could offer spiritual salvation etc.' A copy of one of the programmes, printed in pseudo-Greek lettering, survives on a wall: 'Delphic Festival in Ancient Theatre 9–10 May 1927. Music for Choruses in Ancient Greek Musical Modes. Dances from Ancient Vases and Bas Reliefs. Costumes hand woven. Games in Ancient Stadium. Popular Arts and Crafts. Kleft Songs and National Dances by Shepherds of Parnassus. Trained Archaeologists to serve as guides to Ancient Ruins. Tickets including Automobiles $35.' In the Museum are the costumes for the 1927 production of *Prometheus Bound*, heavily influenced by 1920s fashion. In retrospect, the whole brave, vaguely camp enterprise looked like something from the life of Isadora Duncan, whose marriage to the poet Sergei Esenin somewhat resembled that of Eva and Angelos. It seemed further off even than the original Delphi.

Perhaps it is unfair to compare the high élitist revivalism of the Sikelianos with the earthy conviviality of Melissinos, when Angelos and Eva were no longer there in their fine house to charm me as Stavros had done. Sikelianos was a sizeable figure in his day, considered by Seferis to be the equal of Yeats. A scan of the small library made this hard to credit: 'Sacred stallions, fate / has kept you indestructible . . .'; but the man certainly led the life: worked for Rodin, walked with Nikos Kazantzakis, fought in the Balkan War of 1912.

I called on Stavros on my way home and tried to get him to say something scathing about the patrician, Parnassian Sikelianos, the very essence of 'Katharevoussa'. 'You see he is very *strong*', said

Stavros. 'Very pompous and very strong. Archaic, you see.' I had never heard praise so sweetly qualified out of existence. But did he *love* him? 'Of course!'

[24.9.93]

A Personal Development Holiday

On the ferry to Skyros, where I am teaching creative writing at the Skyros Centre, one of the psychotherapists who is also due to work there asks if the poet taking the writing group is famous. I say I don't know. The Skyros Centre offers 'Personal development holidays for the mind, body and spirit.' I only hope I can go on encouraging this sort of thing for the full two weeks. It is very hot.

'The theme for today is very much arrival', says the community co-ordinator after our first evening meal. 'Whereas the theme for tomorrow will be more or less settling in.' He shows us to our rooms. Mine has a fine view overlooking a valley and the sea. It is rented from a villager and full of her varnished ornaments, which balance precariously on shelves. The narrow alley echoes to the clatter and spatter of extended families, washing lines and yells strung between generations. Village sounds like plates collapsing. 'We only fight in winter', my landlady tells me, 'when we get our houses back from the tourists.' At night, I can hear people breathing in the flat across the alley. Their dog barks when I get out of bed.

Every day follows a pattern. We have a staff meeting from 9.30 to 10.30, at which everyone is asked how they feel and problems are aired. Sometimes we seem to be looking round for these, to fill up time which could be better spent in the bathroom. As the co-ordinator said at 'Demos' on the first morning, 'Water is important in the sense that it is off between 11 and 4, but if you come for the sun, you have to accept this. Remember the first rule of Greek life: put lavatory paper in the bin. At first you will find this hard to do. Eventually you will become addicted to it. One of our visitors bought a bin to take home with him.'

After the staff meeting, we have three or four hours of the writing workshop: exercises, readings, criticism. Then it's a veggie lunch on the large paved terrace overlooking the much-photographed valley. On the low wall, outlined against the horizon, the washing-up bowls, blue, red and green, for wash, rinse and disinfect: a central image of the Skyros experience. Below the wall is the garden where our neighbour Adonis waters his fig trees in the nude, fulfilling the need for a local 'character'.

Of the seventy or so personal developers, only ten are doing the creative writing course, the rest are taking Gestalt therapy, psycho-drama, or psychosynthesis, though what exactly these things are is hard to say from the cries, shouts and pillow-bashings that come from their large, intense meetings. By contrast, we study something like 'Soap Suds' by Louis MacNeice: 'And these were the joys of that house . . .' A certain 'us and them' feeling has developed, reprehens-ible but sustaining. For instance, one of our group came upon the co-ordinator chalking the day's activities on the terrace blackboard this morning and asked waggishly what time the mass suicide was scheduled for. The co-ordinator was not amused, and even went so far as to invoke the siege of Sarajevo. One of the psychodrama students says he is here to give the world one last chance. We watch his face for signs of approval. So far, he's keeping an open mind.

Certainly it is a strange juxtaposition, these democratic healing enterprises alongside élite-aspiring poetry. On the other hand, if writers feel there are never enough books in the world that they must add another one to the store, perhaps wanting to have a psycho-drama made up about your life is not so different. I referred jokingly to their activities as 'amateur theatricals' the other day, and was told that my aggression was a sign of need, which is certainly true.

Woken at night by a donkey's braying, a kind of animal blues, heartfelt and lost, I decide that tomorrow's exercise will be to write a poem in the style of a donkey's bray.

One evening, a woman I don't know comes up to me and says she's heard I don't approve of 'emotion' in poetry: a misunderstand-ing about an argument I'd had about 'self-expression'. After I have a longish drink with her on the subject, the course director sidles up and casually points out that the staff directive does state 'No teaching staff to have sexual relationships with participants.' I hadn't read that far. The large print giveth, the small print taketh away. She tells me the sore throat I caught from the air-conditioning on the plane represents suppressed anger. My cure is to express rage and love myself.

I was discussing psychotherapy with someone and made the mistake of using the phrase 'mental problem'. 'I don't like the phrase mental problem', said the woman. 'I find it unnecessary and aggressive.' I asked her how I should refer to it and she told me, 'I look on it more as an opportunity.' It occurred to me that our two disciplines have something in common, after all. Marilyn, who leads the psychosynthesis sessions, says she 'relates' to creative writing because she often gets her participants to tell their lives as fairy stories. I ask to have a look at the results and say we'll turn them back into lives.

All this may not seem to make for a very holiday-minded atmosphere; it's not exactly bucket-and-spade stuff. All the same, everyone is extremely excited and there is a lot of bonding and hugging going on, including some girl-to-girl snogging on the terrace. I come to the conclusion that bucket-and-spade work is exactly what it is, with the addition of one of those little sieves maybe. The idea being to come up with some gold. Holidays you can take home with you! At any rate, that seems to fit both us and them.

The Poetry Group are to give an after-dinner poetry reading: 'Postcards from the Edge'. The audience is highly responsive. Laughter. Groans. Clapping. Appreciation. 'Supportive'. Some Greek children come to stand on the wall at the back of the terrace to cheer and jeer. At one point a small boy with a strangely adult face reveals an erect, adult-sized member.

[29.10.93]

At the Grave of Rupert Brooke

The town of Skyros is a cubist helter-skelter. At the top stands an impressive, vaguely fascistic monument, dedicated 'To Rupert Brooke and Immortal Poetry': a twice life-sized bronze male nude, shipped to the island from England in the 1930s and said to be of a Belgian male prostitute. On the plinth there is a relief of the poet, showing his youthful profile, flowing locks and 'near-snubbed' nose. The private parts of the statue, a provocative cluster, have been painted green by local wits, a gesture which might also express their feelings for Brooke's latterday compatriots, those pilgrims of 'personal development' who are gathered at the Skyros Centre for a holiday of the mind, body and spirit.

Brooke's actual grave is far away in a wild, inaccessible part of the island now owned by the Greek Navy. Today there is a track leading into the area, but in 1967 the poet Andrew Motion, fresh out of school, nearly died trying to find his way there. He ran out of water and was rescued, twenty hours after setting out, by a friendly shepherd, who showed him the way to the grave. 'I remember seeing a column of ants marching out of a crack in the marble and thinking, there goes the last of Rupert Brooke.'

The grave may soon be cut off for ever by a new naval base, so we feel we should see it while we can. The writers' group, a gang of ten, hire mobilettes for the day and set off for that 'corner of a foreign field', quoting not Brooke but Thom Gunn: 'On motorcycles, up the road, they come: / small, black, as flies hanging in heat, the Boys . . .' It has to be said that we are a somewhat milder-mannered bunch, in our flip-flops and shorts, on our clapped-out Honda 90s. We 'dare a future from the taken routes', but most of them are unsigned and more than once we lose our way, or have to go back for someone who has skidded into a ditch. For some reason, we are having the time of our lives and bonding as madly as the psycho-drama and Gestalt Therapy students back at the Centre.

First stop is the Fountain of the Nymphs for dousings, water-bottle filling and photographs. After an hour, we reach the beautiful Tribuki bay, the largest natural harbour in the Aegean, where the hospital ships were moored in 1915. Looking down on the scene, I am overcome with a feeling of intense loneliness at the thought of those grim vessels moored so far from home. Was it here that Brooke wrote 'Fragment'? How typical that he saw his friends turning to water before his eyes:

> I strayed about the deck, an hour, to-night
> Under a cloudy moonless sky; and peeped
> In at the windows, watched my friends at table,
> Or playing cards, or standing in the doorway,
> Or coming out into the darkness [. . .]
> I could but see them – against the lamplight – pass
> Like coloured shadows, thinner than filmy glass,
> Slight bubbles, fainter than the wave's faint light. . . .

During a picnic ashore, Brooke had remarked on the beauty of an olive grove covered in wild flowers and herbs. When he died a few days later, of septicaemia following an insect bite received in Alexandria, his friends Bernard Freyburg, a New Zealand war hero, and Arthur Asquith, son of the Prime Minister, took him ashore and buried him in the olive grove. They were mindful, no doubt, of the need to find some corner of a foreign field that could be for ever England. It was 23 April, St George's Day, patron saint's day of Skyros, and of England of course. Next day the fleet sailed for the Dardanelles.

The first sight of the grave is from above, a white and green tomb, fresh-painted, alone and alien among the scrawny olive trees. We approach by a line of stones someone has put to mark the route taken by his bearers. At the foot of the tomb is a plaque engraved with the famous poem, the too-perfect epitaph. As we read (and have ourselves photographed reading), a Danish student questions its imperialist flavour. I try to reason that 'richer dust', the offending phrase, is metaphorical, although on reflection it seems to hover about in the middle, getting that off-emphasis from youthful over-excitement. 'Oh I see', says the student.

Excessive photography ensues with a variety of poses, pensive and casual, taken alongside the grave, everyone wielding someone else's camera. The question arises: to smile or not to smile at such times? Examining the results, I see we have decided against. On the way back, we pass a little glass wayside shrine, complete with St George and the Dragon icon and a Lucozade bottle full of oil for the candle. The mangled car that occasioned the shrine has been fenced off like a sort of war memorial: St George's horse gone to the knackers.

We decide to swim and find a deserted beach on Navy property. Through binoculars we watch a naked salt-gatherer wandering about with a sack on a distant island. I find a small, hard, blue jellyfish like a luminous glass lampshade.

Tonight is the half-term general meeting, led by the course director: seventy expectant soul-shoppers sitting round on cushions. Would anyone like to make a public commitment to do something special in the week to come? One person undertakes to visit the nudist beach more often, if someone helps her down the cliff. Another to touch people more often. A third to find more of the wildness he has been talking about in class (God help us!). Asked to share with the assembly anything remarkable that has happened to us during the first week, one girl gives a vivid description of squid-fishing at night. The fishermen let her lower the bait through the hole in the bottom of the boat, but failed to mention that when she hauled it in the squid would douse her with black ink. It is a good story. When she has finished, the director turns to me and asks me to share the experience of finding the beautiful blue jellyfish I was telling her about. I look round at the faces turned in my direction; they must be expecting something remarkable from the head writer. I contemplate describing to them Rupert Brooke's party trick of jumping naked into a cold stream and emerging with an instant erection. I wonder would they be interested to learn, as I was, that he used to hang upside down from a tree to dry his hair? 'Well,' I begin, 'I found this beautiful blue jellyfish on the beach. It was a beautiful luminous blue colour . . .'

[12.11.93]

A Narcissistic Injury

Anyone who thinks I have been unnecessarily cynical or slighting of personal development holidays, from a position of unassailable mental health, will be pleased to learn that I received my comeuppance at the end-of-term cabaret on the island of Skyros.

I have described how a certain 'us and them' feeling had developed between the nine-strong writer's group and the sixty or so psychotherapy students living and eating together at the Skyros Centre. The different psychodrama and Gestalt Therapy classes may have had similar feelings of exclusivity among themselves, but this was not apparent. If they thought anything about the writers, it was probably that ours was an amateurish discipline compared to theirs, whose practitioners could never be qualified members of an important, urgently needed profession, with personal advertising brochures and glowing testimonials to prove it. They probably suspected that what we were doing was itself a leisurely, old-fashioned form of therapy, and I have some sympathy for this point of view.

Why then did it come as such a surprise to hear the words 'poetry' and 'creative writing' being uttered by one of the first performers at the cabaret? This was a charming man who runs the Gestalt classes on Skyros. He was one of the people I most liked at the Centre, and not only because he had asked to see my work.

I suppose it took about ten seconds for the penny to drop that the person on stage was not only talking about the poetry group, he was *me* talking about the poetry group. Suddenly I noticed that he was dressed like me, was standing like me, talking like me, moving like me, moving his neck like me; even his adam's apple stuck out like mine. What was going on? Was this a psychodrama session being put on for my benefit? Was I finally finding out about the content of those screaming, sobbing therapy sessions that had been going on behind closed doors for the last two weeks? At last I understood what it must feel like to be psychologically debagged. Was I supposed to break down in front of everybody? And if so, how was it done?

I wouldn't have minded so much if he hadn't been so good, so committed to his work. He had got my self-deprecating, inverted arrogance to a tee. He had even remembered some of the more conceited modesties I had uttered at the morning staff meetings. How I was not really a community type; how I was not really a teacher; I hadn't even been to university; I knew nothing; how everything I knew about writing could be written on the back of a postage stamp; how writing wasn't something you could teach anyway.

By this time, every face in the house was turned in my direction to see how I was taking it. I was taking it badly, of course, but I was having no difficulty in hiding this fact, since I have been smiling and looking innocent ever since I was seven. Inwardly I cringed; outwardly I took my pillorying in good part. It was not until I realized that this was to be a poetry reading by me that my good-natured grin began to quaver. My tormentor produced a rumpled manuscript from his pocket, bobbed his adam's apple, apologized profusely and began to recite:

> I want my mummy.
> I want my daddy.
> I want my teddy.
> But they don't want me.

Too late, I regretted lending him my poems! After every line, the house collapsed with joyful laughter, all eyes keyed to my response. Other brilliantly witty parodies followed, then he left the stage in a cloud of glory, and I thought it would be appropriate for me to be seen waving a couple of good-natured fingers in his direction, to pretend I hadn't been permanently damaged by the experience.

To my surprise, he came straight over to where I was sitting and began to apologize. He'd been asked to do something for the occasion and I was the only possible candidate because I wasn't a student or permanent staff. Was I furious with him? I mocked the idea. I told him not to be so silly. I told him how good he'd been. He was brilliant! He'd even made *me* laugh! If we could do something, we should do it.

When I got home, there was a letter waiting for me from my impersonator. The letter was affectionate, admiring and regretful: 'All the more, then, are my misgivings about mimicking you at the end-of-term send-up. I know that when I came over to you, wondering – I have to say for the first time – whether I might have sacrificed a friendship with you, you were generous in your bluff assurances. But your very first message was an angry-looking V-sign, and as a working Gestalt therapist I notice such things – often the first remark or gesture is the truer, when all's said and done. If I thoughtlessly, and out to impress with my skill, inadvertently left a bad taste, or inflicted a wound inside, I want to apologize. (In psycho-jargon it is called a "narcissistic injury" – we are all narcissists for this purpose.)'

Whether by psychological accident or artful design, he had enclosed three blank sheets with the letter, so I wrote back at length, truthfully denying hurt and suggesting his mimicking of me had been cathartic of something he found sickly and frightening in himself (art as neurosis). I was out of my depth. It wasn't long before a further interpretation of his actions arrived. 'Yes, there is a lost-in-life's-wash part of me, a would-be writer, and it's intriguing to speculate as to whether I was mocking *him*. I don't think it's that simple – what it feels like, since I did not feel hostile towards you at all, is that I may have wanted to step into the poet's shoes, almost literally in this instance, to *be* him, if only for a few minutes – an act of appropriation . . .'

I had to admit that this had never occurred to me. I wrote back intrigued, and the correspondence continues, with pleasure on my part. I hope he will forgive my recording it.

[26.11.93]

Sitting on Top of My Brother

My brother shut his eyes and clenched his fists, and practised shadow boxing in his transparent oxygen tent. I watched in horror,

195

wondering what he would do if they brought him home. Where would he sleep? Not in my room? Supposing he wanted to ride my bike?

A year later, when I was five, I was sitting on top of him preparing to slay him with a hairbrush when I was arrested by my mother and put on probation. I had discovered that brothers made excellent toys. You could toss them around and you could teach them to say things to guests like 'Are you Itchy-bum the Butcher?'

For the first five years of his life, my brother thought he was a sort of inferior version of me. *I saw you as a kind of twin, a forecast of me. It was very important to have the same T-shirt, and to inherit your clothes was an honour. It came to me very late that I was not your replica, that I didn't have to be like you. I'm still surprised by our differences: motorbikes, jiving, Miles Davis. God how I tried to like him!*

When I was seven, I had to have a governess to fatten me up for prep school. The shadow of this strict world hovered over my freedom. Every morning I was closeted in the schoolroom while my brother bumped his jeep against the door. *The sun rose and sank on you and the demands M.B. made on your time.* I would burst out of the schoolroom with a great yell of 'Down to the rhododendron trees!' and we would charge down to that magical valley where ropes and boards and feathers showed that it was an Indian encampment with facilities for acrobatics (mine) and torture (his). Whatever we were being, I was the hero, the winner, the saviour and conqueror of the world (him), while my brother doubled as victim, assistant and audience. I put him through the most terrible trials, terrified him with my challenges.

When we were Indians, I thought our bravery (his) should be tested in some way. We went to the Indian Meeting Ground, a forest of lopped trees, and my brother got first turn to stand on one of the stumps while I fired an arrow at him. If he blinked or moved, he failed the test. I fired the arrow, and it hit him in the face, causing a scratch. Did I imagine this was a fair test of our bravery, knowing my brother couldn't shoot? Or did I just want to fire an arrow at my brother, because he was there?

In retrospect, I see that he was the true hero of our wars, for he was set against a world not of his making, where everything went my way and to his disadvantage. *I wonder if an elder brother or sister ever really recovers from their power over the younger siblings – and vice versa. Your temper was fearsome and always my fault. I was a battered brother . . .*

We used to watch an early evening series in the 1950s called *The Cisco Kid*. Naturally I was The Kid. My brother was Pancho, his unshaven sidekick. 'Hey, Pancho!' 'Cisco?' 'Fetch de horses, Pancho!' If I look into my heart, I am still clad in black leather from head to foot, a flat, Spanish hat with chinstrap, a thin black eye-mask. What Pancho wears isn't important, so long as he doesn't cry. Cisco is a kind of cool acrobat. Pancho is in charge of comedy. It was the same for Robin Hood and Friar Tuck, the Lone Ranger and Tonto, or just Cowboys (me) and Indians (him). The Indians fell down a lot, or were pushed. My brother got to wear the cardboard sombrero.

When I went away to school, I missed my brother more than my parents or my bike. My parents had certain disadvantages: discipline, punishments, unpredictability, all of which were available in huge quantities at school. My brother was the opposite of school: my younger self, the happy genius of our household. When I wrote home from school, I always asked if they could bring him over, but they never did. By the time he finally joined me there, he was too young, and I was embarrassed by his high voice and high spirits. He too was disappointed: *I thought we'd be inseparable. I hadn't grasped the divided system. Would I ever catch up?*

For certain tribal people, the past lies ahead, stretched out in memory, a place you can see, and will eventually reach. The future is dark and unknown; it must therefore lie behind your back. Having a younger brother meant I was forever looking back at my childhood, playing there, able to visit it whenever I liked because it was there every day, waiting to be rediscovered in the old games, the old inventions, the old innocence. My brother was holidays, bikes, trees, the past. He would put up the banner: 'Welcome Home' and then we would charge down to the rhododendron trees again and put on our papery cowboy suits and talk in funny voices. What did they do to us, these divisions of life into term and holiday, past and future, all-good and all-bad?

My brother grew up and became bigger than me by sheer will-power – to teach me a lesson. There was a moment in 1961, when I was nineteen and he was still fifteen, when one of our routine scuffles took an unexpected turn. Instead of achieving a quick submission with promises of obedience, I found I could barely hold my own, and the bout had to be discontinued before it became embarrassing. It was one of a number of fine readjustments that took place over the years. As my brother grew up, he grew less fond of his old part of adoring slave. A star was being born, and I was cast in the James Mason part, destined to watch my protégé overtaking me.

My father's death changed our relationship completely. I remember the moment when it happened. We were standing in the Edgware Road, wondering what to do about the funeral. The undertaker's was on the other side of the road. It should have been me who crossed and booked the funeral. Up to that moment it would naturally have been me. But I hung back, and my brother crossed the road. The kid brother coronet passed to me forever.

In the years since our father died, my brother has gradually established himself as the head of our family. I have been strangely happy to see this happen, as if I have finally become my younger, freer, happier self, who doesn't have to go to school. That little empire where my brother reflected my desires like the Slave of the Ring still haunts me. For my brother, our childhood was a harder place, a better training ground for the uncongenial world outside. For me, it will always be the future.

[31.12.93]

Margaret Vyner, 1914–1993

I am writing this on some yellowing quarto typing paper I found with my mother's old Olivetti during our recent share-out of her things. This was the machine on which she typed the first drafts of the plays she wrote with my father in the 1950s and 1960s. Yellowing white cat fur clogs the keys. It was the coolest place for her cat to sleep during the long hot Algarve days of crosswords, patience, bestsellers and asthma inhalers after my father died in 1969. She tried, briefly, to sell some ideas for plays after he died, and used to pose as the writer among the framed playbills that were never added to. 'We never ring your mother before twelve,' people used to tell me, 'because we know she's working.' The truth is that ideas for plays are not plays, and she was scared of dialogue.

I tried to write down some of her memories during my holidays with her in Albufeira, but she wasn't keen on that either, believing my interest to be morbid and/or unfair, as she might be needing them herself one day. I now see that her best work was done hiding her distressful breathing problem from her children, who were thus able to go on fondly complaining about her eccentricity right up to her tidy end, when she panted back to England and toppled neatly into her grave.

Her true contribution was self-creation: an apparitional performance switched on for friends, preferably young and passing through, who never failed to be amazed that such a beautiful, gentle-looking woman could be so wicked. The clue to the mystery was the fact that she was Australian, but sounded and looked English. It must have been a shock coming to class-ridden England in the 1930s, and she was always more of an outsider than the rest of us, being three times removed from her roots. I think she was quite chippy when she first arrived. She told me once that she barged into a beautiful young débutante who was walking towards her down the corridor of a nightclub, just because she annoyed her. I loved the story, but the amazing thing about it is not that it happened, but that she told it to her children.

When we were young, we had a London taxi with an open place for luggage beside the driver. She used to encourage the person sitting (illegally) in this area to shout and point at the wheels of cars we were overtaking, the idea being to get them to stop. You had to do it on a straight bit of road, otherwise you missed the fun. 'An image keeps coming back to me', wrote a childhood friend to me recently, 'Dymchurch 1951? I am very excited, waiting for the Williams family to arrive. And suddenly, here they are, in a honking, farting old taxi, Margaret at the wheel, surrounded by children and nannies and grannies and shrimping nets. She looks unbelievably glamorous and happy and blond and outgoing. Hooray, now the holidays have really begun.'

Another friend recalled an incident at tea. 'I, a prissy schoolboy, complained that there was a hair in my cup. Your mother grabbed the cup, stuck her fingers in it and fished around for some time before affecting to remove whatever may or may not have been there. She then handed me back the cup with a "That's all right now". The vision of a grown-up breaking all the niceties and rules of etiquette has stayed with me.' He remembered sitting with us on buses while she told terrible stories in a loud voice for the benefit of people sitting near us: 'I came into the bathroom and there she was, lying naked on the floor in a pool of blood . . .' It was through such intoxicating public-baiting that we learnt our relation to the world.

A total horror of illness and death, her own and other peoples', was her big weakness, so I'm glad she didn't hang around. She never went to funerals, and I can understand why. Cremations are bad medicine. You make arrangements to meet someone you love at a fiery place in the middle of nowhere, then you stand around while something difficult is imagined. As you crunch back to the cars afterwards, you turn and see them spiralling into the air as smoke. A conjurer in peculiar shoes and a damaged opera hat (something has gone wrong with the internal mechanism) slips you a folded envelope in which he has caused to appear their rings and teeth. You clap wildly at this. You wonder why the hearse is a Mercedes. Is it strictly ethical?

I felt strangely at odds with the mood of the people at the service afterwards. Everyone looked so upset, while I was feeling elated, having been depressed for weeks. I think one mourns one's parents in advance, mostly during adolescence, but also during their old age, so that when they do die most of the 'work' has been done already. I couldn't help laughing when I was invited out to dinner the day she died – and only turned it down because I couldn't resist saying why I was laughing. Likewise, when some bold editor asked me to do an obituary, I had the perfect excuse to say no.

I kept thinking of Bernard O'Donoghue's poem 'The Fool in the Graveyard': 'This was his big day and he was glad . . . / Things were looking up / Today he was like the main actor / In the village play, or the footballer / Who took the frees . . .' They even let me read two of my own poems about her during the service, instead of one, as originally planned. I basked in my glory and actually felt she was doing her best to cheer me up, this having been one of her tasks in life. O'Donoghue: 'Outside / It was very cold, but he had on / The Crombie coat his Dad had bought.' As we filed out of the church into the cold afternoon, my brother-in-law loosed a big golden rocket into the wintry sky. That was more like it. That was her, all right.

[21.1.94]

Not so Easy to Accept the Laundry Basket

My grandfather-in-law died recently in Paris aged 102, on the same day my mother died in England, a conspiracy which divided us for their funerals and increased the overall misery. We have just completed the two share-outs, and I am now the richer by several hundred new objects, of which more later.

The division of the spoils is a cultural ritual, and it was interesting to compare the different approaches: awkwardly informal (us) versus the law of the jungle (them). Of course, it's easy to talk. The charm of common human decency diminishes sharply in the face of monetary gain. My mother died poor, at least we think she did; my wife's grandfather was a man of property, a Deputé, a mayor, a business man with numerous descendants, all of whom stood to gain considerably, some more than others. This means that war has been declared. The remarkable thing is that they are fairly forgiving about one another's outbursts. One can only assume that there is some kind of invisible limit to what is being said, rules that are being as carefully observed as our own more subtle ones are.

The way they do it is to divide things into various tiers of roughly equal value – furniture, pictures, ornaments, trinkets – then the family take it in turns to grab what they can within each tier. The game requires cool nerves and lightning decision-making as you frantically compute the relative values of the remaining objects, your own first choice having gone to a rival. The system should work like clockwork, but problems arise when unspoken traditions of owner-ship are broken, causing childlike resentment in the loser and a look of triumph on the face of the inheritor. A doll's desk and chair might be an example of this difficulty, if it had been through more than one pair of hands. Does it belong to the original, or the final owner? If the family is on brittle terms already, a few judders like this will crack it.

Our own method was more flexible, having less to lose. We either gave things to each other which we thought we would like, or modestly held things up and said 'Does anyone want this?' If more than one person did, we tossed for it. A culture of giving away, like that of certain South Seas people, works as well as our own as a system of credit; on the other hand, maybe things have a better chance of finding their right owner if they are fought over. You could even make a case for the keener to possess being the fondest of the deceased. To them that ask shall be given. But some don't like to. I don't know.

The share-out was fun while it lasted, if not afterwards, when we found ourselves alone with our newly acquired goods. All the bereaved LPs, for instance, original cast recordings of *Kiss Me Kate*,

Call Me Madam, Guys and Dolls, Carousel, Wonderful Town, The Pyjama Game, West Side Story, pre-rock Broadway musicals which we grew up with, all unplayable for the foreseeable future as far as I am concerned, unless I become even unhappier than they are. One tries to cure such possessions of their obsession with the past by giving them a new home, a new frame, a coat of paint, but one's affection for their owner seems to support their delusion that they still belong to her and that she is near them still.

Soon enough, one's new things spread out round the house, like children playing hide and seek. They hang themselves in wardrobes, jam themselves into bookshelves, shoulder a place for themselves on your mantelpiece, barge into the scrum of a clothes drawer, add themselves self-consciously to a row of younger-looking shoes. Desired for more than forty years, the objects in a box lose their mysterious power. Old pictures, finding themselves in new places, have to adjust to a subtle change in their status and our appreciation of them; savage satire has become period charm, the romantic has become kitsch.

Eventually they will settle down into their new quarters, I suppose. They will be homesick for a while, but then they will give up hope of going back to their old lives and start getting used to being 'something which used to belong to my mother'. Their presence will prove we are members of the senior generation, the next in line for the chop. It won't be long before they are something which used to belong to us.

Whether we like it or not, they will go on muttering their old owners' names for as long as we have them, insisting on a certain respect. Ownership will go on being deferred backwards until we pass them on ourselves, at which point they will finally become 'ours' – in the eyes of our childen at least. I agreed with my brother when he said he didn't mind who had the pictures and photos, as long as he could see them from time to time. But it's hard to stop yourself grabbing something when it seems to be, literally, the chance of a lifetime.

It is always the trivial things that get you going. It was easy enough to assimilate the Stevengraphs of ancient boat crews and Derby winners, not so easy to accept the laundry basket or the photo of Nureyev my mother had by her bed. Easy to take away the Staffordshire cricketer, not so simple the tape of *A Hard Day's Night*. The powerful sense of madness objects carry about with them – the spider ashtray, the yelling idol, the bust of someone, the submarine lighter, the broken hand, the thing off a boat – makes me wonder what would happen if their owner were to change her mind about dying. What a performance it would be to gather up all this stuff and put it back where it belonged before she noticed it was missing. I've already lost her wedding ring.

It seems I may have made a mistake in taking away the contents of her bathroom and kitchen cupboards: half-empty bottles and jars which she presumably had plans for herself. Recent days have been sweetened by the remains of her marmalade, her raisins, her tomato ketchup, her Branston pickle, her Demerara sugar lumps, things I don't usually buy. But thoughts can go wrong if you don't keep a hold on them. It is dangerous for me to catch sight of her rolled-up tube of glue. Her Badedas bubble bath chills my bones. I ended by wolfing the marmalade with a spoon.

[11.2.94]

Siamese Twins

A poem by Michael Donaghy about Siamese twins appeared in the *Guardian* last week. It wasn't about Siamese twins, of course. Or perhaps it was.

> Like freak Texan sisters joined at the hip
> playing saxophone duet in Vaudeville,
> we slept leaning, back to back . . .
> Inseparable sisters, I watch you every night
> from my half-world, my single mattress.
> You are smoking out back between shows

wearing the teal silk double cocktail dress.
You never speak . . .

The poem reminded me of Paul Muldoon's poem 'Truce', in which his simile for a one-night-stand, a World War I Christmas truce in no-man's-land, is placed first and dazzlingly expanded to take up nearly the whole poem, leaving its 'real' subject, Friday-night lovers who, 'when it's over, / Might get up from their mattresses / To congratulate each other / And exchange names and addresses', to emerge right at the end of the poem. The whole exercise was probably inspired by the chance rhyme of one-night-stand and no-man's-land, neither of which actually appears in the poem.

I visited Michael recently, and he showed me some of the material he had assembled for his poem – all manner of pictures and articles about the strange buoyancy of Siamese twins and their auto-eroticism. The Texan twins in question, Daisy and Violet Hilton, were born in San Antonio in 1909, joined at the hip, but turned slightly away from one another. Dubbed 'The Sensation of Vaudeville', they taught themselves to play saxophone by listening to Rudy Vallee records. 'We are our own jazz band. We have been studying music and we have now reached the point where we can make the big horns moan and whine and cry and gurgle . . .' The girls seem to have had the right idea. They were strikingly attractive apparently, with flowing pin curls, low-cut double evening dresses and a healthy interest in the opposite sex. They even danced. Bob Hope is said to have taught them the bottom-bumping dance, the 'black bottom', although it may have only been one of his sicker jokes.

The twins were promiscuous when they were young. In answer to a reporter's question, 'How do you make love?', Violet said that when Daisy was engaged, 'Sometimes I quit paying attention. Sometimes I read and sometimes I just take a nap.' They learned techniques of 'sexual concentration', and how to turn themselves off to the other's sexual pleasure, from Houdini, who was working the same circuit as them. 'We learnt not to know what the other was doing unless it was our business to know it.'

The story goes that they were in a restaurant once when they got into an argument about whether they had slept with a certain man who was sitting on the other side of the room. Daisy was convinced they had had him. Violet denied all knowledge of the man. To settle the argument, they decided to get up and go over and ask him to his face. They crossed the restaurant and began, 'You may not remember us, but . . .'

In 1932, they won a judgment against their exploiting guardians in the sum of $100,000 and for a while owned a hotel in Pittsburgh. In Hollywood in the 1930s, they made several films together, in one of which, *Chained for Life*, the guilty one is hanged for a murder, leaving the innocent one to a slower death. Just before they died themselves, of Hong Kong flu in 1969, they were working at a supermarket in North Carolina, a double check-out girl, one ringing up, the other bagging.

The original and best-known Siamese twins were Chang and Eng, born in Thailand in 1811. Joined side by side by a 'membrane' at chest level, they resembled one another, but were not identical. They had excellent health, could run like a gazelle, and by all accounts were intelligent and lively company. Their characters, however, were quite different, Chang being gay, Eng morose.

They travelled to America and were soon top of the bill in Barnum's freak-show, which also boasted a giantess and a lion-tamer. This pair fell in love and decided to get married. As their page-boys, the twins sang songs and told dirty jokes, but after the wedding they became depressed, believing they would never attain such happiness themselves. Soon afterwards, they met and proposed to two sisters, Sarah Ann and Adelaide Yeats, and were married on the same day.

The foursome got on well at first. They lived in two different houses, three days at Chang's, followed by three days at Eng's. They had become cotton growers and slave owners and were known as the hardest masters in Carolina. It was now that Chang took to drinking. He was more of a ladies' man than his brother, and this, coupled with his taste for spicy food and dirty jokes, offended and embarrassed the vegetarian Eng. When Chang fell in love with Eng's wife, their fragile domestic harmony came to an end. Emotionally estranged, they decided to be separated physically and journeyed to Scotland where a surgeon named Syme had offered to attempt the operation. Syme enjoyed the publicity, but lost his nerve when it came to cutting the membrane, as did others they consulted in the States. Balked in their bid for freedom, the brothers had no choice but to call a truce. As Mark Twain observed, 'During the Civil War both fought gallantly, Eng on the Union side and Chang on the Confederate. They took each other prisoner at Seven Oaks.'

Following the Civil War, their slaves overran their plantation in revenge for their mistreatment, and the twins barely escaped with their lives. They fled back to Barnum's, expecting to be welcomed with open arms, but times had changed. There were false Siamese twins everywhere by now, and they had to yield star billing to an old woman who had been George Washington's wet-nurse, a girl with no arms or legs, and a black woman with two heads. They were struggling along as second-class citizens in this menagerie when Chang fell ill and Eng was overcome by panic at what might become of him if Chang died. When Chang finally succumbed, Eng asked to be freed from the cadaver, but the surgeon arrived too late. Eng had died of fright two hours after his brother. Between them they managed to father twenty-two children, twelve from Sarah (Eng) and ten from Adelaide (Chang), although the children remained unsorted in the family Bible.

The stories of Chang and Eng, and of Daisy and Violet Hilton, are not particularly tragic in themselves, or even very sad, but as metaphors they crash around like loose cannon and require the strongest will (such as that of Mark Twain) to reimpose order. If they are an image of marriage, for instance, what are we to make of Chang and Eng's treatment of their slaves? Metaphors tend to be over-enthusiastic and sometimes get it wrong altogether. Donaghy's poem is an essay in the control of a metaphor which might otherwise have upstaged him with its puppyish desire to please.

The trend nowadays is to cut metaphors free from their twin

shadow-meanings, and let them have a life of their own. That way you sometimes get two poems instead of one. Humane but boring. Michael Donaghy's poem, remaining true to the image of Siamese twins, reverses the trend. It integrates meaning and metaphor by looking at every decision from both sides of the equation and then judging what is best for the poem as a whole. After all, who would pay to go and see a single Siamese twin?

[25.2.94]

When Prose Talks to Poetry

Reviewing the *Collected Letters* of Thomas and Jane Welsh Carlyle, Volumes Nineteen to Twenty-One, in last week's *TLS*, Daniel Karlin quoted Carlyle's advice to the poet Thomas Cooper, 'to try your next work in *Prose* and as a thing turning altogether on *Facts*, not Fictions'. It was advice he gave to all poets, apparently. One imagines the expression on Cooper's face as he received the message. 'It looks as though Thomas and Jane have been fighting again' may have been his reaction as he sat down to another wasted morning's versifying.

Karlin goes on to describe the Carlyles' marriage as wrung with bitterness, and to marvel at its survival. 'It would be hard to say whether Carlyle was more maddening to live with when he was wrestling with the demon of work or the demon of idleness.' Either way, Jane seems to have given as ill as she got. So it is not difficult to imagine Carlyle venting his rage on the nearest bloody little poet. 'Right,' you can hear him muttering, 'let's see how this one likes it . . .'

And yet there is a residue of good advice here, once you have boiled off the sadistic desire to waste someone else's time with unnecessary labour. Anyone who has ever taken a creative-writing class will be familiar with the students' indifference to, and overall ignorance of, the virtues of prose, which might otherwise have stopped them pulling the poetry over their eyes. In these circumstances, you have to cut back the poetic and nurture the prose, not because it is clearer, but because it is more poetic. If I were a nineteenth-century drawing master, I would make use of the cane, but in a creative-writing 'workshop' everyone's opinion on the subject is equally 'valid', and so I bow my head and swallow the dead metaphors.

As a teenager, I had to put up with a different argument for prose. I was always being nagged to put my talent to more profitable use, to write a play, a novel, anything. I wrote prose as a penance for travelling, but I always preferred poetry, to read as well as to write, not because it was the most rarefied form, but because it was the least. Poetry seemed to tell the writer something, while prose did what it was told. When I failed to produce a blockbuster, a job in publishing was thought to be the solution.

I now see that one of the great strengths of poetry is its indifference to money, or rather money's indifference to it. There is no doubt that prose is the language of money. But if prose equals cash, does cash also equal prose? We shall see when Craig Raine's long poem, *History: The Home Movie*, appears from Penguin later this year and is put up for the Booker. Raine once advised me to write my poems in prose. Had he been quarrelling with his wife, I wonder? I shall be interested to see if he has taken his own advice.

Carlyle was driven away from poetry by 'the base Terror of Beggary'. No such lash drives people towards it, unless it is the lash of laziness, Carlyle's 'demon of idleness'. In my experience, poetry is put aside on such a regular basis for hunger, thirst, masturbation, sociability, deadlines, tiredness, sleep and television that it isn't surprising it wears a broken, ironical expression.

Poor Carlyle. He had to put up with appalling hardships in his flight from Beggary. 'I am sunk in the bowels of Chaos', he wrote to Jane. 'Day after day, I sit here solitary, annihilating rubbish, like to be annihilated by it.'

With her husband 'raying out darkness on all her human attempts at occupation or amusement', there was nothing Jane could do either. The loss of his servant Helen Mitchell was the ultimate irritation. He now had to put up with 'a recalcitrant Edinburgh damsel', whom he finally dismissed with the request that she disappear 'straightway, and in no region of God's universe, if she could avoid it, ever to let me behold her again'. The form of his words is relished by Karlin as 'memorable advice'. Less attractive is Carlyle's own evident relish. In his rounded phrases, one can make out the gloating accents of the powerful speaking to the weak, the rich to the poor, the establishment to the disenfranchised, prose to poetry.

[11.3.94]

Being Entertained for a Living

I have now had over ten years of being entertained for a living – first for the *New Statesman* (television), then for the *Sunday Correspondent* (theatre), currently for *Harpers & Queen* (cinema). In the 1960s I used to write about the odd 'happening' for the *London Magazine*. While the subjects for reviews have plodded upmarket, the journals have plodded down. It won't be long before I'm religious affairs correspondent for *Cosmopolitan*.

Having to be professionally diverted for a living sometimes leaves one at a loss to know what to do for diversion, and I find I watch a lot of television. 'Don't give a damn if it's good or bad. I sit and watch it till it drives me mad. Just so long as it's on I'm glad' (from 'Television' by Dave Edmunds). The only form of entertainment I know anything about is pop music, but so far I have been spared writing about it, which leaves it free to go on entertaining me.

On the whole, I think I was happiest writing about television, or my sentences were happiest, being inclined to bite their own tails. You could say what you liked on the subject in the early 1980s because Clive James had recently annexed the whole area for general larking about; so long as one refrained from anything like a balanced judgement, it was all right. The only thing I ever felt passionately about was that repellent way certain politicians have of smiling when answering questions. Michael Portillo for instance.

If TV reviewing was the easiest job, theatre reviewing was by far the hardest. Plays are more vulnerable beings than tap-water television, and I always sensed my actor father turning in his grave at the idea of a theatre-critic son laying down the law about his profession. This in itself gave the job a certain piquancy, especially as I was getting £300 a week. I thought I could brazen it out for perhaps five years, but as it turned out, the *Correspondent* folded after eighteen months.

It used to amuse and amaze me watching my fellow theatre critics at work, because many of them seemed to have picked up the actor's habit of 'emoting' during the performance they were attending – whether it was the impatiently sprawling figure of Nicholas de Jongh, whose undone shirt buttons exuded disgust at everything, or the fluctuating features of Irving Wardle, which seemed to keep up a constant visual commentary on what was happening on stage, often rivalling it in fascination. There was another one, whose name I forget, who couldn't keep still for a moment. In his mind he was clearly up there on stage with the rest of them.

By far the best thing about the job, from my point of view, was that it happened in the evening, so I didn't waste prime writing time going in to the West End in the middle of the day, as one has to for film previews, which take place at 10.30 a.m. or one o'clock. There were always two tickets waiting to be picked up at the press desk or the box office, and it was pleasant wondering who to take on such a glamorous, yet economical outing, free drinks being also usually available.

It's harder to find someone to go with during the day, partly because they're busy and partly because the films are so far ahead of their publicity that no one knows whether they want to see them yet. 'Oh yeah, what's it about?' they ask, and you have to admit you don't know. One mercy of working for a monthly is that copies of American blockbusters and star-clusters are seldom available early enough to accommodate a glossy's deadline, which is generally three months ahead of publication, so one only gets to see the decent stuff.

There is a certain excitement in going to see a new, unheard-of film. When you get to the viewing theatre (past the commissionaire and down the stairs), a girl with a clipboard smilingly ticks you off on a list and hands you the production notes, which speak of the film's success as if it were a foregone conclusion. No matter how bad the film is, the atmosphere is charged, for this is the last moment when the project is still wrapped in the full glory of its conception, before its secret gets out. Veteran critics exchange loud film-talk in the foyer.

Sandwiches, coffee and a free bar are available. Most people go straight in and put their coats on their favourite seat before hitting the bar. I favour the front row, because it gets more light from the screen. I used to have a 'Write-Lite' torch-pen, but it broke early on in my film-critic career, probably to the relief of my neighbours, and now I find the only way to see what I'm writing is to wait for a brightly lit scene, then scribble like crazy. This was difficult in a recent film like *Germinal*, which was shot mostly down a coalmine. My notes for that film are an illegible palimpsest, which is going to be troublesome later. I seem to have forgotten to move my hand down the page.

People always think you want to dash home to write up your review, but personally I prefer to put it away and forget about it until the deadline comes to my aid. Then I fill my thermos, turn up the music and go out shopping a lot. My difficulty in writing reviews is not so much remembering the film (which usually comes back to me if I can decipher my notes), but in writing sentences and working out what order to put them in. Having written out my various comments in longhand, I type them on to separate strips of paper and move them around on my desk until the right air of rational thought is achieved, then I staple them into place and type them out again.

It seems just a short time ago that I was getting on my motorbike to deliver my copy to wherever it had to go, loitering pleasurably in some office while the editor read my article, maybe abusing the photocopier to pass the time. All that is a thing of the past, alas. Like a jealous wife, the new fax machine keeps me indoors. I don't get around much any more.

[25.3.94]

We've Got a King Who Cares for People

The last time I went to the British Embassy church in Paris was in January 1960. Off the leash for the first time, aged seventeen, and totally out of my depth in the 'Cours de Civilisation Française' I was supposed to be taking, I was looking for some English-speaking warmth to tide me over, but I wasn't optimistic.

The congregation, as I remember it, consisted mostly of a pink cloud of pre-débutantes from Madame Anita's finishing school, all wearing white gloves and little hats and carrying shoulder-bags. They floated out into the street afterwards, and in the chattering conglomeration I learnt that they were going to the vicar's tea party that afternoon. At this shrilly pastoral affair I made my first 'grown-up' friends, among them the seventeen-year-old Lucy Lambton, who was one of those people who makes things happen, and still is.

Lucy had access to the jet-set world of fifteen-year-old Guinness heir Tara Browne, then living in Paris with his mother Oonagh Guinness and her current husband, a *louche* Cuban shoe designer called Miguel Ferreras. Tara was familiar with such things as amethyst cuff-links, brocade ties, menthol cigarettes, Bloody Marys, Phil Spectre singles, Le Club de L'Etoile and a chauffeur-driven Lincoln Continental to take him there and get him home by three in the morning. Before long so was I. I never looked back.

Well, I did, of course. I never stopped looking back. Otherwise I wouldn't have been hanging around in the Rue d'Aguesseau thirty-four years later, scuffling around in the past, steeplechasing the years, expecting what? Tara was killed in a car crash in 1966. Did I expect him to appear out of the stones?

I found my way to the church more by feel than map-reading. It seemed to have disappeared completely, making me think I'd got the wrong street, until I noticed the sign saying 'St Michael's' on the plate glass door of a new office block. The old church had gone, swallowed up by Mammon, but some sort of space had been allotted to it inside or behind or underneath the new block. Feeling sorry for it, I entered a rather bleak area and saw rows of chairs, a cinema screen and a traditional altar. A young man wearing old jeans and a gingham shirt was sitting in a big chair near the altar. A girl stood behind the altar wearing a turquoise stole. She smiled at us as we took our seats.

Before long the young man stood up and announced that this was the day when Jesus entered Jerusalem on a donkey: 'Which means that it must be . . . ?' He threw up his arms encouragingly like Bruce Forsyth in *The Generation Game* and I could almost make out the words 'Nice to see you' on his lips. 'To see you, nice', I wanted to shout back, but the right answer was 'Palm Sunday', of course, and we had to shout it several times before Bruce was satisfied. I looked round to see if there were many children present, but they were all grown-ups of a certain kind, who seemed to find nothing strange about all this.

Bruce emphasized that it was a donkey on which Christ had entered Jerusalem and wanted to know what sort of vehicle we thought the Queen of England might have used. Someone suggested a Rolls, and Bruce got us to impersonate the crowds lining the Jerusalem streets, shouting 'Her Majesty's got a new Rolls Royce'. What sort of vehicle would the President of America have used? This time we had to sing out 'Clinton's got a new Cadillac and Hillary chose the carpet'. And what about the President of France? Mustn't forget him! 'Peugeot–Citroën–Renault, Mitterand drives them all'.

While we considered the image of a Deux Chevaux bumping over first-century cobblestones, Bruce came to his point. 'But we don't have a king who drives a Rolls or a Cadillac or a Citroën, do we? We've got a king who rides a donkey.' This last phrase turned out to be the first line of a rewritten version of 'What shall we do with the drunken sailor', the words of which now appeared on the screen, via an overhead projector. 'We've got a king who cares for people', sang the congregation, accompanied by a flute and guitar. 'What shall we do with our life this morning?' The answer came to me across the years: 'Throw him in the scuppers till he's sober'.

'Now, while you're all still standing up', said Bruce, 'I think it would be a nice idea if we gave Jesus a Mexican Wave to welcome him into Jerusalem'. I had never done a Mexican wave before, but I soon learned that it involves putting your arms above your head and then bringing them down just after your neighbour, creating a ripple effect. Bruce was quite pleased with our efforts here. Tucking his shirt back into his jeans, he said he was going to leave us in the capable hands of Kirstie, who now came from behind the altar smiling her friendly game-show hostess smile.

It seemed that it was now Kirstie's turn to compare the Queen unfavourably to Jesus. 'She's got a little wave that goes like this', she said critically, and she waved to us like the Queen. A cartoon of the Queen waving appeared on the screen, followed by other would-be amusing drawings. 'When I went to see the Queen as a little girl', said Kirstie, 'I wondered whether Jesus was like that. What do you think?' We paused here for a thought-provoking song, the words of which appeared on the screen. Then Kirstie came back and explained that Jesus had wept because he could see the people in Jerusalem were doing wicked things and knew he was going to be blamed for everything. 'We need to learn to say sorry to Jesus, and especially God, because then Jesus will stop crying. He wants us all to say we are sorry so that we can all be his friends . . .' Kirstie smiled her game-show hostess smile and left the stage.

'Now', said Bruce. 'Is there anybody here who'd like to lead the prayers this morning?' It was an opportunity for Satan to step in and smarten up the proceedings, but nobody volunteered. As it turned out, they needn't have worried. To modernize an old prayer, all you have to do is change 'thee' and 'thy' to 'you' and 'your', as in 'Your kingdom come, Your will be done', and Bob's your uncle. Anyone could have done it. The girl in the turquoise stole smiled at the man in jeans, and an atmosphere of pure 'Jackanory' trickled over the scene.

215

I thought of the rows of seventeen-year-old pre-debs in their white gloves and little hats, singing 'Dear Lord and Father of Mankind'. That hadn't been religion either, but it didn't seem to matter so much then. What a strange coincidence it is that everything always changes for the worse during the course of a single lifetime. Watch this space in a fortnight's time for my Easter Sunday conversion to Rome.

[22.4.94]

My Conversion to Rome

Photographs should not be looked at too much or they lose their transparency. They should be kept in plastic bags under the bed and forgotten about for a decade or two so that they can get mixed up, regather their resources and spring their ambushes on us when we are least expecting it. I am a dedicated scrapbook maker, but I cannot resist looking at my beautifully laid-out pages until I undo the project with familiarity. Perhaps I only do it to tame the sadness of time. It doesn't work, because there is always the odd photo or postcard which will suddenly appear to keelhaul me.

One such is a wedding photograph of my wife taken in the garden of her grandparents' house at Sacy-le-Petit in France, where we were married. She's examining her wedding-ring and laughing. I'd had it engraved with 'kawan-kawan', the word for 'friends' in Malay, which she'd been studying when we met. She's looking inside the ring and asking why I've put the Malay word for a herd of elephants. In another photo, taken in the church earlier, I can see her grandmother scowling at the cheap brass ring my wife is putting on my finger. The sequence covers our entire wedding-day, from the moment my wife gets up in the morning, cleans her teeth and has her hair done, through the church service (presided over by her grandmother), the civil service (presided over by her mayor grandfather), the garden party and our departure in a Citroën DS taxi ordered by me at the last moment. The final shots show the car

216

gradually disappearing into the flat Oise countryside on its way to Paris, the Hotel d'Angleterre, a train to Venice and a future in London.

That was in 1965 and I hadn't been back since. It came as a shock, then, to hear recently that my wife had decided to take the place instead of the money when the old people died and that she wanted to try and make use of it creatively. I was extremely apprehensive about the project at first, and still am — second homes are not for *TLS* columnists. The charm of Sacy-le-Petit, my wife explained, was its peculiar charmlessness, a comprehensive absence of shops, cafés, or any other kind of distraction. I would grow to like it in time.

We spent Easter there this year as the new owners of 'le château', and something about the birds singing, the trees coming out, the nearby church tolling the half-hours and the baker's van hooting at the front gate with fresh croissants has converted me, although I must admit I had no choice.

I was quite looking forward to seeing the church, which I hadn't been into since we were married, but unfortunately it wasn't Sacy's turn to do Easter this year and the church was locked. Instead, we decided to go to a choral mass being held on the Saturday evening in the neighbouring village of Grandfresnoy. Not having a car, we set out on foot, just as the sun was going down. It looked an easy walk. The countryside is rich, flat and hedgeless, like Norfolk, with a gentle wooded rise on the horizon known locally as 'La Montagne'. The roads head off in the direction of steeple or tower, but they never seem to arrive. Grandfresnoy looked about a mile away, but it kept ducking and diving behind unsuspected folds, keeping us at a distance. We must have been walking an hour when we entered Grandfresnoy rather footsore and saw our first café and mini-market for a week.

As the church bell began its last peals, we took our place in a pew at the back and I couldn't help comparing the austere décor with that of the lamentable British Embassy church in Paris, which I'd been to the week before. No jarring hymn numbers in racks, but dim-lit Stations of the Cross. No nursery rhymes projected on a screen, but a cardboard cross hung with children's drawings of flowers. No game-show hostess, but a bunch of red roses in a bowl. No Mexican wave to Jesus, but an old statue of a saint carrying a sword and a starfish.

We had barely settled into our places when we were invited to process out of the church again and on to the church steps, where a sizeable fire was blazing in a metal bowl. The last time I saw a fire on church steps was in Mexico, where its origins are acknowledged to be pre-Christian. The sight was unmistakably pagan and boded well for the production, I thought. We huddled round in the freezing wind while the fire was blessed, a symbol of everlasting life which would be proved on Easter Day. A big candle with a red cross on it was also plentifully blessed, but when it came to lighting it from the fire so that eternal life could be carried into the church, the slender tapers proved no match for the wind and an unforeseen hitch threatened to upset our enlightened priest's stage-management. Acolytes tried repeatedly to light the candle, as jokes and laughter began. The priest even tried to light the candle directly from the fire, but thought better of this indignity. Luckily someone had a little bunch of Palm Sunday *buis* (boxwood) and she used this to transfer a flame to the candle. Now we lit our own tapers and began to escort the big candle back into the darkened church while the choir sang Jubilate Deo.

The mass that followed was two hours long, but of such total theatricality that it held me spellbound. The cast was enormous. Aside from the well-rehearsed forty-strong choir, complete with demented musical director, there must have been six priests and as many boy acolytes, all with some tiny, specific task to perform, involving fetching and carrying various receptacles, covered by or resting on embroidered cloths. A faint air of amateurishness added spontaneity to the proceedings. From a distance it looked like a slow-motion cookery class, or possibly a Japanese tea ceremony. Bells tolled. Rattles sounded. A gong boomed off-stage to mark the different movements. At one point the entire congregation was rebaptized with holy water from a shaker. At another, the church filled with incense from a burner. No expense had been spared. All we had to do was look on and be amazed at this wonderful celebration of meaninglessness, the triumph of form over content.

At the height of the service, at the blessing, as the host was held high, the church bell started chiming again, as if to summon us elsewhere. I thought of the silly songs and cartoons in the British Embassy church, and wondered how the two performances could possibly be part of the same thing.

When it was all finally over, we were approached by France, a former retainer and prominent member of the choir, red-faced and excited, wanting to know how we were going to find our way home in the dark. 'Vous êtes montés à pied?' she asked incredulously. 'Je peux vous redescendre à Sacy, si vous voulez.' We smiled at the local habit of imagining mountains in this flat land, but we were glad of the lift home.

[13.5.94]

What the War in Bosnia is About

My niece Hilary Dunn, a researcher and scriptwriter at the BBC, is married to a Bosnian Muslim, Jasmin Dizdar, a budding film director and author of a book about Miloš Forman. They met in a disco in 1987 during a film festival at Karlovy Vary, a Czech tourist resort. Hilary was there with a film she had written while at the North London Polytechnic. The two found themselves sitting at a table and began talking. When they got up to dance, they had to laugh because he's six foot three and she's five foot one. The great 'distance' between them, as Dizdar says, was the first bond between them. They agreed to meet next day – her last in Karlovy – but he overslept. He went to the Festival centre in time to see a downcast Hilary receiving her diploma. After various romantic trysts in Prague and Paris, they were married in London in 1989, since when their life together has been overshadowed by the war in Bosnia.

Jasmin hasn't seen his parents since 1988. They live in the Serbsurrounded enclave of Zenica, a modern steel town now given over to arms production, where all the Muslim people who have been cleansed from other parts of Bosnia have wound up 'in a huge ant's nest, everyone walking on other peoples' shoulders'. Every morning his mother joins a car boot sale as long as Oxford Street where she sells bits and pieces from the house in return for seeds for her husband's allotment. 'The Serbs don't want the town because it isn't a tourist attraction. They control it economically anyway, just as the Germans control Yugoslavia with the mark.'

Jasmin sends what money he can, if he finds a way, but he isn't finding it easy to work in this country. He would like to make a film about Bosnia, but draws back from turning their suffering to his advantage. 'I don't want to show my country as a battlefield just for the sake of showing Englishmen the ways of killing.' He was asked by the BBC recently to make a drama documentary about his brother's Scarlet Pimpernel-like escape from Zenica (details suppressed to protect the route). He responded with enthusiasm, only to discover that the producer's true interest lay in heroism, not only his brother's but that of England, the good and safe haven. 'Escape to England', he mocked. 'Like James Bond. Put some music on it and everyone's happy.' As soon as he started talking about the feared-more-than-death amputations in Bosnian hospitals, routinely performed without anaesthetic, he detected a cooling on the other end of the line. 'My film would have appealed to the conscience of this so-called civilized Europe. But you cannot sell a conscience to people interested in propaganda.'

It would be insufferable to pretend to understand the conflicting emotions of an exile in time of war, but among the guilt and fear there is undoubtedly shame for his country. 'When I was in Paris in 1988 everyone would melt when I said I was Yugoslav. Now you're the most worthless creep on the planet. Something dramatically changed and I'm not the man I used to be. You can say "I'm English" – but I can't say I'm Yugoslav any more. I'm nothing. I'm downgraded. When I go into a hairdresser's, I can't say I'm Bosnian or they all look at you. They can't read their newspapers, thinking you must be some stupid Muslim fundamentalist. I say I'm from Holland now.'

The tragedy, as he sees it, is that five years ago this unique country, this unique blend of differences, had it made. With their brand of 'self-rule socialism', not unlike that later achieved by Solidarity in Poland, they would have been first into the Common Market after the Iron Curtain came down. 'Now the Serbs are only the Serbs, the Muslims are only the Muslims. It'll be 500 years before we enter.'

And yet the war, according to Jasmin, is nothing to do with nationalism or even nationhood, since all the sides are from the same ethnic origin and nothing can change that. 'There is more ethnic difference between the Scots and the English.' Nor is it about religion: Orthodox, Catholic, or Muslim. 'All that was forgotten long ago under Tito. We say "Fuck God" now as easily as you say "Bloody hell".' Rather it is a series of local scraps invariably to do with economic jealousy. The insult, for instance, of guest-workers returning from Germany with fast cars and building big houses in the middle of nowhere on the back of a currency devaluation. 'To a certain extent, it is a class war, provincial squabbles masquerading as national determinism as a means of dragging the superpowers into the traditional Balkan game of embarrassing the neighbours. "Look, I've got a bigger boy behind me than you." We persuade ourselves we'd be better off under a certain patronage, and the superpowers are only too happy to extend their sphere of influence.' He passed me a dictionary. 'Open it anywhere. Put your finger on a word. *That's* what the war in Bosnia is about.'

It is a game which got out of hand when all the talented minds lost interest in these family squabbles and left them to it. But like all family squabbles it won't last. 'The warring sides are not enemies', says Jasmin, stabbing the sofa with his forefinger. 'Cut my throat if I am wrong. They will be friends again within five years. Less. Look at Mostar. The Muslims and Croats destroyed it. Now they are friends again. Who cannot say it won't happen with the Serbs?'

The ambiguity of his thesis emerges when Jasmin goes on to describe the different family characteristics: friendly, wholehearted,

221

naïve Muslims; civilized, perfectionist Croats; stubborn, go-getting Serbs. Might these not be proto-nationalistic characteristics after all? His is a heartfelt, necessary point of view, but you sense that it is this strain of optimism, mixed with aloofness, that he clings to in the midst of his privileged, guilty happiness in London with Hilary. For the time being he must remain silent, but when the dust settles, 'when the dust settles in *me*', the pair are surely destined to make a great film about their once and future Yugoslavia.

[3.6.94]

Telephones

With my right hand out of action, I notice that no one dials a telephone number with their left hand. They pick up the phone with their right, swap over to dial, then swap back again to speak, the way the French swap their fork over after they have cut up their meat. People don't trust their left hand to perform such an intimate task as dialling, any more than they trust it to perform adequately in bed, unless it be for some mild perversion of habitude. If one hand ever had cause to be jealous of the other, it is surely the underprivileged left of the pushy, over-confident right.

Sex and the telephone are so intricately bound up with one another that the gesture of making a call unconsciously mimics those of sex – menial left arm rounding up and gathering in, while the élite right hand explores and enjoys. As a teenager, I would take my girlfriend to the cinema in order to put my arm round her shoulder. I didn't know then why I wanted to keep my right hand free – something to do with the bridegroom keeping his sword-arm free – but I knew I felt backward, off-balance, ill-prepared if I was trapped into sitting on the wrong side: sinister instead of dexterous.

When I rang up, weeks in advance, to arrange one of these early fumbles, I would make a list of amusing things to say, a name, a joke, a query, to have by me in case the displacement chatter suddenly ran dry, suspending me over the gorge. Lawrence Durrell once wrote that telephones were the symbol of communications that never take place. This was certainly true in my case, but it didn't stop me shaking. The sound of a person's voice takes a truer picture of them than any camera, and as the medium of this print-out, the telephone was as close as I could get. It was the thing I held when I spoke to her, holding it close to my face, almost kissing it, while I whimpered my shamefaced lust barely disguised as film talk, school talk, a story of a hot-air balloon that had come down in our garden.

Telephones in those days were any colour so long as it was black: powerful squat images of fear and fulfilment, their flex snaking away across the floor on its urgent journey to the loved one. The ring of those old phones still operates like Pavlov's bell on my responses. If I find I have someone's telephone number by heart, I know I'm in trouble.

The postmodern, post-useful proliferation of telephonic styles and facilities, most of them cancelling one another out, has managed to diffuse the sexuality of the telephone, to the point where not having one carries a greater erotic charge. 'His two tongues sought her two mouths', wrote Martin Amis. By this analogy, the dialling finger is a third tongue, performing a discreet but essential foreplay. But instead of seductively twirling the sensitive instrument with a hooked index finger, the modern would-be communicator must peck briefly in a style we all know to be wrong.

The new one-piece consoles have lost the powerful image of the old phones; they look like chocolate biscuits; they lack the essential doubleness of cradle and receiver, the mysterious way in which their separation heralded contact. In modern phones, the receiver does not copulate snugly with its partner, it seems to take pride in being a single piece of equipment, the dial tellingly transferred to the handset in an image of auto-eroticism. For telephones nowadays more often than not connect someone to no one – the recorded voice of the desired person, or that of someone else altogether; I recently had Lauren Bacall, murmuring 'You know how to whistle, don't you? You put your lips together and blow.'

Am I alone in feeling a force ten cold wind coming off these machines? It is as if a curtain had been lifted on another side of the person you are calling, revealing them as they really are. I hang up before a betraying gap can appear on the answering tape and rarely come back for a second dose.

I still feel a nostalgic erotic twinge when I see an old bakelite phone, monumental and authoritative, sitting like a miniature mountain on its plain, its slanting chrome dial looking like one of those mysterious images cut out of the hillside. Surely the modern equivalent of a chalk giant with an erection would be a rudimentary telephone dial, so much more evocative than ten buttons, although I suppose its meaning is lost already and it would soon have 'origin unknown' against it in the dictionary of historical images.

[8.7.94]

Answerphones

The telephone is like Catullus's sparrow: 'My lady's pet, with whom she often plays whilst she holds you in her lap, or gives you her fingertip to peck'. The answerphone, on the other hand, reminds me of nothing so much as God, with one of His dodgily recorded maxims on the answering tape: 'Blessed are the meek', 'Thou shalt not commit adultery' – polite ways of saying 'Thank you so much, we'll let you know'. You offer up your halting, heartfelt prayer and it is forgotten about for centuries. Gradually you come to the conclusion that there is nobody there. You decide not to make any more calls yourself, but to let other people call you. You install an answerphone and become a god yourself. Peter O'Toole, in *The Ruling Class*, when asked how he knew he was God, replied, 'Because whenever I pray I find I am talking to myself'.

It is interesting to note that people who have made the transition to an answerphone are rarely satisfied with their new toy. They seem to need to get calls more than their friends need to make them, which makes one wonder if God himself is like this. Owners of answer-phones apparently play back their messages over and over again,

224

especially those from lovers, trying to squeeze a significance, a giveaway commitment from our stammered, shamefaced blurtings. Why is he so confused? That nervous cough, why did he think he had to call back to say who he was? What does it mean?

A friend tells me that when he comes in he checks his messages even before he has closed the door, before taking off his coat, before saying hello to the cat. If the little red eye isn't winking at him, his day is ruined retrospectively and he goes into decline. The week his answerphone was out of action he felt reinvigorated, as if his life had been given back to him. No longer was he aware of something nasty lurking behind the door, waiting to mug him with bad news whenever he came in. He talked about a new reality. Ours perhaps. In his new-found confidence he had discovered my own favourite device of taking the receiver off the hook.

Once upon a time people knocked on your door and you were either in or out or hiding behind the curtain. Then came visiting cards and the possibilities of social embarrassment multiplied. To call or not to call? To leave a card or not leave a card? How many cards? Signed or unsigned? With one corner turned down, or two? And what to expect in return? Cards gave way to the telephone and once more we were either in, out, or busy. Then came the answerphone, and the possibilities for suffering once more proliferated. One's disappointment at finding someone out was increased rather than ameliorated by the wincingly unfunny messages such machines seemed to call for. 'This is the Battersea Dogs' Home . . . It isn't really', 'This is me, so that must be you' etc., as if someone were holding a gun to their head and commanding them to be witty. One had the strange sensation of being the cause of some-one's embarrassment and they of yours. Perhaps you weren't so fond of them after all. Whatever made you think they were so amusing?

It seems one should refrain from leaving one's personality in the charge of these traducers. I favour the approach of an American record company boss who has a barked 'Well?' on his voicebox, or the straightforward 'What's in it for me?', even if that was from a firm of that name. Harold Pinter's answerphone says simply, 'Speak after the pause'. Fats Domino's would have a rhythmical 'One, two, you know what to do . . .' Woody Allen once tried to imitate the answerphone voice, but was soon rumbled when he started arguing.

The duration of the recording is important, for it is now that one must make up one's mind whether to speak and what to say. Once a syllable is out, the aural photograph is clocked, and the callee is empowered to humiliate you by not calling back. Because, of course, you never know if they are there or not, laughing amongst themselves, checking out your amusement value, deciding to wait and see what you have to offer, or who's on the other line, before committing themselves.

How often have I yearned to obliterate the soul-revealing message that was bluffed out of me by a cute recorded voice, or even redraft it in more dignified terms. To paraphrase Larkin: Man hands on messages to man. / They deepen on the telephone shelf. / Get off as quickly as you can / And don't leave any messages yourself.

[5.8.94]

Male Model

Nick suggests I do up the top button of my Zegna Soft charcoal-grey waffle-effect sports shirt (£85), maybe pull it out of my trousers, make it look casual. And why don't I hunch my shoulders, let everything go loose? I could bunch up my gold cashmere single-breasted Zegna Soft jacket (£595), shove my hands in the pockets, treat it disrespectfully. I might like to lean right forward with my legs wide apart. Try a big smile. 'Turn your head away, but leave your eyes where they are, if you see what I mean . . . That's it, hold that, I like that one . . .'

Everyone knows poets will go anywhere and do anything in order to get out of the house. They'll go to Scotland, and go through a whole special kind of humiliation in a hall, providing there's a drink and seven people in the audience, only four of whom are friends of the organizer. Sometimes they don't have to go so far to make fools of themselves.

The last time I was asked to model clothes was in 1962. The twist had just arrived, followed by twist clothes, or what someone thought might be twist clothes, brightly-coloured jumpsuits with contrasting hoops at elbow and knee to accommodate the pivoting movements. Julian Mitchell was doing the copy for the *Sunday Times* and asked me if I'd like to model. I seem to remember being very coquettish about it even then; certainly that is how Mitchell remembers it. At first I said no, fearing to look foolish, then I said yes, imagining the girls, finally deciding against it out of laziness, a decision which I regretted, but didn't feel I could go back on. Thirty-three years later, I am being given a second chance.

As soon as I hear that a handful of male poets (I wonder would the women be so willing?) are being asked to model clothes for *Esquire* magazine, my vanity is stirred, and in my excitement I don't even ask if there is a fee, only where I should report and when. My contact asks if I require a car and I instantly decline, lest she imagine that I am getting too big for my boots already. I tell her I can get there just as easily on my motorbike, with the result that, when the morning comes, I have to put on my crash helmet over freshly-washed hair, which always gives it a flattened, unnatural look. I imagine I'll be able to fix it when I get there, but as soon as I walk into the cramped studio, I know this is going to be impossible.

I get there early, but Glyn Maxwell and Simon Armitage are there ahead of me. This is their last engagement before going off to Iceland to be Auden and MacNeice. (Stephen Spender will be modelling later this afternoon.) Glyn is already posing in a big literary pullover, while Simon utters wisecracks from the sofa, waiting his turn. There is a certain kind of competitive self-satire that poets go in for when they meet, and the form is exaggerated on this occasion because of the mortal danger we are all in of blowing our cover. By the time we have finished going 'Nothing to do with poetry? No money? How early shall I be there?', there is no time left for the mirror-work I have been relying on, unless I do it in public in the full-length mirror leaning against a wall, which seems impossible. I can see that a greater problem is going to be the clothes, which we are allowed to choose for ourselves.

Just inside the door of the studio is a clothes rail groaning with what at first sight looks like the most awful tack, but which on closer inspection turns out to be made of things like silk, cashmere and alpaca. Everything is crushed and battered-looking from sheer quality, limp with cash, but still managing to give out powerful signals of what used to be called 'commonness': silk-knit jumpers, safari collars, jackets with five buttons, suits made of 'interesting' material, with 'original design features'. Would I like to pick something out? What did he take me for? Did they have any twist jumpsuits by any chance?

I'm told it is the trendsetter Versace with his taste for chronic East End glitter fashion and gold appliqué who is responsible for this wallow in 1970s naffness, but photographer Hugo Glendinning has a more charitable angle on it: 'I think the autumn season has something about it which people of our generation are going to have some difficulty with', he tells me with euphemistic accuracy. He must be twenty years younger than me and probably loves the stuff. In desperation, Nick the stylist has started holding up more and more awful things for my approval, and I am aware that time is passing and that several people here have livings to earn, including theoretically, me. What to do?

Eventually I pick out a black shirt and lighter coloured jacket out of 'Crossroads' and present myself, rather condescendingly, for approval. There is a pause and disappointed faces all round. I have chosen a Versace jacket and an Armani shirt, but unfortunately the two golden boys of Italian tack are not in love with each other and have issued strict orders that they do not wish to appear on the same model. It's back to the clothes rail for a sulky compromise.

I heard afterwards that Alan Jenkins had warned the crew in advance that I would be easily the most fussy about the clothes, which was why they were more amused than impatient with my performance.

A week later, I got a call from *Esquire*, asking for a poem to be included in the layout, presumably by way of a fee, because nothing else was forthcoming. I faxed them one including the exchange: ' "You should be with someone a full minute / before you realize they're well-dressed" . . . "Suppose you realize before that?" . . . "Probably queer," said my father.' They liked the poem, they said, but it was on the long side. Had I got something shorter?

[30.9.94]

Return to Skyros

The island of Skyros. Another Personal Development holiday. I'm sitting on my balcony overlooking the little white town, watching the sun go down between two mustard-dusted mountains. The sky turns heliotrope. Eagles wheel. Two jets on a near-collision course leave sunset vapour trails. A fizzing, popping streetlamp shorting on and off outside my window and a lovesick donkey braying hopelessly at unpredictable intervals keep me awake most of the night, so the following morning I set my students to reproduce in words the heartfelt longing of a donkey-cry. I explain the exercise nine times, then most of them write poems about donkeys, which is fair enough. 'My donkeyness calls to your donkeyness' is the best line. A quiet-spoken participant describes a voice workshop she attended in London where the facilitator led her down through the register until she was producing sounds like Paul Robeson. She found this extremely satisfying, but was unable to reproduce the sound on her own and the workshop closed down soon afterwards. She was hoping to rediscover the secret on Skyros, so far without success. When encouraged, she manages quite a convincing donkey-bray. This frivolity suddenly careers off into a revelation of a near rape, which freezes everyone solid.

It's odd how quickly one's silent, daily, internal life can be replaced by a sort of twelve-hour disjointed word-exchange with a lot of affable, holiday-minded strangers. There are gaps for sleeping and shaving (if there's any water), but basically you're part of a larger babble which effectively suspends thought. Perhaps this is the purpose of the family. One of the male holiday-makers is convinced that an elderly woman on the course is keeping his bag in her room. I try to reason him away from this delusion, but there is no other explanation for its disappearance, he says.

Demos. This is the after-breakfast announcements and appreciations session, led this morning by an American volunteer. 'I am heaven and earth', she begins, making the signs, 'I produce Yin and Yang and combine them into one. Thus I create everything and I destroy everything. Then I resurrect it again . . . and I destroy it again. . . .' A male student leans across to me and whispers, 'Sounds like a tough date' – a welcome note in what is essentially an irony-free environment.

Every day, volunteers are required for the next day's Demos. Usually I try to disappear into my muesli, but I have been considering doing one about certain New Age words such as 'sharing', 'energy', 'space', 'permission', 'supportive', 'interaction' 'empowerment', saying what I think they all mean. I could take as my text part of the blurb for a course called 'Becoming the Warrioress': 'As we learn to set our personal warrioress free, we reach new heights of self-expression and discovery, and begin to merge with the Divine Feminine Essence in a truly empowered way.' I mention the idea of compiling a New Age dictionary to Hazel, our dance and movement facilitator, and she is so taken with the idea that she brings it up at a staff meeting. Luckily, I manage to stop her before she can get very far – 'I wanted to talk to you about that, Hazel.'

Hazel has asked to join my course, which means that now I have to be truthful at staff meetings about what goes on there. The truth is I have had a crisis of confidence following an exercise I got out of a book and didn't read properly beforehand: 'Listen to a poem as it is read out, then write down all the evocative words you can remember. Now imagine a journey you might make and use your chosen words to guide you into a poem. Let the borrowed language propose ways to break through your familiarity with the landscape, by suggesting details, mood, narrative, and diction.'

As the full horror of this exercise (by Cleopatra Mathis) dawns on me, I realize that I do not have the guts to disown it and have to pretend what a groovy exercise it is and what a great help it has been with my own work. Hazel makes her excuses and leaves, followed by Sheilah. Slowly, everything dies. As a diversionary measure, I put on my trusty Larkin cassette in which he reads all his most Larkinish poems: his fear of death, his love of work, his dislike of other people. It would be hard to imagine anything less appropriate, less New Age. Nobody likes him, and their suspicions are confirmed that I, too, am an old-type fouled-up guy in need of therapy. I should never have made Larkin leave the UK.

A torch-led moonwalk. Sage-green spongelike things in a submarine light. Vicious pale edges of grey scrub and lighter grey meadows are etched with motionless lead sheep as we progress across a valley to a lone oak tree on a hillside opposite the town. I look up and see on a bank above my head a silent, bright grey donkey looking down on me, outlined by stars. At the tree, we turn and contemplate the lights of Skyros on its helter-skelter of a crag, outlined against a rippled, moonlit sea. Someone tries to photograph this with a flash. Someone else plays flute. Another woman makes her move on a man, but from behind, I'm interested to see. Rather daring that, or would be for a man, but it seems to work, and they go off together. Now it is time for holding hands round the tree and the spell is broken. It is getting cold, and I realize I am squeezing the hand of Mike, our personal development therapist.

A Greek evening in Thomas's beachside taverna. Counting the steps for Greek dancing gets increasingly difficult as the retsina flows, and I soon have to choose whether to drink or dance before I pull everyone down with me. I do a lot of leaning with one hand against the toilet wall. Later, one of our party runs amok through the village, smashing bottles and screaming obscenities. She disappears completely for two days, then emerges with her hair scraped back and a martyred expression, having made a successful transition into middle age.

A news item. Something possibly symbolical has happened in the Personal Development course. After nearly two weeks of Regression, the participants are just about to take their souls back into their hearts prior to Reintegration when a vast framed tapestry made by an earlier therapy group falls off the wall with a loud crash and hundreds of moths fly out. The leader plays down the significance of this, while admitting that there may have been some disturbance in the air.

The last evening. As I am coming up from the beach, I hear a little boy shouting out what sounds like 'Hu-ko, Hu-ko'. He runs up and offers me a large photo of a woman. I try to take it, but he snatches it back, expecting a different response. The people I am with cannot believe I do not know the child and look at me strangely. It strikes me that this is the sensation of being foreign: you're totally out of touch most of the time, but trying desperately to catch up. As in writing, you're trying to express yourself, but more than that you're trying to find something out, like what does 'Hu-ko' mean. Is it me? And who is the woman in the photo? No one I ask has a satisfactory answer, and I suppose I'll never find out now. When I hug the director goodbye (these things are catching), he makes an attempt to turn me upside down. 'What are you doing?' I ask. 'I just think it would be good for you to stand on your head sometimes', he says.

[28.10.94]

A Short Bad Film about Violence

Everyone has their favourite row, the one they do best, the one they feel expresses some underlying truth. It doesn't, but they think it does at the time and that's what inspires them, what fires their imagination. The words may vary with the subject-matter (the least important aspect of a row), but the basic format (length, texture, outcome) will remain the same. A favourite row may become confused with a partner's favourite row over the years, but your own will always be distinguished by that extra sense of commitment, of coming *home*. When people recognize they are in the presence of their very own row, their hearts leap up, they throw back their shoulders at the world, they feel themselves capable of anything. And unfortunately they are.

If they'd had a tape recorder running during some of their rows they would have written something genuinely spontaneous by now. They would find out what their thoughts sounded like speeded up to the limits of pronounceability. They would discover how good their grammar really was, how articulate they remained under pressure. They might not like what they found. If they were unlucky, as I once was, they would find out what they were thinking about the moment before a scream, or a punch. If they were lucky, as I was, they would get a chance to rewrite their row before the general public were invited to give their verdict on it.

Rows with my daughter follow the same pattern as rows with her mother, so (I reason) they must have something to do with me. What happens is this. I protest at some minor outrage. Instead of mollifying me briefly and changing the subject (all too easy, but also cheap), they up the stakes by leaving the room.

Falling for it every time, I run after them, begging forgiveness. It isn't long before money is mentioned by me, along with the difficulty of working at home, reviewing a travel book for £70. After that, it is downhill all the way, with tears (mine) at the bottom.

The row is basically a star vehicle for a time-honoured performance. I do all the talking, but my wife or daughter gets the best part and all the notices, being free to react visually, without encumbrance of hackneyed speech. A critic would point out that this row of mine wasn't really a row at all and that that was where it was flawed. I would answer that this was an intrinsic part of its creation, the thing that spurred me on to ever dizzier heights of self-justification.

How's this for a short, bad film about violence? My daughter and I were drawing up our troops at the battlefield of the lunch table. There followed an explosion and an exit. I ran after her and with a solicitude that was really anger, asked what was the matter. She flew at me with fists flying and I cuffed her round the top of the head. I wore my watch on my right hand in those days and as I lashed out the bracelet expanded and the watch hit her in the mouth. Blood began to flow. Moments of horror followed as I realized it was not just her lip that was broken: I had chipped one of her precious new front teeth. It occurred to me suddenly that one should be able to decide against anything so grotesque, in the way that one decides not to poke a pen in one's eye. But no. There it was in my hand, a piece of my daughter's body that would not grow back again.

The horror increased as the three of us sat in a taxi on our way to University College Hospital. There was a bus strike that day and like the blood in our veins the traffic was frozen solid. For one terrible hour we sat murmuring and bleeding into handkerchiefs in the back of that taxi, which seemed to be transporting us gradually to hell.

Does one grow up suddenly at such times, or down? I remember wanting to turn away into the darkness, yet knowing that I had to fumble forward, pretending there was light up ahead, pretending I was still me. Later, a man at UCH would stick a little false piece on to my daughter's tooth and slowly colour would seep back into the world, words would be tried out like very thin ice, we would buy a teddy bear and a duvet in the Reject Shop and by some twist of irony my daughter would thank me. I remember we went to see some terrifying film about violence in a post-holocaust wilderness. Magic-ally, she enjoyed herself. A smile was attempted. A mirror was looked in without undue horror. Tea was made.

I had further to go before getting out of that darkened hall, that endless taxi ride, that crowded waiting room. After a year I would cease to think about it every day and start to think about it every other day. Writing about it now may be the last twist of the guilty knife. In a strange way I hope it isn't. When it happened I remember casting around for a pin-hole of light back into the real world where everything was as it should be and I was still good old me. Living now in that familiar world I want to be able to look back through that pin-hole occasionally to a time when such feelings were still alive and tender and I seemed to be carrying something precious and breakable in my arms towards some achievable goal. I suppose it is through such shocks and shake-ups that one learns how unimportant ends are compared to means, that the best we can do is try to stay cool and muddle through. I gave the offending watch to the TV repair man. I wear my watch on my other wrist now, in memory of that day.

[*Guardian*, 9.1.92]

Merry Stories and Funny Pictures

The 'Merry Stories and Funny Pictures' in *Struwwelpeter* – author lost in translation, believed to be Heinrich Hoffmann, who also wrote *The Nutcracker* – aren't merry or funny so much as grotesque, cruel and horrific, hence their enduring charm for children. They presumably came from Germany one merry Christmas long ago, but the date, too, has been lost or blurred with successive efforts at republication. The stiff, stylized images exist in a sort of eternal Regency, which prevents them dating much. The boys wear belted smocks, leggings and Eton collars, which make them look as if they are dressed specifically for the punishments and suffering they are about to incur. The girls are rounded teenagers in three-quarter-length dresses with provocative, frilly pantaloons showing. The terrifying stories of sadism, disaster and revenge are couched as cautionary tales for nicely brought-up little boys and girls, but the illustrator's relish for what happens to them when they slip up was not lost on me aged six or so. I was only glad it wasn't me who had his thumbs cut off by the 'Great, long, red-legged scissorman', because I was a big thumb addict and had to be weaned to go away to school.

Opening my battered copy now, I note that there are fewer rhymes than I had thought, only eight, and that they are printed on only one side of their flaky, creamy, falling-out pages, leaving the other free for early signature practice and other punishment-risking transgressions. I was lucky not to have had my eyes put out for writing 'Hug' all over the place. The curiously unreal pictures, with their blocks of smudged colour printing and sub-classical line decorations depicting elements of the tale, are still weirdly impregnated with horror for me and I shiver again at the unreasonable punishments meted out for all the things I used to do myself. 'Mama had scarcely turned her back, The thumb was in, Alack, Alack!'

Presumably this was how Germans learnt their manners in the good old days of discipline, duelling and war. It isn't difficult to see how a world which produced Struwwelpeter had to go on to produce Sigmund Freud, who would doubtless have insisted that little Conrad's thumb was his penis, that he'd been masturbating and that the red-legged scissor-man was his castration complex. Personally, I think it's an association one can either make or not make. My thumb was my thumb.

One of Freud's 'patients', Paul Shreber, who believed the sun shone out of his anus (surely one of Freud's own dreams), was the son of the inventor of a useful restricting harness for maintaining children in an upright position at table. The device was invented too late to save Fidgety Philip. His villainous-looking mother, growing fatter in each picture, regards through lorgnettes a virile teenager who 'wriggles and giggles and then I declare / Swings backwards and forwards and tilts up his chair', until he brings the entire heavily-laden table crashing down round his ears and with it the civilized world.

There is a paradox at the heart of Struwwelpeter which is a paradox of society and of Christianity itself: 'Naughty romping girls and boys / Who tear their clothes and make a noise, / Such as these shall never look / At this pretty picture-book.' Just as the meek shall inherit the earth and the good go to heaven, so the ignorant, over-sexed or bookless shall be damned. Worst of all these sinners is the eponymous 'Shock-headed Peter' himself, an impressive straw-haired youth in a red smock, green leggings and a Bob Dylan afro. This delinquent stands defiantly on top of the box of the poem indicting him for his uncivilized behaviour. Legs splayed, he holds out for our inspection his bizarre foot-long yogi's fingernails, like Christ showing his wounds to Thomas. Clearly this proud one is going to have to be made an example of. Already there is a certain Christ-like dignity about him.

Struwwelpeter! Surely there was a 1960s heavy rock band named after this proto-hippy, a rival to Steppenwolf? Turn the page and we come to an even worse offender, Cruel Frederick, the epitome of Punk, the original Sid Vicious, who sadistically 'Caught the flies, poor little things, / And then tore off their tiny wings. / And oh! far worse than all beside, / He whipped his Mary till she cried.' Frederick makes the mistake of whipping his dog Tray, who isn't as long-suffering as Mary. 'At this, good Tray grew very red / And growled and bit him till he bled.'

Most influential of the rhymes from a literary point of view is Little Johnny Head-in-Air, the dreamer who falls in the river, which seems to have given rise to at least two of World War II's most famous poems: 'Do not despair / For Johnny-head-in-air' by John Pudney and 'When a beau goes in / Into the drink' by Gavin Ewart. In the Struwwelpeter original, the dreamer is rescued, while three little fishes chant 'Silly little Johnny, look, / You have lost your writing-book' – a cautionary tale to poets everywhere.

I feel sure the book has had some subliminal influence on my own work, perhaps in my exaggerated interest in hair; the artist has a peculiar way of drawing it up into (no doubt phallic) points, which then become the most memorable part of each picture, or did for me. I don't know if any of the cautionary aspects of the book got through to me, because I still tip my chair and fiddle with matches, but perhaps they did subconsciously, because I very rarely whip my wife.

[*Sunday Times*, 30.1.94]

237

Lucky to Be Alive

I met a woman at a party who told me she always remembered people's hands. I followed her glance downwards and made a mental note to stop biting my fingernails. A couple of days later, one of my hands was in plaster, and I seemed to have lost my appetite.

My wife had a lawyer's meeting in Beauvais on the way to her newly inherited house near Compiègne, so it seemed that ferry and motorbike were the simplest way of travelling. The lawyer cancelled the appointment the day before, because of a funeral. By then it was too late to change our plans. We got up early and drove down to Newhaven for the 8.15 ferry. It was raining when we reached Dieppe, but we enjoyed the heroism of placing our gleaming crash helmets on the bars of cafés and talking about the weather to anyone who looked at us, postponing the moment, over *croques monsieurs*, when we would have to broach our wet saddle again.

For a couple of hours we steamed along quite happily through the folds of domestic Normandy, empty wet roads shining white between stubble fields, rainbows all over the place, the occasional war cemetery raising ranks of white hands at low black clouds. Then, at Beauvais, the little roads we favoured ran out, and we started suffering the spray of overtaking lorries. We stopped to change our socks, then soldiered on, our thoughts locked on the wonderful idea that it would all soon be over.

The last mile or so of RN17 before the turning to Sacy-le-Petit is a notorious speedway, and now it was rush hour and dark. There seemed hardly enough space to position myself between the opposing streams of traffic prior to turning left, so I had turned into a little bay on the right, which seemed designed for the purpose, and waited for a gap before crossing. Nothing to the right, distant lights to the left, cautiously I set out . . .

My wife says she felt like Cassandra. She saw our ill fortune coming in the shape of two headlights, but due to the suspension of responsibility one has to practise on the back of a motorbike, thought she must be mistaken. The first I knew that anything was wrong was her voice crying my name, but by then it was too late.

The noise – outrageous, loud, metal-damage noise, prolonged and various – was followed by an inexplicable imbalance, an unfamiliar propulsion, the body's cringing apprehension of invasion – I remember thinking 'so far so good' – then impact, silence and a furious scrabbling for safety.

While faces and headlights gathered round our little piece of chaos, I was jumping up and down jibbering 'What have I done to you? What have I done to you?' But my wife seemed to be all right and calmly ordered me to get the bike off the road. I would have liked to have kicked it into the ditch, but when I tried to lift it, I discovered my left hand wouldn't work. I pulled off my glove and saw two fingers pointing in wrong directions. The ambulance arrived, and I found it important to tell one of the orderlies that he looked like Tom Cruise and to have a long conversation with him about Cruise's films, none of which he had seen.

The hospital was all too familiar – desultory corridors turning corners into other corridors, swing doors with metal strips, wheel-chairs, hatches, ether, a room to do lots of waiting in, where we duly waited, while a boy in a coma took precedence over my measly broken fingers. In X-ray the nurse got quite impatient, telling me to spread my hand flat on the X-ray plate or she couldn't do her job properly. She changed her mind when she saw the results. 'Il est bien cassé', she told me reassuringly. Seeing an X-ray is like seeing a photograph of the future. I had met my skeleton for the first time – an image which would return to me in the coming weeks.

To pin or plaster? For reasons of cowardice I was all in favour of plaster, but either way it meant an operation. On the way to the theatre I asked what had happened to the boy and was told he'd tried to hang himself. He was thirteen and was going to survive. After that, nothing seemed to matter very much.

A couple of days later, my wife and I went to evening mass in the church at Sacy-le-Petit where we were married almost exactly twenty-nine years ago and offered up the usual gratitude for what was, in reality, a piece of bad luck, but which the human spirit seemed to need to call a blessed escape. I had made the local newspaper: '*Hugo William, sujet britannique de 52 ans en vacances à Sacy-le-Petit, a été heurté par une voiture alors qu'il se trouvait au guidon de sa moto . . .*'

And indeed, everyone seemed to agree that I was lucky to be alive. The road was a death trap. Four people had died there last month. *Le bon dieu* etc. After mass, I was surrounded by nuns, who told me I had been lucky because it was the month of the Virgin and I remembered we had stopped on the way at Neufchâtel-sur-Bray to see a little gilt statue of the Madonna, standing on tangled snakes. The snakes obviously represented my mangled motorbike. The Virgin had plucked me from the wreck. On the other hand, if we hadn't stopped there we would have been ten minutes earlier and might not have . . .

Narrow escape or bad luck, what really bothered me about the whole business was the lacuna which seemed to have opened up in my ability to look after someone else's life. The answer seems to be that your guard is lowered just before you reach your destination, your thoughts go on ahead, which is why so many accidents happen near home. I remembered being thrilled at the prospect of imminent arrival, so much so I couldn't wait. In my mind I was sitting with a drink beside the fire. If we die, perhaps we just carry on with what we are doing, and everything is all right forever.

I made my way back to London by train and have been giving dozens of different versions of the accident – from PG to 18 – to people with varying degrees of need to know about it. The plaster is a great social advantage, like having a little dog or a funny hat. Women place their hands on my arm, and their faces betray their pained identification as they glance downwards at my sunset knuckles, my fingertips swathed like babies in soiled swaddling clothes. They want the details, and I never tire of giving them – the flashing lights, the mobile phones, the ambulance in the night, the motorbike and us scattered over the hurtling country road. I don't mind describing it, because each time I tell the story the noise gets fainter, the lights recede, the whole thing becomes less . . . unexpected. When I think of it now, I am almost ready for it to happen, braced for impact, able to take evasive action.

As for my hand, it is a trophy, a talisman, a lucky charm, a symbol of survival. I hold it up in triumph like that mutilated beggar in Fellini's *Satyricon*. Any day now I will be Walter Mitty, who, it will be remembered, set the bone himself.

[18.11.94]